The Thief, His Wife and The Canoe

David Leigh is an award-winning British investigative journalist and author living and working out of Miami. He is a member of the UK Crime Writers' Association. Before moving to Florida to work as Senior News Director for a celebrated news and photographic agency, Leigh worked for British newspapers, including the *Daily Mirror*, where during his twelve-year tenure he worked as a Senior Reporter, News Editor and Foreign Editor covering news stories across the world. He then spent three years as Assistant Editor (Head of News) at the *Daily Express*, where he oversaw coverage of stories including the 9/11 terrorist atrocities, the Second Gulf War and the fall of Saddam Hussein.

He won two prestigious awards, the National Association of News Agencies' News Story of the Year and the London Press Club's Scoop of the Year, for his reporting on the incredible 'John Darwin; Canoe Man' story. He later ghost wrote a book for Darwin's wife Anne, *Out of My Depth*.

Tony Hutchinson – Months after completing his 'A' Levels in 1978, he was pounding the streets of Hartlepool wearing a police uniform and dreaming of being a detective. By the time John 'Canoe Man' Darwin walked into a London police station in December 2007 and uttered the immortal words, 'I think I am a missing person', Tony had gone from a fresh-faced 'bobby on the beat' to Head of Cleveland Police's Murder Team. Thirty years of hunting thieves, killers and every type of criminal in between, nothing catapulted him in front of the worldwide media like John and Anne Darwin. Now retired, he has had four novels published in his Dark Tides thriller series.

The Thief, His Wife and The Canoe

BY DAVID LEIGH

With Tony Hutchinson

HODDER

First published in Great Britain in 2022 by Hodder & Stoughton
An Hachette UK company

1

Copyright © David Leigh and Anthony Hutchinson 2022

The right of David Leigh and Anthony Hutchinson to be
identified as the Author of the Work has been asserted by them in
accordance with the Copyright, Designs and Patents Act 1988.

A CIP catalogue record for this title is available from the British Library

Paperback ISBN 9781529395167
eBook ISBN 9781529395174

Typeset in Bembo by Hewer Text UK Ltd, Edinburgh
Printed and bound in Great Britain by Clays Ltd, Elcograf S.p.A.

Hodder & Stoughton policy is to use papers that are natural, renewable
and recyclable products and made from wood grown in sustainable
forests. The logging and manufacturing processes are expected to
conform to the environmental regulations of the country of origin.

Hodder & Stoughton Ltd
Carmelite House
50 Victoria Embankment
London EC4Y 0DZ

www.hodder.co.uk

Contents

PROLOGUE

April 2003

THE BALDING, MIDDLE-AGED man with a rounded face and a slight paunch is standing in the bay window of the second-floor bedroom of his imposing sea-front home in the north-east of England, watching the waves roll ashore.

It's a bone-chilling morning in early April. Spring has yet to arrive in Seaton Carew. It's often late. Old Big 'Ead Brian Clough described it as the coldest place in England when he became manager of the then Hartlepools (sic) United in 1965 and discovered the beach was the training ground.

Occasional passers-by are hunched over, heads bowed into the biting wind, hands buried deep in their pockets, oblivious to the heavily bearded face of a man in the big Victorian house across the street contemptuously staring out to sea as if he had conquered the world.

The sea looks cold and grey that morning, much as it always does at this time of year. The good old North Sea. He has plenty to thank it for.

He's stood next to an old brass spyglass, pointed seawards. His hands are planted on his hips. And he's stark-bollock naked.

Dripping in arrogance and vanity, he throws his head back and laughs. *I bloody well did it*, he congratulates himself.

This is John Ronald Darwin in all his glory. A dreamer and schemer feeling as pleased as punch with himself, having twelve months earlier pulled off something truly outrageous. In the years to come, it will bestow upon his shoulders a notoriety he will accept with glowing pride.

FOUR YEARS LATER

I

'I Think I'm a Missing Person'

'SORRY SARGE, THERE'S some crackpot in the front office. Says he's a missing person.'

The young cop shrugs his shoulders, an apologetic look on his face.

Sergeant Craig Clark-Darby averts his eyes from the rookie officer standing at his desk and looks at the white plastic clock on the station wall. It's been on a go-slow all day. The time is now 5.40 p.m., Saturday 1 December 2007. Twenty minutes until he's due to go home after a dull twelve-hour shift.

'For fuck's sake,' he mutters as he begrudgingly heads out to see who it is who has wandered off the street with the sole intent of ruining his Saturday evening.

'Yes sir, how can I help you?' he asks with minimum enthusiasm.

'Ah, good evening officer. As I just told your young colleague there, I think I'm a missing person.'

Clark-Darby looks dubiously into the eyes of the strangely suntanned man standing across the counter.

He takes a deep breath, puffs out his cheeks and slowly exhales.

Right, he thinks to himself. *And I'm the Lone bloody Ranger . . .*

He just wants to go home.

'What exactly makes you think you're a missing person, sir?' he asks courteously.

'Well if I knew that I don't think I'd be here now, would I?' is the smug response.

'Right,' says the officer, hoping the false smile hides his irritation. The last thing he needs right now is a smart arse.

Another deep breath.

'Don't think I caught the name, sir?'

'Darwin. John . . . Ronald . . . Darwin.'

He speaks slowly. North-easterners have a tendency to speak fast and outsiders can struggle to keep up. In case there's any doubt, the man spells out the letters of his surname 'D . . . A . . . R . . . W . . . I . . . N. From up north . . . Seaton Carew. Hartlepool.'

He smiles, delighted with his delivery. Not even a hint of the Hartlepudlian tendency to h-drop. Locals stay in 'otels and turn up the 'eating when it gets cold.

A second, longer sigh from Clark-Darby. This oddball has been here five minutes, but the uniformed section sergeant at London's West End Central police station is already weary. There's something extremely annoying about the man.

He looks to be in his fifties and is wearing walking boots; dark blue, ill-fitting cargo trousers; a blue shirt, still showing the manufacturer's packing creases; an off-white, crew-neck cricket jumper; and what looks like a fake leather jacket. Some of the clothing still have the Asda labels showing. Maybe he's a shoplifter . . . but not a very smart one.

The man claims he isn't quite sure where he came from or even how he arrived at the police station.

Fifteen minutes earlier he had been found wandering 'dazed and confused' around a Top Shop in Oxford Street, telling a store assistant he'd mislaid his wife, children and Rottweiler dogs. The baffled girl had called a security guard, who somewhat reluctantly, given the icy weather, walked him around the corner to the drab, grey-stone police station at 27 Savile Row, W1.

'I was wondering, why are all the Christmas lights on when it's only June?' he asks.

'Wait there one moment please,' says the sergeant, avoiding the question and returning to the back office.

Maybe he's on drugs; they often are.

'Right oh,' the man cheerily responds, peering through the Perspex screen and shifting awkwardly from side to side.

He looks around, examining his surroundings. The walls are decorated with tinsel, though it looks tired and has lost most of its sparkle. John shakes his head, appearing bemused at the faded festive trimmings.

'Keep a close eye on that one while I make some checks,' Clark-Darby instructs his young colleague. 'And don't let him leave.'

The sergeant is in for a surprise.

On checking missing persons records he quickly discovers there is indeed a John Darwin who disappeared off the Cleveland coast a little under six years earlier in the spring of 2002.

But he isn't missing – he's *dead*.

Strangely, there's no photograph attached to the file, so there's no way of knowing if it's the same man. He picks up the phone and calls Hartlepool police station to see if anyone there can throw any light on the curious case he's found himself dealing with three weeks before Christmas.

'We've got a right one here,' he tells the officer at the other end of the line. 'Either this guy has lost the plot or we have a Christmas miracle on our hands and he's come back from the dead! Says his name is John Darwin and claims he remembers nothing since a holiday in Norway in 2000. Claims to think it's still June and asked why all the Christmas decorations are up.'

The sergeant has already established 'John Darwin' has no form of identification on him, simply a brown leather folding wallet containing £140, comprising eight crisp notes, six twenties, and two tens, and a key-ring with several keys attached. He claims not to know what any of the keys are for.

'Blimey,' says the cop at the other end of the line. 'I remember that job very well. The bloke disappeared in a canoe off the coast of Seaton Carew. Caused a right hoo-ha. There was a massive search but I don't think a body was ever found. Let me see if I can contact a member of the family for you.'

Clark-Darby is perplexed. He's not buying this back-from-the-dead story for a second. The mysterious stranger is guilty of something, he's just not sure what. He returns to the front counter and advises the man that he is being arrested under section 136 of the Mental Health Act for his own safety. With no evidence to suggest any wrongdoing – as yet – he doesn't want to let the self-styled missing person disappear into the night. Bang goes Clark-Darby's evening.

'If you could come this way sir,' he says, escorting the man, who raises no objections, to a small detention room, similar to a cell, off the main corridor.

There's a concrete bed with a mattress, sheet and a pillow, all tear-proof, for obvious reasons, and in the corner a toilet without a seat. The once-white paint is yellow and peeling, walls permeated with the stench of body odour and urine from the visits of countless past miscreants.

'Have a seat and we'll see if we can contact someone for you.'

The man claiming to be John Darwin accepts the offer of a cup of tea to warm him up. It's close to freezing outside.

He sits on the bed, alone with his thoughts.

2

'But . . . Me Dad's Dead'

MARK DARWIN IS partying at a friend's wedding blessing in Balham, south London, when his mobile rings. It's just gone 9 p.m. and the function is in full swing, making it difficult to hear over the beat of the music. He can just about make out that the woman is a police officer from Hartlepool, close to his mam's home. He anxiously moves outside.

'I'm sorry to surprise you like this,' says duty inspector Helen Eustace. 'I got your number from your grandmother. I know this will come as quite a shock, but we have someone in custody saying he's your dad.'

Mark is bewildered. Did he hear correctly? An icy shiver runs down his spine.

'But . . . but . . . me dad's dead,' he stutters. 'He died five years ago.'

'Well, he's pretty adamant,' the inspector continues. 'He turned up at the West End Central police station in London. Appears to be suffering from amnesia. Anyway, you can make your way there love to see for yourself.'

Mark is rooted to the spot, his world grinding into slow motion. His heart is pumping. What the . . .? Dad? No . . . surely . . . it can't possibly be true? Can it? His whole body is shaking.

His mind flashes back to the traumatic call he received from his uncle Michael five years earlier saying that his dad was missing at sea; to dashing north to comfort his heartbroken mother; to her sobbing uncontrollably as she greeted him at the drawing-room door. He shudders as he recalls her red-raw eyes, her running nose and her inconsolable grief.

Silence.

'Are you okay love?' asks the inspector.

'Yes, yes, I err, think so,' Mark finally responds. 'I just don't understand . . .'

Inspector Eustace asks a few questions about his father's disappearance and all the painful memories come flooding back. Looking out of the window and seeing the flashing lights of the search-and-rescue helicopters in the distance and lifeboats trawling up and down the coast searching for his dad, who had vanished in his red canoe. Mark had closed the curtains to try and shelter his mam from the heartbreaking spectacle, their worlds shattered.

He keeps telling himself it can't possibly be true.

Still on the phone, he rushes back inside and grabs his girlfriend Felicia, known to everyone as Flick, and tells her what's happening. Flick calls her uncle, who drives them to the nearest station. By the time they get on the Tube, Mark is in tears. Flick hugs him tightly. It's impossible to find the right words.

Inspector Eustace calls Anthony Darwin. She asks who he's with and if he wants to sit down.

Mark's younger brother, who's at home with wife Louise, steels himself for the worst. Maybe one of his grandparents has died or there's been a terrible accident. All sorts of dark thoughts are racing through his mind. He feels sick to the stomach.

But there is no death – quite the opposite.

The officer repeats the story she's just told his brother. Anthony is dumbfounded and asks her to repeat what she's just told him. It can't be true. Who is this person purporting to be his dad and playing some sort of sick game with their lives? He tries calling Mark but he's on the Tube and there's no signal.

Anthony had been in Canada on the holiday of a lifetime and planning to propose to Louise when he received the call five years earlier. Mark had been the one who dialled his number, but he had been unable to get the words out, so had handed the phone to his Auntie Christine, Anne's younger sister. Silly bugger, Anthony initially thought; Dad's got himself washed down the coast. But then the seriousness of the situation had hit home and he and Louise had cancelled everything and flown back immediately.

When he arrived in Seaton Carew two days later, his mam was still shaking and sobbing. The house was a hive of activity for days as police, family, neighbours and his mother's work colleagues came to show their support. They were all on tenterhooks waiting for news, their hearts stopping every time the phone rang. But there was no news. Dad had gone. Their hearts were broken.

As Mark and Flick hurriedly walk past the flickering blue Metropolitan Police lamp on the corner of Boyle Street and arrive at West End Central, Anthony is on the phone to an officer trying to get more information. Told that his brother is on the phone, Mark asks to speak to him.

'I know this is all so crazy,' says Mark.

He tells Anthony to stay put until he has seen the man purporting to be their father, to see if it really is him.

Mark and Flick are led into an interview room by Clark-Darby, who explains that the man has been arrested for his own safety. He tactfully chooses not to mention the fact that he doesn't believe the man's story for one second, or that he reminds him of a wooden actor from a 1970s sit-com.

'He remembers your name and date of birth,' the officer tells Mark. 'He's reasonably smartly dressed but *seems* to be suffering from amnesia of some kind.'

A psychiatrist who has been called to the police station to assess the man enters the room and tells Mark and Flick that in his opinion he is fine to leave. He doesn't pose a danger to anyone as long as he has someone to look after him.

'Would you like to see him?' says Clark-Darby. Mark's heart skips a beat. 'Just go easy, as maybe he's had a bump on his head or something. He seems a bit fragile.'

Mark, lean and clean-cut, with short, slightly spiked black hair, takes a deep breath and braces himself. He is gulping down water but his throat is still dry. His heart is pounding, such is his terror that this will turn out to be a cruel hoax or that the man has simply assumed his father's identity.

But neither is the case.

The man led into the room and standing there in front of him looks older, thinner and with a little less hair than he remembers, but it's his dad all right: the man who was so cruelly snatched from his life more than five years earlier.

'Oh my God, Dad!' he exclaims, his voice trembling, tears welling in his eyes. He feels numb.

'Oh, hello son,' John says casually. 'I can't find your mam and the dogs anywhere.'

The two men hug. Mark doesn't want to let go. He is overwrought – euphoria and disbelief combining. The last time he saw his father was at his parents' sea-front house in Seaton Carew in February 2002, three weeks before his life was shattered irrevocably when he vanished into thin air.

Now here he is – very much alive.

Mark is bewildered, a million questions racing through his mind. But the officer has advised him to tread carefully, so the conversation is a little stifled. Sipping water from a polystyrene cup, he can't believe what's happening. He explains that Zena and Meg, the beloved Rottweilers, are dead.

'They were good, loyal dogs,' John responds rather vacantly.

He looks at Flick, a pretty, bespectacled girl with her auburn hair tied back in a ponytail. She is beaming from ear to ear at her boyfriend's happiness.

'I don't know you, love,' he says.

A little belatedly, given the extraordinary circumstances, Mark introduces her.

'I've missed you so much, Dad,' he says, unable to take his eyes off his father as the latter formally shakes hands with his girlfriend.

His dad is clean-shaven and tanned. He looks a picture of health. Mark wonders where on earth he has been. For all he knows he could have a new life with a new family. He is thrilled beyond belief but feels totally disorientated. So many questions. But now's not the time. He calls Anthony, who has been anxiously pacing around his house for nearly half an hour, and tells him that, yes, incredibly, the man is indeed their long-lost dad.

'It's Dad . . . but I don't know what to tell you,' says Mark. 'You'd best get here as quickly as you can.'

Anthony and Louise jump in their car and head towards the city. But the younger Darwin brother is in such a state that he gets lost in central London. He ends up having to call the police and, after explaining his predicament, is given an escort to the station.

Anthony is as stunned as his brother when he first sets eyes on his father. They too embrace.

'I can't believe you're here, Dad,' says Anthony.

'It's good to see you, son,' says John, as if he hasn't seen him for a month or two.

Anthony, an inch or two taller than his brother but with the same dark hair and intense eyes, sits down and stares at his father in disbelief. It's beyond spooky.

The boys know they need to share the amazing news with Mam. She is going to find it hard to believe.

But their dad is also in for quite a shock.

Six weeks earlier, after selling up in Seaton, Anne Darwin stunned everyone by leaving the UK to start a new life in, of all places, Panama, Central America. She was fifty-five and known as a homely, family woman who had never shown any great desire to travel abroad, let alone to some far-flung place on the other side of the world. And why Panama, a somewhat intriguing country that gave its name to hats, cocktails, spy books and a very famous canal. Anne didn't even speak Spanish, though she had bought half a dozen teach-yourself books.

She told her nearest and dearest that the family home held too many unhappy memories, and each day she would find herself vacantly gazing out of the living-room's bay window towards the spot from which John had set out to sea on his ill-fated canoe outing. With that and the wet and miserable north-east weather, she was constantly depressed and had decided, after several holidays in Panama, to sell up and make a new life for herself in the sun.

Although greatly concerned and wondering if their mother had lost her marbles, the boys had agreed that if that was what she really wanted, she had their full support. They were desperate for her to be happy again and would visit her as soon as they could. Now they would have to explain that little bombshell to their dad.

Clark-Darby leads them all to an upstairs room where there's a telephone. It's early afternoon in Panama, five hours behind the UK. Mark's fingers shake as he punches in the numbers. He doesn't have to wait long.

'Is everything okay?' says his mother as she picks up the phone after several rings and hears her son's voice.

She glances at her watch. It's 5.15 p.m. and getting late back home.

'Don't panic, Mam, I have no bad news, everybody is all right,' says Mark.

There's no easy way to say this.

'Mam, brace yourself . . . you're not going to believe this . . . but I'm sitting here with Dad!'

Silence.

'What on earth do you mean?' his mother eventually responds.

Mark is shaking like a leaf in a hurricane.

'He's . . . turned up in London . . . he's okay . . . he's alive, Mam.'

'Oh my God,' his mother responds and starts sobbing.

Mark asks if she's all right and if she'd like to speak to him.

'Of course I would,' she says, and he hands the phone to his dad.

'Hello love, is that really you?' says John. 'I'm confused. I was in a shop and I didn't know where you and the boys and dogs were.'

It's all totally surreal. The pair chat for a couple of minutes and then his dad passes the phone back to Mark.

'I'll call you later, Mam,' Mark says.

He can hear his mother sobbing down the phone as he ends the call.

The police say they have no good grounds to detain John, so he's free to go. They'll be in touch the next day, Clark-Darby tells them, advising the boys to keep a very close eye on their father. The two of them leave West End Central protectively walking either side of him. Neither can quite believe this is happening.

It's quickly decided that John should stay with Anthony and Louise, as they have more room than Mark at their three-bed-semi, so all five head to Hampshire in Anthony's car. When they arrive, they sit chatting in the living room looking at old family photographs until the early hours, hoping something will jog John's memory. Anthony shows his dad photos of his wedding to Louise the year after he disappeared. Initially they'd been forced to postpone it – because it coincided with his inquest – but Anthony doesn't mention that.

'I so wish you could have been there, Dad,' he says.

Louise's father had even made a poignant toast to absent friends.

John's recollections are strange to say the least. He recalls working as a teacher (a job he'd left many years earlier), owning a yellow sports car and hunting rabbits, but he can't seem to remember a lot more than that.

Anthony takes a photograph of his dad sitting on the sofa, looking slightly dishevelled, and emails it to his mother. She replies saying, 'Dad has lost a lot of hair and looks older', and sends back a picture taken, she says, a few weeks earlier, of herself riding a horse in Costa Rica. The boys *assume* the photograph must have been taken by a fellow holidaymaker. Mark and Flick decide to stay over and John is shown to the spare room.

No one gets much sleep that night. Questions whirr through the brothers' minds. Where on earth has their dad been these last five years and what's he been doing? Neither can quite believe it to be true that he's back with them.

Early the next morning, after breakfast, Anthony drives his dad to the nearby Asda supermarket. There is a brief moment of panic when Anthony turns around and can't see John, who has wandered off into another aisle. Terrified he has disappeared again, Anthony runs from aisle to aisle until, mightily relieved, he finds him.

'Dad . . . please . . . you need to stay close to me!' says Anthony.

He buys his dad jeans, several t-shirts, three pairs of underpants and some socks. John insists he wants to pay, but Anthony won't hear of it.

Later that day, Mark and Flick return to London, as Mark, who's thirty-one, is starting a new job as a software engineer the following morning. It's left to Anthony and Louise to continue gently trying to coax information from John. Bizarrely, he says he doesn't know what baked beans are and can't recall whether he takes sugar in his coffee, yet he remembers Mark and Anthony's dates of birth. He again speaks to Anne, and this time they chat for longer.

Anthony, who's twenty-nine, speaks to his mam and is puzzled when she says she can't return straight away because she is sorting out some problems with her visa. But, surprising though it is, he doesn't push her.

He's just thrilled to have his dad back.

3

'Amnesia? Bollocks More Like!'

As word of John Darwin's reincarnation spreads like wildfire throughout Cleveland Police, Detective Superintendent Tony Hutchinson is enjoying a Sunday at home in the picturesque North Yorkshire village of Osmotherley when he receives a 'you'll never guess what?' phone call from Detective Sergeant Iain Henderson. The men have been friends since working together at Hartlepool in the early 1990s. It's the first Hutchinson has heard of Darwin's incredible reappearance and he's taken aback by the news. Two thoughts race through his mind: shit-storm . . . and con artist.

Hutchinson, or 'Hutch' as he's known to everyone, is a formidable 6-foot 5-inch giant of a man. Head of Cleveland Police's murder squad, he's a plain-speaking, old-fashioned cop who has risen through the ranks and, by reputation, is respected by everyone, friend and foe alike. Bald, with inquisitive blue eyes, he's a tough, no-nonsense larger-than-life detective, known for his great sense of humour and not someone to be messed with. He looks like he could have been a heavyweight boxer.

Back in March 2002, when John Darwin was 'lost at sea', Hutch had just finished one murder trial, was finalising the case file for another murder that occurred in January and was preparing for an impending trial. A busy man, he hadn't been concerned with the missing canoeist. At least not from a policing point of view.

Coincidentally, he was living in Seaton Carew at the time of the disappearance.

Seaton, as it is commonly known, is a typical northern seaside town; its beach is a three-mile arc of sand, sheltered to the north by Hartlepool's headland and to the south by Coatham Sands. At the end of the sea front, before the town peters out into the sand dunes, offering up a hazy vista of the belching chemical plants and the power station, the dull metallic sea is blocked from view by the flat slab of the bus station, clock tower and public toilets. The symmetrical Grade 2-listed Art Deco building opened in 1938 and was the first building ever to use curved concrete. It's quite something.

Like many English seaside towns, it has a history to be proud of. Its grander cousin Scarborough, further down the coast, might be able to boast of its spa, but Seaton's heyday was no less fondly remembered.

Originally a fishing village, it was adopted by the wealthy Quakers of Darlington as their seaside resort, and a regular coach service between Stockton and Seaton Carew began in 1783 with 'The Diligence', as the coach was called, operating on Tuesdays and Fridays in the summer months.

In the decades after the war, the intoxicating excitement of the town and its myriad attractions like the wooden helter-skelter proved an irresistible magnet for workers and their families from the surrounding pit communities and the crowded terraced streets of Stockton, Middlesbrough and Hartlepool.

Hutch's parents met in the town on August Bank Holiday 1953 on a day trip from Newcastle organised by his maternal grandmother. He often joked that Lizzie Casey had a lot to answer for!

On the morning after the disappearance, as discarded carrier bags whipped against the railings and the waves boomed on the ugly black rocks that prevented the sea from sucking the road into oblivion, the talk across every fence, in the bars of The Staincliffe, The Marine and The Seaton Hotel, and in the fish-and-chip shops and the sea-front stores selling candy floss and brightly coloured sticks of rock, was about the man who had mysteriously vanished at sea.

'Any news on that bloke who went out in his canoe?' was all anyone was asking.

Even the members of Seaton Carew Golf Club, the tenth oldest in England, temporarily forget about their handicaps. Coastal communities have always spoken about those lost at sea.

Now, five years on, the good folk of Seaton are amazed at the news of the back-from-the-dead canoeist. Everyone knows Hutch – man mountains tend to leave a marked impression – and they expect him to have the 'inside track'. He does not. But it's occupying his thoughts.

Although on the surface of it, John Darwin's re-emergence appears to be a heart-warming, if baffling, turn of events, Hutch already knows that this strange canoe-man caper is far from the medical mystery it's being billed as. Cops, like journalists, are cynical creatures at the best of times.

He remembers the huge search operation . . . and the mutterings of how calm the sea had been that day. Questions will be asked of the original investigation, so he bounces around some of his own. As a detective, you never switch off.

He has vague recollections of Darwin being spotted sitting on the beach with his canoe before paddling out. Was he enjoying the view, or was he there to be noticed? How had he been lost in reasonable sea conditions? Why was he not seen once out at sea? How experienced a canoeist was he? Were the Darwins' finances thoroughly examined? And where the hell had he been for five and a half years before walking into that London police station?

Amnesia, thinks Hutch. *Bollocks more like!*

Then he remembers Darwin had two sons. If this turns out to be the crime he already suspects it to be, surely they must have been involved? If they weren't, how could any father do that to his own children? Could there be anything more despicable than lying to your own sons about your 'death'? All these thoughts and more are rushing through his mind.

But he shrugs his shoulders. *Not my problem.* The investigation will be undertaken by the CID at Hartlepool, not by the murder team. Shame really. It would be an interesting inquiry, probably his last before retirement and a nice one to go out on. He had joined Cleveland Constabulary in 1978, and next year his thirty years were up. After more than forty murder investigations, cases of serial sex offenders, abductions and arsons it was time for something new.

***

That evening, Simon Walton, crime reporter on the *Evening Gazette* in Middlesbrough, is making one last round of calls to his local police force, checking for any late-breaking stories before finishing his shift. Regular calls to the police, fire and ambulance services are part of a local reporter's daily routine.

The duty inspector at Cleveland Police mentions she has something that may be of interest.

'Does the name John Darwin mean anything to you?' she asks.

The name rattles around Walton's brain.

'Canoeist. Seaton Carew,' continues the inspector.

'Ahhh, yes, of course, I remember,' replies Walton.

'Well he's turned up in London, alive and well but suffering from memory loss,' he's told.

'Bloody hell, you're joking!' says Walton, who nearly drops the phone in amazement, knowing he has a front-page story on his hands.

There is going to be an announcement in the morning, but as he's called, the inspector decided to give him the scoop. More than five years earlier he had been a cub reporter on the *Hartlepool Mail* and covered the story of John Darwin's disappearance. He remembers his stomach being in knots after being sent on a dreaded 'death knock' to try and speak to the man's wife, only to be told that she and her two sons were far too upset to talk to a journalist. It's about the toughest assignment that can be asked of a young reporter. You either get the door slammed in your face or, very occasionally, are invited in by a grieving relative grateful for someone to talk to. The foreboding of the knock never leaves you.

Sure enough, the astonishing tale is the 'splash', the lead front-page story as journalists call it, in the following day's paper. It isn't long before it is being followed up by just about every news organisation in the country. Journalists are desperate to unravel the mystery of where John Darwin has been for the last five years. And vitally, where are his wife and family?

4

'The Sea Was as Smooth as a Millpond'

BY MONDAY MORNING, Anthony already has several reporters and photographers camped on his doorstep, all desperate to discover more about the incredible story. As far as the press is concerned, this is the story of the day. What's the truth here, everyone is asking? There has to be more to it than meets the eye.

Reporters want to know if they can talk to the man already dubbed 'Canoe Man' and what Anthony has to say about his dad's reappearance. He's totally overwhelmed and saying nothing. Where is your mother, they all ask? Anthony's silence is not going to deter journalists. The race to find Anne Darwin is well and truly on.

TV crews start descending on Seaton Carew to report from the scene of the disappearance. Reporters are busy seeking out anyone who remembers the story, the huge air and sea search, and the poor wife left behind. It's the lead story on local, then national news bulletins. The former prison officer is the talk of the town, just as he had been five years earlier when he vanished.

'I always wondered about this fella,' Tug Wilson, the now retired RNLI station controller for the watch station at the mouth of Hartlepool Dock, tells reporters.

In some quarters 'this fella' is already being described as the 2002 World Hide and Seek Champion. The jokes are coming thick and fast and it's not long before the town is christened *Seaton Canoe*. Humour is a way of life in the north-east.

'The sea was as smooth as a millpond that day, like glass,' adds Wilson. 'We always wondered whether there was maybe a little more to it than met the eye.'

Station mechanic and second coxswain, Gary Waugh, remembers being as baffled as anyone that there hadn't been a single sighting of either the missing man or the wreckage from his canoe for days.

'You couldn't have picked a better night for searching,' he says. 'It was flat calm, lovely sky at night, excellent for searching. Conditions were perfect, you could see quite a way with normal eyesight. Basically, you couldn't have picked a better night.'

He remembers the massive search being launched after the man's wife returned to her home to discover that her husband, along with his pride-and-joy canoe, were both missing. In a total panic after calling the prison where he worked and discovering he hadn't turned up for his shift, she had dialled 999 and reported him missing.

Police had quizzed neighbours and quickly established her husband had indeed been seen leaving his home earlier that morning, carrying his canoe and taking off from the shore in the direction of Teesmouth.

A full-scale search-and-rescue operation had sprung into operation. In all, some sixty-five RNLI volunteers were involved in one of the biggest rescue operations off the north-east coast of England in years. Ten rescue boats had used tried-and-tested search patterns, methodically criss-crossing 200 square miles of ocean for any trace of the local man last seen paddling out to sea in a red canoe.

Worryingly, he had apparently been heading towards the mouth of the River Tees – one of the busiest shipping channels in the United Kingdom. The possibility of a gruesome death, being sucked into a ship's propellers, could not be ruled out. No one wanted to admit it, but they all knew that the outcome of the rescue mission was looking bleaker by the minute. The spotters screwed up their eyes in the vain hope it might help them see something. But there was nothing to be seen: nothing at all.

Everyone was puzzled. It had been a textbook operation in what the men considered ideal rescue conditions: only partly cloudy, with a 'sea state' of two to three, meaning only a gentle swell, with no hint of the mountainous waves or icy conditions they so often had to contend with. It was, they all agreed, the perfect day for a rescue. So, where was he?

The operation, coordinated by the Humber Coastguard, had grown steadily in scale throughout the day. Three aircraft had been called in to assist: a bright yellow Royal Air Force Sea King search-and-rescue helicopter, a small fixed-wing Cleveland Police spotter plane and an RAF Nimrod reconnaissance aircraft. Even a Royal

Naval warship, HMS *Explorer*, which happened to be in the area on exercise, had joined the search, all surely adding, rescuers felt, to the chances of success. Dozens of RNLI and Coastguard shore teams were combing the coastline for debris . . . or worse. Nothing had been left to chance.

The following day, shortly after lunch, there was finally a break-through when a double-ended paddle, typically used by canoeists, was retrieved from the sea near North Gare, just a mile or two along the coast from where the missing man was seen paddling off the previous day. If, as feared, it was his, it could mean he had been left at the mercy of the sea and the notoriously strong tidal currents that could quickly have dragged him out towards the shipping lanes.

It wasn't until four days after John's disappearance, on Monday morning, 25 March, that coastguards terminated the search-and-rescue operation, admitting that the chances of the missing man being found alive had passed and he was presumed drowned at sea. Some of the lifeboat volunteers, who had by then spent eighty-five hours searching for him, spoke grimly among themselves that the next time anyone would likely see him was when his body was washed ashore.

For others, though, the niggling doubts had always remained. And now, learning of Darwin's reappearance, it all comes flooding back to Waugh.

'Finding the paddle was fishy, wasn't it?' he says. 'It was the cat among the pigeons for us. We reckoned it to be a place where a person, or an object, would never get washed up, especially the paddle without the canoe. A million to one chance; it just didn't add up at all. That's when we thought there may be a bit more to this disappearance.

'When I saw on the morning news that he had turned up, my first thought was good, that it was a life saved for us. It's not someone missing.

'Then it was . . . yeeaaahh, but bit of a sod like.

'But we in the lifeboat fraternity tend not to criticise people, because you never want to deter someone from calling the lifeboat out of fear of being criticised later.

'When something like this happens, thirty guys will always say,

"Told you so, told you so." But at the time you treat it like any other job, no matter what you're thinking.'

John's ninety-year-old father, Ronnie, is contacted by journalists at his home in the former pit village of Blackhall Colliery, six miles north of Hartlepool, in County Durham, and makes his feelings very clear. The pair had fallen out years ago, though no one was ever quite sure why.

'I always said to the police that there might be more to this than it appeared at first,' he says. 'When his canoe was found but he wasn't, it didn't seem right.

'He had ideas above his station. He had big dreams and ambitions, and I sometimes think he was in too much of a hurry to make money.'

John's aunt Margaret Burns, eighty, is even more forthright.

'Most of the family believe that the trauma of nearly drowning was enough to make him lose his memory, but I'm not so sure,' she says. 'I'm a cynic. To be honest, I don't believe he ever got his feet wet.'

Someone else was in for an almighty shock that morning.

'FUCKKK my old boots!'

Although he is the only one in the car, John Duffield begins talking, almost shouting, out loud. His mind is racing so fast he only narrowly avoids swerving off the road. *For Christ's sake man, get a grip*, he tells himself.

The man who bought No. 3 The Cliff from Anne Darwin four months earlier is driving to work along the A19 towards Middlesbrough when he hears a news flash on BBC Radio Five Live about a canoeist from the north-east who has suddenly turned up after being missing for five years. Hardly believing what he is hearing, he pulls over to the hard shoulder and calls his girlfriend to see if she has heard the news. He knows it could only be one man: John Darwin.

When he arrives at work he starts telling everyone about the guy who used to live in his house coming back from the dead. A million things are racing through his mind. He is struggling to take it all in. He even wonders whether Darwin might have some claim on his house. His colleagues think it's hilarious and are killing themselves laughing and cracking jokes about him being left up shit creek without a paddle. But Duffield isn't sure it's quite that funny. He can think of nothing else for the remainder of the day. He's in total panic.

Early the following morning, as he's getting ready for work, he starts receiving phone calls from reporters. And when he opens his front door there is a barrage of photographers and TV satellite vans already parked outside on the gravel driveway. The enormity of the story starts to dawn on him. He steps back inside to collect his thoughts.

Then he remembers there's a pile of unopened mail for Mrs Darwin. He hadn't been given a forwarding address, nor had his estate agent, so he had just stuck the post away in a drawer. There's a letter from the Banco Nacional de Panamá and another from the HSBC, also in Panama. There is a letter that he had inadvertently opened; a shipping note giving a residential address for Mrs Darwin in Panama City.

Best ring the Bobbies he thinks. He calls and mentions that among the letters are some from banks and relocation companies in Panama. Within minutes several police cars pull into his drive like something out of *The Sweeney*. Among the mail are letters addressed to a Mr John Jones. No one is quite sure who he is.

'I just stuck them away thinking sooner or later she would be in touch,' Duffield tells detectives.

He was amazed how much stuff she had left behind.

'There was a globe with white pins stuck in it, one showing Canada and the other Panama, although at the time I didn't give it a second thought,' he says.

'I spotted a couple of teach-yourself-Spanish books lying on a desk and remember thinking to myself that perhaps she was emigrating to Spain.'

There were three double beds, five singles, lots of bedside tables, two television sets and two computers. Also, a multi-gym in the cellar and, in the downstairs front room, a dining table, wall unit and three-piece leather suite with a matching footstool. In the kitchen, she'd left a washing machine, tumble drier, a chest fridge and even a soda syphon, a relic from the 1970s.

'I had to get three skips to get rid of all the junk,' he says.

Cleveland Police issue a bland statement. Suspicions are running high but there's still a lot of work to do here.

'Mr Darwin is fit and well and relatives have been informed of his whereabouts,' says the statement. 'It is not known at this time where he has spent the last five and a half years.'

The police detail a short recap of his disappearance, saying the broken-up remains of Mr Darwin's canoe were washed ashore at Blue Lagoon Sands at the mouth of the River Tees six weeks after he vanished.

Searchers found no trace of the man, who was fifty-one and worked at Holme House prison in Stockton.

He was missing, presumed dead.

Now, suddenly, here he is again. And Anne, his wife of thirty-three years, has recently sold her home to start a new life in Panama. *Panama!* A middle-aged woman from Seaton Carew selling up and starting a new life on the other side of the world is not normal in anyone's book. Fishy, to use Gary Waugh's words, doesn't even go there.

Detectives are already checking if she applied for life insurance payouts after her husband's disappearance. Which of course she would be perfectly entitled to . . . providing he was dead.

She had. With the Norwich Union and American International Group (AIG).

Things are getting interesting.

5

'I Suppose You'd Better Come In'

'**M**ORNING MATE, IT'S Gerry.'

It's just before 5 a.m. and I recognise the distinctive voice of Gerry Hunt, the *Daily Mail*'s respected and long-standing Foreign Editor. It's 10 a.m. in London and, in truth, he's already tried a couple of other journalists living in the United States but can't raise them. It's why I always sleep with my phone on.

'Morning Gerry, what's up?'

'Sorry, I know it's early David, but are you free to go to Panama for us? We'll need a snapper too.'

'Sure,' I say, coming around from my slumber at my home in Coral Gables, a leafy residential suburb on the outskirts of Miami.

'Panama Beach on the Florida Panhandle?'

'No,' Gerry responds. 'Panama, Central America.'

My ears prick up.

'Of course. What's going on?'

Gerry quickly fills me in on what is so far known about the remarkable story making the morning headlines. Apparently, this 'Canoe Man' chap John Darwin has suddenly turned up five years after being reported missing, presumed dead, and everyone is chasing the story. Finding his wife Anne is the prime objective. She has only recently emigrated from her home in the north-east of England. It's all very mysterious.

Gerry explains that details are sketchy at best and, despite reports that she's been seen in places as far afield as Australia, Barbados and Jamaica, he's pretty sure from the *Mail*'s sources that Panama is the right location. The Foreign Desk secretary has already checked and found there's an American Airlines flight leaving Miami International Airport, twenty minutes from my home, at 11.15 a.m., giving me plenty of time to pack a bag and get to the airport.

'All good – leave it with me Gerry,' I respond.

Gerry cups his phone as he shouts over to the picture desk. 'David Leigh's going to Panama for us and has got a photographer who can go with him. Yep, . . . will be there early evening.'

Then back to me.

'Right, good stuff, keep in touch young man. The boss really loves this story – I'm sure you'll crack it for us!'

The boss is Paul Dacre, Editor-in-Chief of Associated Newspapers, publisher of the *Daily Mail*, the *Mail on Sunday*, the *Metro* and the *Mail Online* website. Love him or hate him, and there's plenty on either side of the divide, he is a brilliant no-nonsense journalist respected and feared in equal measures by everyone from government ministers to those working under him. And what Mr Dacre wants, he expects to get.

Just that little bit of extra pressure. Thanks Gerry.

I call Steve Dennett, the photographer who three years earlier had moved to Miami with me to open up a Florida bureau for an international news and photographic agency, Splash News & Pictures.

'Morning Steven,' I say as I wake him at his South Beach condo.

Tall and lean and a dead ringer for footballer Gareth Bale, Steve is twenty-seven (sixteen years my junior) and originally from Burgess Hill, West Sussex, where he cut his teeth working as a news photographer for a picture agency in Brighton. By complete coincidence, fifteen years earlier I had worked with his reporter dad Phil on the *Brighton Evening Argus*, where I'd spent three years before heading to town to try my luck in Fleet Street. Steve wanted to see the world so applied for the job in Miami: the bright lights of star-studded South Beach are not a bad life for a young British photographer wanting to make a name for himself.

'Get your bags packed – we're off to Panama. The Central American one. Flight's at 11.15. See you at the airport.'

It's common practice for reporters working on big news stories to travel with a photographer. Only two things matter when it comes to your travel companion; that they're good at their job and fun to work with. Steve ticked both boxes.

I had lived in Miami since bailing out of Fleet Street and moving to the Florida sunshine with my wife and two young daughters after fifteen years working relentless hours on the news desks of national papers. I still missed the camaraderie and the electrifying buzz of a frantic news room when a big story broke. Working with amazing teams of journalists during both Gulf Wars, the 9/11 terrorist atrocities, the death of Princess Diana and every other major news story that happened during that period were experiences of a lifetime. As was being blown out of my chair as I sat at my desk on the twenty-second floor of the *Daily Mirror*'s Canary Wharf offices when the IRA decided to bomb London's Docklands in 1996.

Living in the Sunshine State had its perks. It was the perfect base for jobs in the Caribbean and Central and South America. I'd travelled extensively, covering stories on most of the islands, and been sent on assignments in Colombia, Argentina, Chile, Mexico and Costa Rica. But never Panama. It sounded interesting, maybe slightly mysterious. Visiting new countries is always an adventure. And this story felt like it was going to be a fascinating one to work on. There was just the small matter of keeping Gerry and his very demanding boss happy.

I got up, made a cuppa, then went online to read up on the story making the morning headlines before calling a cab to the airport. Miami is just a two-hour, fifty-minute flight from Tocumen International Airport, fifteen miles outside the capital, Panama City, but I didn't have an awful lot to go on in my quest to find a woman in a country covering 29,157 square miles, roughly the size of Scotland, and home to four million people. I hooked up with Steve at the airport and we spent much of the flight pondering what to do when we arrived, hopeful that more information would come to light while we were in the air. Unfortunately, that was not to be the case.

'Anne Darwin' and 'Panama' was literally all we had to go on.

Where the hell did we start?

***

Tocumen airport, like many of its Central and South American counterparts, is noisy and chaotic and we are in a seemingly never-ending, snaking queue to get through immigration when Brian Peters* from the *Mail*'s night Foreign Desk, calls my mobile.

---

* Name changed.

'Have you found her yet?' he asks, deadpan, and although I'm not entirely sure, I hope he's joking.

'Err, no Brian, I haven't,' I respond, trying not to sound too indignant.

'I was hoping you were going to have some more info for us.

'We've only just landed and Panama is quite a large country. Wouldn't hold your breath if I were you. I haven't exactly got much to go on.'

And that was a massive understatement.

'Fucking idiot!' I say to Steve as I end the call. 'Wanted to know if we'd found her yet!'

Steve rolls his eyes.

In the back of my mind I keep thinking that surely if this woman was starting a new life in a foreign country she would be living in an attractive little coastal town. Not here in the heart of the capital city. And if her husband has just turned up after more than five years, surely she would already be on a flight home to be joyfully reunited with him? Regardless, we had to press on. Maybe there'd be a neighbour who might know something and could at least give us a bit of a story.

We discuss staying put and staking out likely flights to the UK. We are aware that Anne Darwin could easily already be somewhere over the Atlantic, but if she hasn't yet left, it's probable she would have to pass through Panama's only international airport. We soon discover, though, that there are no direct flights to the UK, and to make matters even more difficult, there are many different possible routes home to England. What's more, we don't have a clue what Mrs Darwin looks like.

We decide to get a rental car and head towards the city centre. With zero information to go on, our friend Google provides us with a name and address of a British pub, The Londoner, in the heart of Panama City. A massive long shot, of course, but we figure it is bound to have ex-pat Brits as patrons and someone just *might* have heard of Anne Darwin. Bars are usually a mine of information and often a good starting point for journalists working overseas, especially when trying to find the proverbial needle in a haystack. A nice cold pint wasn't a bad prospect either.

It's already dark, lightly spitting with rain, and the traffic-choked roads, with vehicles seemingly coming at us from all angles, are chaotic to say the least. Like *The Wacky Races* on steroids. It's also horribly hot and sticky, there's no satellite navigation, and the large-scale map provided by the rental company is proving worse than useless. Even trying to work out which way we're headed is a nightmare. Horns blare as we slow down, then miss a succession of turns. Steve turns towards me and grins inanely at the bedlam we're adding to. He's not one to get easily flustered; his unflappability helped make him the great photographer he is.

'Glad you find this funny,' I say, glancing back at the map.

'You do realise we're fucking lost?'

There's another issue. All the road signs are in Spanish and the rain has worsened into what feels like a tropical storm. With the wipers going at full pelt it's hard to make out anything. My mobile rings and, seeing it's an overseas call, I groan and ready myself to tell the *Mail* that, no, I still haven't found Mrs f'ing Darwin. But it's not who I had been expecting.

'Hello maaaate. Got someone in Panama?'

The call is from my old friend Anthony Harwood, News Editor of the *Daily Mirror* in London. He uses his customary elongated greeting.

'Might have,' I respond somewhat guardedly.

'What's up?'

Of course, I know full well the entire British media is now frantically trying to track down the wife of the canoeist who has mysteriously come back from the dead sporting a suspiciously golden tan and claiming a bad dose of amnesia. But I'm working for a rival newspaper. And good friends or not, British tabloids have always been fiercely competitive when it comes to securing an exclusive story. Right now, all everyone wants is a talk with Anne Darwin.

I explain that I'm already in Panama but on assignment for the *Daily Mail*, and I joke that he'd better be quick as I'm just about to do the full sit-down interview with Mrs Darwin.

'So you've got her address?' says Harwood – and I immediately sense the man from the *Mirror* might well have the information I am so desperately looking for.

'Well, actually no,' I respond. 'Have you?'

'Yep,' says Harwood. 'Want it?'

'Err, yes please,' I answer.

My heart skips a beat. The beads of sweat on my forehead are suddenly not all down to the humidity.

'That would be quite helpful,' I add, trying to keep my excitement under control.

Harwood continues: 'We have it and so does the *Sun*, and they've got a reporter on a flight from New York that's due to arrive in about three hours.'

I swallow hard. Three hours plus the snaking queue at immigration. Maybe that's all the head start I'll need? Suddenly I can taste the scoop.

'We're told there are several journos from other papers, the *Express*, *The Times*, onboard as well. My problem is that I haven't even got anyone in the air yet. How do we work this one out?'

We went back years – Harwood having been my deputy when I was News Editor at the *Mirror* six years earlier. We are good mates and although now working for rival newspapers, I know the only sensible option is to try and strike a deal with him quickly or risk being beaten to Mrs Darwin's doorstep. The *Mail* had been ahead of the game in getting me to Panama, but the *Mirror* has the crucial information. If another reporter beats me to her door, regardless of the lack of information, the *Mail* will be seriously pissed off.

'Tell you what,' I say, 'give me the address and I give you my word that if anything comes of it, I'll square it with the *Mail* that you both get whatever I get.'

'Okay, you're on,' says Harwood and a gentleman's agreement is struck. Trust goes a long way in this business.

Steve senses my excitement and momentarily takes his eyes off the road. 'Well?'

I bring him up to speed. He grins, again.

'That's handy.'

He's never one to overstate things.

A few minutes later Harwood calls back, explaining that Jeremy Armstrong, his paper's north-east correspondent and another long-time friend and colleague, had come up with the address '4-B PH Riazor', in an area called El Dorado.

Nice one Jezza!

I hastily check my, until then, useless map and to my amazement discover we are only about fifteen minutes away from the part of town that I seem to remember shares its name with a doomed 1990s BBC soap opera. My luck has changed beyond my wildest expectations. Now all I have to do is find the address.

Please make this easy.

But, of course, it isn't. Riazor is simply the name of a building and there's no street name. It's incredibly frustrating. So near and yet so far. After circling aimlessly for fifteen minutes we pull up behind a stationary taxi. I jump out and show the driver the name Riazor on my phone. He smiles and gives me the thumbs-up. I pull out some dollars.

'*Si señor!*' and he indicates for me to follow. Within a few minutes we pull up outside an anonymous four-storey stone building set back from the road on a street called Calle Archangel. If I ever needed to call my very own archangel, this is it.

I push the outside buzzer for 4-B hoping for the best but, predictably, there is no response. After half a dozen more attempts are greeted with a deafening silence, I can't help thinking that my initial reaction that Mrs Darwin is already long gone must be right. What a fucker.

It's just gone 8 p.m., pitch black and there is no one about. It looks pretty hopeless. Then, through the glass front doors, we spot a smart, professional-looking woman coming out of the lift inside the building carrying an umbrella. We stride over to catch her attention by knocking on the entrance door, presuming she must be a resident. The woman, who looks to be in her mid-thirties, comes over but doesn't speak a word of English.

Despite having spent three years living in Miami, a city where well over half the population is Hispanic, neither Steve nor I had quite got around to mastering the lingo. Typical lazy Brits. Let everyone speak our language.

We needed help: my hands and eyes plead with the woman to stay put and I quickly call my Spanish-speaking colleague, Matheus Sanchez, in Miami. I ask him to see what he can find out and thrust the mobile into the confused woman's hand. I feel my hopes rising as she talks animatedly, smiles, talks some more, then, with another huge smile that displays her perfect white teeth, passes the phone back to me.

'You old charmer,' I say to Mat and eagerly ask what he has found out.

'Bugger all!' is the response.

'Seriously?' I ask, having just witnessed the most excitable 'I know nothing' conversation imaginable.

'She hasn't got a clue. Says they're mainly Colombians living there and she doesn't know of a British woman. She's a Colombian lawyer.'

Damn. But having now inched my way a few steps inside the foyer, I can see over the woman's shoulder what looks suspiciously like a list of residents pinned to the wall under a glass frame. I need to check it out and hastily walk over. And there, listed in capital letters as the occupant of 4-B, is the name I am looking for: ANNE DARWIN. Bingo!

'*Gracias, gracias,*' I exude, draining the remainder of my Spanish vocabulary as Steve and I wave 'thanks' at the woman who has unwittingly let us into her apartment complex and is now standing staring at us. *Hope she doesn't call security.* We bound up three flights of stairs and hammer on what we believe to be Mrs Darwin's door. There are no numbers.

Our joy as it opens is short-lived as we are greeted by what we can only assume to be another Colombian, a youngish guy wearing blue-and-white-striped pyjama bottoms and a white vest. He looks blankly at me as I fire off a succession of questions. *I really must get to those Spanish lessons.* But on hearing the words 'English woman', something clicks and the man smiles, excitedly repeating the word 'Engleesh, Engleesh', and points up the stairs to the next floor.

We race upstairs. There are four doors. The one in the right-hand corner helpfully does have a number: 4-B. I knock several times: nothing. Crouching down on all fours, I can see from the slight gap under the door that the apartment appears to be in total darkness. I knock again: nothing.

'Mrs Darwin, are you there?'

I knock again and again and again, with slightly more force each time. There is obviously no one there.

'Shit,' I say out loud. 'I bet she's long gone.'

'Not looking good, David,' says Steve.

Thanks mate!

But we have nowhere else to go and it is way too early to give up, so we stand there, knocking every few minutes, with me repeatedly asking, 'Mrs Darwin, are you there? I've come with news about your husband.'

None of the neighbours are answering their doors, although we sense people are home in at least two of the other apartments on the floor. They must be wondering what on earth is going on and obviously have decided that opening their doors to find out isn't a good option; parts of Panama did have a fairly lawless reputation. I try not to think about it.

For forty minutes I knock repeatedly, calling her name as I stand there, all hope of anyone being in disappearing with each rap of my knuckles. I turn, rest my back against the heavy white-painted wooden door, look up at the ceiling and sigh. And then, a faint voice. I jump to attention and turn to the door.

'What do you want?'

'Jeez!' I mouth to Steve, heart racing. 'She's in there.'

'I've come about your husband, John. I thought you'd be relieved that he's turned up safe and well in England? Presumably you know about it?'

There is no response. It doesn't take Einstein to work out that there is something incredibly strange about a woman who could well be Mrs Darwin still being in Panama while the rest of her family celebrate the astonishing return of her husband in the UK.

'Aren't you pleased your husband is alive and well?' I ask.

We strike up a strained conversation, but her voice is so soft it's difficult to make out exactly what she is saying.

'Perhaps I can help you in some way?' I say.

'You can't, nobody can,' she says, which is a weird response to say the least.

There seems to be a frightened desperation in her voice. All incredibly strange. I just have to persuade her to open that door. She has obviously heard me talking to someone, but through the spyhole she can only see me. She asks who's with me.

'It's my photographer, Steve,' I tell her. 'He can go if you want?'

She doesn't want any pictures, so I nod to my colleague to disappear and tell the woman who I am now confident to be Mrs Darwin that if she looks out of her window she will see Steve getting into our rental car parked across the road.

Another brief silence. I'm getting close, but I'm not there yet. I glance at my watch. There's still time. My rival journalists won't land for another ninety minutes. Just a few words from Mrs Darwin will give me a great scoop, possibly a front-page story. Mr Dacre will be happy.

But I want more than that. I want the entire story. That's why reporters do what we do. Best not be greedy: one step at a time. *Come on Mrs Darwin, . . . open that freaking door.*

'How do I even know who you are?' she asks.

I pull out my press card from my wallet and slide it under the door. I tell her who I am, how I have been sent by the *Daily Mail* in London from my home in Miami, even about my wife Sue and two young daughters, Georgia and Charlie, as I try desperately to gain enough trust for her to open that door.

Again, silence.

Then finally, I hear the key-chain sliding off the latch and slowly the door starts to open. I take a step backwards, a little nervously, not quite sure whether I am about to be greeted by a crazy woman with a gun in her hand (it is Panama after all), but standing there is a small, bony, woman, with silvery-white hair, who introduces herself in an unmistakable north-east accent as 'Anne'.

'I suppose you'd better come in,' she says.

6

'Let's Get as Far Away From Here as We Can'

THE APARTMENT IS small, clutter-free and spotless, with two white leather armchairs at either end of a matching sofa, surrounding a glass-topped coffee table. There are several large and not overly attractive prints of the Panamanian countryside adorning the walls. The floor is white tiled and cold, and the whole apartment has an empty, clinical, unlived-in feeling. I am obviously intrigued to have a look around, but know a guided tour isn't really on the cards.

'You must be incredibly relieved about your husband?' I ask, as Mrs Darwin, who insists I call her Anne, motions for me to sit down opposite her, having somewhat reluctantly invited me into her apartment.

But she *has* let me in and that is intriguing in itself. I'm over the first hurdle.

'Of course I am, yes,' she responds, not sounding altogether convincing.

'But I have to ask,' I continue, 'lots of people are wondering why on earth you haven't dashed back home to see him?'

There is a brief pause and Anne looks down at her hands, carefully considering her answer.

'I am going back, but there are things here I have to sort out first,' she finally responds.

Come on Anne, I think to myself, this isn't making much sense. What sort of 'things' could be more important than being reunited with your husband? But I have to tread carefully. This woman is incredibly flustered – that strange 'no one can help me' line – and she later admits that having a reporter turn up on her doorstep caught her totally off-guard. At this stage I wasn't sure what contact she'd had with John and their sons. She tells me a friend back home told her that Sky News and the BBC were already reporting she was in

Panama, but she is astonished anyone has been able to find her quite so quickly. *She's not the only one.*

She continues to speak, slowly and thoughtfully, saying she has been trying to contact her local lawyer because there is paperwork she needs to sign regarding her visa application to stay in Panama and, in two days' time, her lifetime's belongings are due to arrive on a cargo ship from the UK. She has to be at the port in Colon to personally sign for her 20-foot container. Both quite possibly true, but there is still something very odd here.

She offers me a drink and, parched from standing in a stifling corridor with no air-conditioning for so long, I readily accept a cold glass of water. Although intensely guarded, she seems in no hurry to kick me out and, if anything, appears pleased to be able to establish what is being reported about her husband's sudden – and remarkable – reappearance.

The more we talk, the more she starts to relax and open up. I tell her what I know, how everyone is amazed by the story and desperate to hear her reaction. I keep it very upbeat. It's important to try and gain a bit of trust before asking too many probing questions.

'Yes, I can understand why everyone could be so curious,' she says.

'I'm finding it pretty hard to take in myself.'

As well as trying to get her reaction to the news, I am acutely aware that within an hour or two, Anne will be besieged by other British reporters and TV crews, desperate, like me, for an interview. Harwood from the *Mirror* told me about the journalists on a flight from New York, but for all I know others might already be on the ground. It's entirely possible they already have Anne's address. If anyone turns up, my chances of a great exclusive are gone. It's a race against time. But I have to stay calm. Somehow I have to get Anne out of her apartment and away from the area.

Trying to make it sound as natural as possible, I suggest that while she works out what to do next, she might perhaps be better off moving to a hotel where she won't be found or bothered. I tell her, truthfully, that journalists will soon be camped outside around the clock, making life pretty miserable for her. She won't be able to go anywhere or do anything without being followed and having cameras watch her every move. That sort of pressure is not easy to deal with and I'm not sure Anne could cope.

'I promise you I'll look after you and keep those nasty journalists away,' I say with a smile, well aware we both know I am one of the very people I am promising to protect her from.

I'm hoping a smile and a little humour will go a long way. The clock is ticking. I need to uncover the truth about John Darwin's remarkable reappearance – and get her the hell out of there.

Anne says she is going to call a relative in England to seek their advice, and I feel my hopes of persuading her to come with me slipping away. Naturally, I try to talk her into making the call later, but she is adamant and there is nothing more I can do.

She enters her bedroom, closing the door behind her, and I hear her talking on the phone for about ten to fifteen minutes. Each passing minute brings the chasing pack closer. I force my brain to think of something else, but it's not easy. I sit there, looking around the spartanly furnished two-bedroom apartment, wondering what a middle-aged British housewife is really doing living here in a drab city suburb of Panama, on the other side of the world to her family and friends.

Lots of things don't make sense. But of two things I am already quite sure: Anne Darwin is alone and very, very nervous. I am convinced any minute the door will open and she will politely ask me to leave, quashing all hopes of getting the kind of scoop all journalists spend their lives dreaming about. I have a story, but not much of one, and crucially I don't yet have a photograph of her. There is so much more I want.

The door finally opens and I am staggered to see Anne standing there clutching a small black suitcase.

'Are we going?' I ask, knowing she must have seen the look of amazement on my face.

'I've just got to get a few things together and I'll be ready,' she says.
Bloody hell.

My brain kicks into gear, years of experience coming to the fore; I need to get her as far away from here as possible. I really did not expect this. I text Steve telling him to drive the car up to the front door of the apartment block, as we are coming out in a couple of minutes. He later admits he had assumed I was joking about Anne leaving with us.

'How the hell did you manage that?' he asked.

'Not really sure,' I answered honestly. 'I'm as amazed as you.'

I have no idea why Anne agreed to leave with us. It's not unusual for what journalists call 'buy ups' – someone paid for their exclusive story – to be spirited away and put up in a hotel to keep them away from rivals. But despite a number of reports in broadsheet newspapers suggesting I had paid Anne thousands of pounds to tell her story, she neither once asked for or was offered a penny. Money wasn't her motivation. I assume she was terrified at the prospect of lots of journalists on her doorstep. Maybe my honesty played a part. I didn't hide the fact that the press pack was charging towards Panama, and she was aware from what her friend had told her that the news channels knew where she was.

Whatever the reason, I am not complaining.

We leave the apartment, me carrying Anne's small suitcase while she tightly clutches a black leather document folder, as if guarding it with her life. We take the lift to the ground floor and as I open the back door of the small black Seat Ibiza rental for Anne, I feel a huge sense of relief. Incredibly, I have my catch and, from a journalist's point of view, a prized catch it is at that.

Two important things got me here: sleeping with my phone on and the dogged persistence that had been drummed into me by a number of great mentors, especially my reporter dad, Don, in whose journalistic footprints I had followed. Three if you count Archangel.

It's dark and the roads are still choked with traffic as we drive to the nearby El Panama Hotel, which Steve and I had checked into and dumped our bags in a few hours earlier. While Steve sits in the car with Anne, I dash up to our room, grab our luggage and pay the bill for a night we will never enjoy.

'Where to?' says Steve.

'No idea,' I reply. 'Just drive. Let's just get as far away from here as we can.'

I know rival journalists will be hot on our heels, so getting as far away from Anne's home is my most pressing objective. The adrenalin always kicks in when the pack is in pursuit.

Anne seems anxious to assist and says she vaguely recognises one of the main roads out of town. With no better plan of our own, we take that and head off into the unknown. Using her *very* limited Spanish, Anne asks for directions at the first toll booth we arrive at, but the response is a completely incomprehensible series of rapid gestures and instructions, so we all smile politely – and cluelessly drive on into the night. *It was some years before I finally saw sense and took Spanish lessons.*

It's nearly 2 a.m. and we are still on the road. Everyone is shattered and what had earlier been a busy dual carriageway is now a totally deserted one-track road. We spot what looks like a backpackers' hostel, brightly lit and welcoming, on the other side of the road and decide to pull over and seek a bed for the night. I ring the bell and eventually a sleepy receptionist, who we have obviously woken, opens the door.

'*Dos habitaciones, por favor,*' I say, holding up two fingers in case she hasn't grasped what I'm asking.

She nods and leads us up a short flight of marble-tiled stairs to what resembles a school dormitory. It may well have been that Anne was expecting a night at the Ritz or another luxury hotel when she accepted my offer of a bed for the night, but what she got was a hostel costing, in total, about £12.50 for both rooms, one for her and one for me and Steve. Nothing like living the high life.

The rooms are basic but clean and the beds rock solid: like lying on concrete blocks. Using my Blackberry, which I was amazed to find had a signal out there in the middle of nowhere, I file off quick emails to both the *Daily Mirror* and *Mail*, telling them the score; we have Mrs Darwin, we have escaped the 'pack', and things are actually looking pretty good. I knew they would be ecstatic.

I'm exhausted and fall asleep virtually as soon as hitting the pillow. But I wake early, just a few hours later, a little panicked that Anne may not still be there. Hardly surprisingly, she had been in a slightly agitated state when we left her, and Steve says he hopes she hasn't done anything stupid, which sends a shiver down my spine. I go out into the corridor, gently tap on her door and, needless to say, am hugely relieved to hear her voice, saying she is already up and will be ready to go in about fifteen minutes.

So far, so good. Now all we need is to get Anne to open up a little, expand on what she really knows about her husband's reappearance and agree to have her photograph taken (the papers are desperate for pictures to see what she looks like) and we are in business. It's just a matter of treading ever so gently and the papers will have the story they crave.

It's a warm, sunny morning, with cloudless blue skies as we set off, heading north-west away from the hostel and further still from Panama City, on the Inter-American Highway. The landscape is breathtaking, with wide-open plains disappearing into the distance with a mountainous backdrop. It is still early and conversation is sparse. Anne sits in silence, blankly gazing out of the window and seemingly lost in thought – no doubt wondering, among other things, what on earth she has got herself into – as we speed along. No one has any real idea where or in what direction we are even going, as overnight we had somehow managed to lose our pathetic map.

'Just keep driving,' I tell Steve; it's becoming a familiar instruction.

After about an hour on the road and conscious that deadlines are approaching for the papers in England, with the five-hour time difference, we pull up at the first decent-looking hotel we come across, the Hotel Coronado and Beach Resort, just outside the small town of La Chorrera, sixty miles from Panama City.

We wanted to put some distance between ourselves and our journalistic rivals in the capital, but know time is of the essence as we have a story to file that will almost certainly be on the front pages of the following day's papers. It's a delicate balancing act between trying to get as much information as we can from Anne, as quickly as possible, but without losing the trust we are starting to gain. I desperately need more information but am anxious not to do or say anything that will blow the whole thing.

I leave the others in the car and walk over to the reception lobby to check on availability. Fortunately, it seems the hotel is virtually empty. I book two rooms and, mindful that Fleet Street's finest will be desperately trying to find us, make up an excuse about why we have to check in using false names – names that are different to those on our requested passports. I know journalists from other newspapers will be calling all the hotels in the area trying to track us down by asking if they have guests named Darwin, Leigh or Dennett, and

– other than interviewing Anne – staying one step ahead of my cunning colleagues is my most immediate concern. *Two days later an eagle-eyed rival located where we were staying by matching a photograph of the wicker chair Anne was using on the terrace to one on the hotel's website. Fortunately, by then we had moved on, but it highlighted the ingenuity we were up against.*

The hotel is quiet, save for a few American holidaymakers, and Anne says little as she picks at a fruit plate and sips a cup of strong local coffee over breakfast. I explain that we really need to have a brief chat and take a few photographs so everyone back home can see she is fine and looking forward to being reunited with her long-lost husband. Anne nods and says okay, but first wants to freshen up and change out of her shorts and t-shirt into something a little less casual.

We are now tantalisingly close to securing the interview, but, as can so often happen, she begins to have last-minute nerves and asks how she can be sure we will accurately report what she tells us. Having had their appetites whetted by my overnight email, the *Mirror* and the *Mail* are, by this time, chomping at the bit for 'copy' and there is no way I can afford to slip up now. I assure Anne I will run through exactly what I've written before hitting the send button. Not giving her full copy approval, simply offering to let her see the quotes that will be attributed to her in my article.

The reassurance seems to steady her nerves and she says she is ready to proceed.

7

'I Can't Make Any Sense of it All'

STEVE FINISHES HIS coffee and wanders outside. He strolls around the hotel terrace checking the light and backdrop. He wants somewhere that will portray a suitable tropical vibe. The story will be huge and he doesn't want his reputation damaged by producing photographs of Anne squinting, cast in shadow or with a plant 'growing' out of her head.

He locates a good spot, but as Anne sits in the aforementioned wicker chair to have her picture taken, Steve quickly discovers we have a problem. As soon as she's in the sun the lenses of her reactor-light glasses darken. Shades are a complete no-no for portrait photographs. People want to see the subject's eyes. Anne moves into the shade and they gradually clear again. She has an idea. She puts the glasses in her pocket, sits down, puts them back on and Steve quickly fires off as many frames as possible before they darken again. We're all laughing at the dilemma. We repeat the routine in several different locations, as papers always want variety: head shots, full-length, half-length, standing, seated – the design of the page will dictate how the pictures will be used.

With the photographs taken care of, Anne, wearing a blue-patterned top, khaki trousers and brown sandals, says she's ready for the interview. The tape recorder is on the table as back-up and my pen poised to take shorthand notes of the interview.

Anne starts to open up about her remarkable – and not altogether believable – story.

'You've got to understand, this is all so amazing and hard for me to take in,' she says. 'This is the moment I always prayed for.'

Really, well why haven't you dashed home to be with your husband then? I'll sit on that for a minute.

Anne says the timing of her husband's reappearance is incredible. She had only recently moved to Panama after years of agonising about

43

how best to pick up the pieces of her life. Now, just as she is starting out afresh, her whole world has again been turned upside down and she is struggling to take everything in.

'But it is the most wonderful news, it really is,' she says, labouring the point like an amateur thespian overplaying Miss Marple.

I ask about the moment she discovered her husband was still alive and how she had felt. She tells me how Mark had called three days earlier, Saturday afternoon, to break the astonishing news.

'I had been out shopping and on the way home had posted my Christmas cards,' she recalls.

'Late afternoon I got a call from Mark. It was getting late in England and at first I thought something terrible must have happened. He explained things, as best he could, and then he put John on the phone.

'He sounded a bit strange; there was something a bit different about his voice. But there I was, speaking to my husband.

'It was the day I had always dreamed about but never really believed would happen.'

She said John claimed to remember absolutely nothing about the last few years and had no idea where he had been or where he had been living. After he'd hung up, she was left in a complete daze and lay awake all night wondering whether it was all a crazy dream. It was so surreal.

Anne falls quiet. Steve is already back in the hotel room editing his photographs, so it's just the two of us sitting there in the tropical heat, an overhead five-pronged rattan fan offering some relief from the intense humidity. I'm thinking about Anne's words and her demeanour. There is little or no emotion. Everything is so matter-of-fact. *And totally unbelievable.*

She says they had spoken again on each of the following two days, and the more they talked, the more normal his voice became.

'But what happened, I just don't know,' she says. 'I can't make any sense of it all. I know there must have been an accident that day he went out in the canoe and he must have hit his head or something. But I know there are so many unanswered questions. It is a complete mystery to me.'

I listen intently, taking down every word she utters. But now I need to starting pushing a little, getting to the crux of the story.

What's she hiding? Her words are too rehearsed. I apologise but say it's very difficult for me to comprehend why she hasn't caught the first flight home. Her response is that she has 'visa issues' to address, before repeating the line from the previous evening that her furniture and other belongings shipped from the UK are arriving the following week. Once that's sorted, she'll rush straight back into her husband's arms.

'I want to see John and my family and try and see if I can put the pieces of my life back together again,' she says.

Try? Is there someone else in the picture? Although Anne is opening up a little, her answers don't ring true. Nothing does. But now, having at least got a version of events that gives me a decent story to file, it's time to turn up the heat and put to her some accusations that everyone at home is asking. I know she's not going to like them.

Here goes. I ask outright if she knew all along that her husband had been alive.

'No, I did not,' she snaps, infuriated at the question. 'I'm as amazed as anyone.'

She obviously knew it was coming, but it's interesting that there's no composure or thought to her response, just anger that I had dared to suggest such a thing. I'm not done yet.

'People are already suggesting that John may have faked his death because of some financial problems, and even that you may have been in cahoots with him,' I continue.

Another flash of anger.

'People can think what they want, I know the truth,' she fires back. *I had no doubt about that. I just wasn't sure I was hearing it.*

Again, I ask if it was possible that her husband might have planned his disappearance, even if she hadn't known about it, but she regains her composure and shakes her head.

'No . . . John just wouldn't have done that,' she says. 'If there were problems, we talked about them.'

I ask if they had been in debt at the time of his disappearance, but Anne is having none of it, insisting that is nobody else's business. She does, however, admit to having received some money from life insurance policies paid out after a coroner had declared her husband dead the year after he vanished.

'Of course there is a possibility they may now have to be repaid,' she says, admitting that money has been playing on her mind. 'It is one of the many things I am struggling to come to terms with.'

'They [the insurance policies] were claimed in good faith when I believed I had lost my husband and now he has come back from the dead. If that happens, of course it won't be easy, but I'll deal with it.'

The phrase 'good faith' re-enforces my doubts about everything she says. It is already starting to sound like a criminal defence. Maybe she senses my scepticism.

'It is not the money I ever wanted – it was having my husband back,' she says. 'It took a long time for the insurance companies to pay me and I'm sure they'll be looking closely at the situation.'

I ask if she will be able to repay the money or if she has already spent it.

'My finances are no one's concerns,' Anne replies, irritated at my persistence. 'They're a private matter.'

Again, I apologise for having to ask such tough questions, but explain it is what everyone back home is asking.

'I can understand everyone wants to know,' she admits. 'Maybe all the speculation is to be expected. There was a lot of speculation after he disappeared. People speculated about our finances, all sorts of things, but that's all it was, speculation.'

I decide to move on and the conversation turns to Panama. Why, I ask, has she moved here? Without doubt a beautiful and exotic country, but so far away from loved ones. It's a curious choice in anyone's book.

'I'm sure it came as a surprise to many people that I decided to move here to Panama and start a new life for myself,' she responds. 'But I moved here for me, to try and start afresh. I came here two years ago for a holiday by myself, as I had always wanted to see the Panama Canal. It was breathtaking, and I fell in love with the country and its people straight away.'

You always wanted to see the Panama Canal? It may be an engineering marvel and one of the seven manmade wonders of the world, but it's not everyone's usual must-see destination. Perhaps she has a fascination with huge container ships or canal locks . . .

'I came back a couple of times after that and decided it was where I wanted to live,' she continues. 'I love the climate, everything about the place. I've been learning Spanish and starting my life again.'

But it's over eleven hours from your beloved family in the UK, Anne. Your parents, sons, siblings and friends. If you wanted a bit of sunshine, why not start life afresh in Spain or Portugal and be closer to all of them?

Anne says she now has to work out what the future holds. It's hard to know what she feels is more important: her new life or having her husband back.

'I will fly back and see John and hopefully he will be able to move back over here with me and we can start afresh,' she says. 'I really don't want to live in England any more. I don't like the cold, but whether John will want to come here remains to be seen.

'There are many, many things we have to talk about. I know it's not going to be easy.'

Over the next hour, Anne reminisces about her life and marriage to the boy she met on the school bus in their smoky pit village of Blackhall Rocks, six miles north of Hartlepool. The north-east was a tough industrial area where coal, ship-building and steel provided much of the employment.

'When he was young he loved the outdoors, splashing about in the waves and anything to do with boats,' she says.

That was when he first developed his love of canoeing.

At school, John's lack of height earned him the nickname 'Dinky', and with his stick-out ears she didn't initially find him attractive. But he was persistent. The nods at the school bus-stop morphed in later years into visits to the local sweetshop where she worked.

'He would come in and out of the shop and pass the time of day,' Anne recalls.

'He asked me out several times and each time I declined. It was pretty much John's nature – he was a persistent man. He could be very persuasive and charming, and eventually he wore me down and I said yes and we started seeing each other.'

John eventually became a maths, science and religious studies teacher at English Martyrs School in Leadgate, near Consett, County Durham, after studying in Manchester.

'I was twenty-one when he proposed and we married later that same year at St Joseph's Catholic Church in Blackhall, where we lived,' Anne says.

'It was a nice, small wedding, just family and friends. It was a lovely day.'

The date was 22 December 1973. Anne wore white lace with a veil and headdress and carried a bouquet of red roses.

'That was how it all started,' she says.

Steve comes back to check on our progress and to say his photographs are edited and ready to send. I ask Anne if she'd like to see them but she declines, saying she hates any pictures of herself. Steve has email addresses for the picture editors handling the story at the *Mirror* and *Mail*, and I say he might as well send them. We take a short break, ordering coffee and water. It's approaching 11 a.m. and the heat has intensified. Four p.m. in London – the papers will be getting anxious to see some copy. I have to crack on. The pressure to file is mounting.

'Tell me about the day of John's disappearance,' I say.

Anne spells out how her life had changed for ever on that fateful day, 21 March 2002.

She returned from work after stopping to pick up some shopping and immediately noticed John's car was on the drive. He should have been at work. But he wasn't at home and she picked up the phone and dialled 1471 to see if anyone had called. She recognised the last number received as that of HMP Holme House, where John worked as a prison officer.

She called the prison and asked to speak to her husband, but was told he hadn't reported for work. Panicked, she claims, she called 999. No mention of whether she tried calling his mobile.

'I told them John hadn't turned up for work and that wasn't at all like him,' she recalls.

When two police officers arrived at her house a short while later, she told them it was all a bit of a mystery and although she was trying to reassure herself everything would be fine, she was growing increasingly worried he might have had an accident.

She said at first, when she saw his car, she assumed that a work colleague must have passed by to give him a lift, as had happened once or twice in the past. She had been greeted at the door by their two Rottweilers, so assumed John couldn't be at home or the dogs would have been with him. Then she spotted his red canoe was missing from the hallway and assumed he had taken it out and perhaps got into some kind of difficulty.

It seemed to me to be a huge assumption.

A search-and-rescue operation had begun almost immediately. She had called her brother Michael, but decided against alerting the boys that night as she was sure John would turn up at any minute and she didn't want to unduly scare them.

But come morning, after what she described as a fraught and sleepless night, she was told by the police there was still no word of John or sightings of the canoe. She again called Michael and asked him to call Mark, who would be at work in London. Letting Anthony know was a different matter altogether. Her younger son was on holiday in Canada, visiting Niagara Falls, where he planned to ask his girlfriend Louise to marry him, and she couldn't contemplate how to break the news to him, ruining what was meant to be the happiest time of his life.

Mark had been at his desk when he took the call from his uncle Michael, informing him he had some very worrying news about his dad, who was missing. Michael, a former Met police officer who lived in Berkshire, told Mark what he knew and said if that he caught the Tube to Heathrow, he'd drive there, pick him up and they could travel north together. Struggling to take in what his uncle had told him, Mark rushed home, hurriedly packed a suitcase, then jumped on a Tube.

Anne continues: 'The media turned up outside my home and the search continued, but there was nothing for days, and then, weeks later, they found the canoe, which had been smashed to pieces.

'That was a devastating blow. I just believed there must have been an accident. Some people said the sea had been quite rough, although I'm aware other people said it was calm.

'It was difficult to do anything or get on with my life, as I was frantic with worry. Normal life just sort of stopped. They were very difficult times.'

I nodded. *Maybe the difficult times are just beginning?*

'Every day I'd pray for some news, but there was nothing. It was as if he had just disappeared off the face of the earth.

'About three months later, I decided to go back to work. That was very hard. The people I worked with had given me a tremendous amount of support and they were all very understanding. But there were days when I just couldn't cope and had to go home. I couldn't have got through without the support of my family and friends. Everyone was so kind.

'The hardest thing for me was just not knowing what had happened.'

The question of 'why Panama?' is perplexing. I again ask for an explanation. She reiterates that visiting the Panama Canal had been a lifelong dream and in 2006 she booked a trip and immediately fell in love with the country.

'I think my family was happy for me and happy that I was trying to get on and make a new life for myself,' she recalls.

'I guess some people were shocked when I decided to visit Panama by myself. I know it's not your everyday holiday destination, not the norm. But it was where I wanted to go, so I made the arrangements and did all the tourist things. I think I fell head over heels in love with the country straight away.'

Anne returned to windy Seaton Carew, but said she knew in her heart she needed to make some drastic changes to her life. Over the next eighteen months, she flew back to Panama for two more visits before taking the plunge and deciding to start her life afresh on the other side of the world. As you do . . .

'The place gave me such a buzz, I loved Panama City,' she continues.

'I found an apartment that I liked in a quiet part of town and took the decision to make it my new home.'

Quite a giant step, I think to myself. A fifty-something-year-old woman from the north-east of England upping sticks and moving to a part of the world where she doesn't know a soul and can't speak the language. I ask if there is someone new in her life, but she insists there could never be anyone to replace her husband.

About six weeks later, after selling up in England, she flew back to Central America to start her new life in the Panamanian sunshine. *Extraordinary.*

'I took some Spanish lessons at home and started trying to teach myself a bit, although there are lots of people here who speak English,' she says. 'I got such a buzz from being here. I loved walking down the street and into town. I never felt threatened. I felt in some way like I had been reborn.'

Conscious that time is ticking away and deadlines are fast approaching, I decide I have more than enough of a story to file. It's a long way short of what I really need, but it will suffice for now. I call the papers to give them a run-down on what I will be filing and about an hour later the papers have the copy.

On top of the story is a note marked 'strictly not for publication'. It reads: '*This is what Mrs Darwin is claiming – but she's obviously lying though her teeth.*'

Within an hour or two, early editions of the papers, with my story wiping out both front pages, and the copy carried over four pages inside, are being put to bed. Wednesday morning's *Mirror* carries the front-page headline in bold capital letters, SECRET LIFE OF MRS CANOE, while the *Mail*'s, again in capitals, is YES, I DID POCKET THE LIFE INSURANCE.

Both carry Steve's pictures of Mrs Darwin's smiling face behind only slightly tinted glasses.

But our job is far from done.

8

'Panama is My Home Now'

WHILE THE FOLLOWING day's papers are going to press with front-page headlines revealing Anne's reaction to her husband's dramatic return from the dead, it is still only lunchtime in Panama.

After the interview is over and Steve has put away his cameras, Anne is a lot more at ease. She seems pleased to have given her side of the story – and blissfully unaware that we haven't bought a word of it. She probably also thinks all 'the fuss', as she sees it, will now start to die down. It is obvious she has no real grasp of what a big deal the story has become or the headlines it is making at home in England. But if she thinks it is now about to go quietly away, she couldn't be more wrong. There is a voracious appetite for more.

I know she is lying but to what extent I'm not sure. The most important thing at this stage is not to appear too dubious or push her to the point she no longer trusts me. It's still early days and I feel the best way of getting to the truth is by gently chipping away. Twenty years as a journalist had taught me to trust my instinct and not rush things. I now had time on my side and nobody, including me, knew exactly where we were!

Anne is hungry and asks if we can get a bite to eat. With her 'photo session' over, she changes into khaki shorts and a white t-shirt and the three of us drive off in search of food. We are about fifteen minutes' drive from the town of La Chorrea, on the Gulf of Panama, a little agricultural community that is slowly being sucked into the highly profitable tourist trail engulfing the area. Seeing its potential, many ex-pats have purchased cheap second homes in and around the town, which, rather idyllically, is known for its cattle, oranges and coffee.

Among the area's main draws are spectacular waterfalls along the Caimito River. The town is famed for two local dishes: chicheme (a cold drink prepared with milk, corn and cinnamon), and bollos (boiled cornmeal sticks with a filling of meat, pork or chicken). On the surrounding agricultural land, crops of sugar cane, bananas and maize are plentiful.

Steve spots a restaurant and villa complex and is about to turn in when Anne suddenly says she'd rather not go there and asks if we can find somewhere else. It's a weird request as we are in the middle of nowhere, but she obviously isn't going to offer an explanation so I decide not to push her. I make a mental note to return later, have a nose around and show people her picture, to see if it rings any bells.

We drive on and find another restaurant, which is little more than a wooden shack with a dozen rickety tables scattered about the premises. It is completely deserted. Anne decides to skip the local delicacies, instead choosing a lunch of grilled fish and salad and bottled water. The food is fresh and tastes good. Steve and I opt for locally caught herring.

Afterwards, Anne says she'd like to stretch her legs, so we follow a winding lane towards the coast and take a short stroll on the first beach we come across, which turns out to be in a picturesque bay. It is pebbled and not the easiest to walk on, and it isn't long before Anne stops to look out over the water, gazing wistfully at the mountains in the distance. She remarks on what a beautiful country it is.

'I do love it here,' she says. 'It's so peaceful and unspoiled. Certainly a bit different to Seaton Carew!'

I nod and agree, although I've never actually been to Anne's home town. In fact, I'm not sure I'd heard of it before this assignment had come up. I discover that Seaton Carew came under the administrative control of Hartlepool in 1967. I had heard of that place. Local lad Jeff Stelling and Sky Sports Soccer Saturday were responsible for that.

It is my first visit to Panama and the countryside certainly takes some beating. Out there in the middle of nowhere, with just the odd whitewashed building dotted about the wooded landscape, there is very little to spoil the beauty of the surroundings. Guide books tell you how the country is unusual in that not only does it sit on the Isthmus of Panama, the narrow bridge of land connecting the continents of North and South America, but its famous canal connects the

Atlantic and Pacific Oceans. The forty-eight-mile long waterway that lured Anne here in the first place. Or so she claims.

I keep thinking to myself that all this scenery, spectacular as it might be, can't possibly be the real reason behind Anne's decision to emigrate. There has to be a darker side to her Panamanian adventure . . .

We make our way back to the hotel, a collection of cubed, breeze-block buildings, painted white but softened by the deep purple and red bougainvillea vines trailing from wooden trellises at every corner. Anne returns to her room, saying she is going for a lie-down. She has black rings under her eyes and looks exhausted. It is obvious she hasn't had a proper night's sleep in days. It's impossible to know exactly what is going on in her mind, but she looks to be carrying the weight of the world on her shoulders.

At about 7 p.m., I knock on her door to see if she wants dinner. Fifteen minutes later, with her hair still wet from the shower, Anne and I head down to the hotel's La Caretta courtyard restaurant. Dressed in a full-length white cotton skirt and short-sleeve patterned blouse, exposing her sun-tanned arms, she smiles and politely nods good evening to the dozen or so other diners as we make our way to a table.

Anne tells the waiter she'd like water and a glass of wine, a dry white. Good idea.

'The same, *por favor*,' I say, and tell Anne that Steve is tired from driving and is taking a nap so won't be joining us. In truth, he has returned to the restaurant she had so mysteriously not wanted to visit earlier that day to see if he can establish exactly why she had been afraid to show her face there.

While trying not to push my dinner companion too hard, I am acutely aware I have so far only scratched at the surface of the story and have a long way to go to get to the truth behind her husband's disappearance and why she had upped sticks and moved thousands of miles from her beloved sons, her elderly parents and her lifelong friends. The pieces of the jigsaw don't fit together.

But maybe feeling she has said more than enough for the day already, she gives little else away as she tucks into a chicken salad, skil-fully skirting around any probing questions. She is, however, at pains to point out how keen she is to get back home and be reunited with her husband – while seemingly being in no rush to do so. She also talks openly about how hard it is going to be to pick up the pieces of their life together.

'I really don't want to live in England any more,' she says, but that only leaves me wondering why she seems so worried about where she is going to live.

Surely, with her husband back from the dead, she should be the happiest person alive?

'Panama is my home now. But whether John will want to come here I really don't know,' she adds.

'I don't even know where he's been all this time,' Anne continues. 'Everything is so confusing. I really don't know what I'm going to do.'

And there lies the crux of the story: exactly where has John Darwin been for five long years? And why isn't Anne just a tiny bit more intrigued? Can she really have known nothing? Or is she lying to protect him, maybe herself and the boys as well? She's certainly lying about something. Yet she proffers no theories as to where he might have been all that time or what he might have been up to. Those are the most natural questions to be asking. I decide not to push things.

Anne is obviously very worried about something – it's just a case of figuring out exactly what that is.

And, of course, I have my suspicions.

9

'We'll Get Him When We're Ready'

WITH JOHN DARWIN back from the dead, speculation on the story has reached fever pitch. The lifeboatmen's niggling doubts were, indeed, far from unfounded.

Hordes of TV crews, photographers and reporters are swarming outside Cleveland Police headquarters desperate for news on the inquiry. When it becomes apparent that the media is going nowhere, Hutch is called into a meeting with an Assistant Chief Constable and other senior officers.

'Right, what do we do here?' asks the ACC.

Hutch's view is that Cleveland Police should hold a press conference. Asked exactly what it will achieve, he suggests two things. One, get the press off our backs; they won't be happy until they get an update on the investigation. And two, it will provide a good opportunity to seek witnesses as to where Darwin has been and what he's been up to. Key questions everyone is asking.

'Give the media something and use them to get information in return,' says Hutch. 'Job's jobbed.'

The thinking is sound and the press conference is sanctioned. And with a distinct lack of volunteers, Hutch, one of the county's most senior detectives and vastly experienced at addressing the media, agrees to front it. He suggests that if he's handling the media he may as well be appointed Senior Investigating Officer (SIO) and his team from the murder squad should conduct the investigation.

Hutch leaves the meeting, ambles across the deep-pile green carpet outside the Chief Officers' rooms, and back onto the lino floors on the corridors used by lesser mortals, lines of inquiry already forming in his head.

The role of SIO is to develop the investigative strategy and all its various strands. Contrary to popular TV dramas, it is not their role to interview suspects, speak to witnesses and make 'house to house' enquiries while driving a gleaming vintage sports car. As Hutch always told senior detectives of the future, 'the SIO is the conductor, not part of the orchestra'.

He summons his deputy, Detective Inspector Andy Greenwood, and a few others to meet him in his office.

'We've got the Canoe Man job,' he announces.

The others nod and smile, there's the odd wisecrack, and somebody says, 'That was always going to happen.' Hutch fires off the instructions that have been percolating in his mind.

'We need the original coroner's file. What was done at the time? We'll do a press conference tomorrow. Let's see if anyone out there can help. I want to know where this fella has been and what he's been up to. We need all the financials, details of life insurance policies. How much was paid out to his wife? Where is she? What were their finances like before he went missing? What is this really all about?'

Back in 2000 when a forty-three-year-old female schoolteacher, loved and respected by everybody who knew her, was found dead and her partner 'unconscious' in the house they shared, Hutch questioned whether the crime scene had been staged. Both had multiple stab wounds, caused, according to the now conscious male, by an intruder, but the detective never 'bought' the existence of a third person. His investigative intuition proved correct and the man was convicted of murder and sentenced to life imprisonment.

That same antennae now has the Darwins in its sights.

With retirement now just a few months away, this is going to be the detective superintendent's swansong. He had joined the CID in 1981: it was all he ever wanted to do. His investigative antennae built over years at the coalface of crime screamed that Darwin's death was faked to claim the insurance money and pay off his debts. He had been desperate, and desperate people do desperate things. Hutch just has to prove it.

Addressing the detectives in front of him, he reveals that unbeknown to all but a few, a 'cold case' review into Darwin's disappearance has already quietly been underway for several months. The news creates a buzz about the room.

'Apparently, the Economic Crime Unit has been looking into it,' he says.

It's revealed that Anne's behaviour in the run-up to quitting her job at a doctor's surgery in Gilesgate had raised eyebrows with her work colleagues. One, in particular, had grown very suspicious about her regular whispered phone calls with a mystery man – Anne didn't seem the type to have a secret lover. The colleague just happened to be married to a former Cleveland police officer. She told him that she had begun to wonder whether it might be Anne's 'dead' husband on the other end of the line.

'Something is just not right here,' she said to her husband.

Convinced that her long-time colleague was hiding something, she was suspicious but had no evidence.

Her husband passed on his wife's concerns to the police and the regional asset recovery team was instructed to formally begin re-examining the case under the direction of a detective inspector and a superintendent from Hartlepool CID. Hutch tells his team that Detective Constable Gary Dolan from the ECU is already digging into the Darwins' finances, specifically a number of recent money transfers made by Mrs Darwin involving offshore banks in Jersey. He's also been tasked with seeing what else he can discover about her strange decision – for a woman who had never previously shown any interest in travelling – to quit her job and emigrate to Panama, where she was reportedly looking to buy property.

In fact, a meeting to discuss the case had been held just a few days before John's miraculous resurrection. Had he somehow got wind of the new investigation and dreamt up the amnesia story to pre-empt police coming looking for him? Was Mrs Darwin visiting her husband, who has perhaps changed his identity and started a secret new life overseas? He is extremely sun-tanned for an English winter and doesn't look the sort to visit tanning salons. Nothing can be ruled out.

There are already stories in the press quoting neighbours as saying there was always something odd about both John and his disappearance, particularly as a body had never been found. Civil servant Gary Walker, who bought the Darwins' former home in the County Durham village of Witton Gilbert for £72,000 shortly before John vanished, is quoted as saying: 'When he disappeared, which was shortly after we moved in, everyone around here said, "He's done a

Reggie Perrin'" (the character who faked his death, played by the late Leonard Rossiter in the hit television series of the late 1970s).

'It sounds ridiculous,' Mr Walker continued, 'but some of them told me they thought there was something not quite right. We had the bailiffs around a few times after he moved out and kept getting letters about debts. The loft and cellar were full of junk, including thirty to forty porcelain frogs, bike wheels, clothes and numerous documents. We heard he dabbled in shares, bought property and traded at car boot sales.'

The life insurance companies who had paid out after John's inquest were also very interested.

Cleveland Police issue a brief statement, giving little away.

'This man cannot remember anything about what has happened to him,' it says. 'He has no memory at all. But he has been somewhere for the last five years and a lot of questions need answering.'

With the story making headlines and knowing that a bucket-load of information will be coming their way, Hutch decides the inquiry will be run on HOLMES – the Home Office Large Major Enquiry System, a computerised database that is used in the investigation of major crimes where large amounts of data have to be processed.

It was developed after the hunt for Peter Sutcliffe, the Yorkshire Ripper, who despite being interviewed nine times during the five-year investigation was allowed to slip through the net because it had been impossible to have a complete overview of the vast quantity of information collected and stored.

The murder squad detectives are relaxed. Typically, their investigations are marked by a huge sense of urgency as they collectively seek to identify and arrest a killer in a community gripped by fear. This is very different. On the surface it looks to be more a fraud investigation. No massive haste. Slow and methodical is good.

'There's no rush here,' Hutch tells them.

'Darwin's with one of his sons. Leave him there. We'll get him when we're ready.'

But slow doesn't last long.

10

A Picture from Panama

THAT EVENING, URGENCY bolts into the police investigation due to the existence of a quite extraordinary photograph. Hutch's instructions for his team to take things slowly and methodically fly out the window.

He's at home working on tomorrow's press conference when his mobile rings. It's just after 7 p.m. It's one of the detectives from the HOLMES room and he knows from the tone in his voice that something is up.

'Hutch, you need to look at this website,' says the officer, struggling to get the words out quickly enough.

Hutch inputs the web address into his laptop and sees a jaw-dropping photograph of a smiling John and Anne Darwin together in Panama, standing alongside a real-estate agent. The photo is embedded with the date it was taken on: 14 July 2006 – four years after John disappeared and eighteen months before he came back from the dead.

It is emphatic proof that the Darwins' fanciful story is a pack of lies. It is a truly astonishing find.

Just as former neighbours had suspected, John Darwin had indeed done a Reggie Perrin, faked his own death and buggered off to Panama.

Hutch bursts out laughing.

'Stupid bastards!' he exhales, knowing everything is about to go into overdrive. 'Not that clever are you.'

Still staring at his computer screen, he asks how the photo has been found.

'Some woman rang it in,' he's told. 'Wouldn't give her name. Described herself as a bit of a geek.'

Turns out a young, single mum who had been following developments on the story with interest was highly dubious about lots of things, just like the police and the media. She had then used the wonders of the worldwide web to blow John and Anne Darwins' story to smithereens.

It was simple but brilliant.

While researching the story online, she entered the words 'John, Anne and Panama' into Google and hit 'images'. She pressed the return key and, in the blink of an eye, up popped the astonishing picture. Its existence has exploded the story into a whole new level of drama. Talk about a grenade being tossed into the room. Hutch knows they have to act quickly.

'If this woman has told *us*,' he says, 'we have to work on the premise she's told the media. That photograph will be on the front pages tomorrow. And in London, the papers are on the streets in the early hours. We need to arrest Darwin now before he does another runner.'

Today there would be an immediate inquiry into why the police had not discovered the damning photograph themselves. But the way people connected in 2007 was very different to how it is now. Interrogating the Internet was not at the time a go-to investigative strand of the CID armoury.

The iPhone was the new kid on a block dominated by Nokia, Blackberry, Motorola and Sony. Facebook and Twitter were just taking off and our lives were not stored on hand-held computers capable of making phone calls. 'It's all about contextualisation,' Hutch says. 'It's rather neatly summed up in the opening line of L.P. Hartley's 1953 novel, *The Go Between*: "The past is a foreign country: they do things differently there."'

Hutch was right. Four hours after informing the police, the woman calls the paper she takes, the *Daily Mirror*.

It's 11 p.m. and Stewart Maclean, three months into his first staff job on a national newspaper, is on the hated 'dog watch' as late-duty reporter. He has another four hours before his shift ends at 3 a.m. It's rare for anything even remotely exciting to happen so late at night.

When the news desk phone rings, he answers, expecting it to be the usual late-night crank call. It isn't. It's the sleuth, who explains how she has just discovered the mind-boggling picture from Panama. Maclean listens intently and puts the same three words into Google, hits images and is equally as astonished.

'Gosh, you're right,' he tells the woman. 'This is incredible!'

'Yes, I just blinked – and there they were,' the woman, who asks to remain anonymous, tells him. 'I've always been a sceptic. Nobody can simply vanish in this day and age. I knew there had to be something, some sign.'

Maclean clicks on the image of Darwin, wearing a burgundy short-sleeved shirt, and his wife, sporting a white vest top and giving a toothy grin. It takes him to a Panama relocation website, MoveToPanama.com. There's a number for the owner, Mario Vilar, who is also in the picture.

Thrilled at a massive story falling into his lap, he instructs the woman not to tell other papers in order to protect his scoop. He then calls Vilar, who answers the phone and confirms the story about the 'nice English woman Anne' and 'her friend John' looking to buy property in Panama.

Maclean, now Deputy Editor of the BBC's flagship current affairs programme *Newsnight*, recalled: 'I couldn't really believe my eyes at first. Mario told me how John and Anne had been looking to buy property in Panama. It was a slam dunk. It proved the Darwins' story was a complete fabrication.'

The handful of journalists still left in the *Mirror* newsroom on the twenty-second floor of the fifty-floor pyramid-topped skyscraper Canary Wharf, in the heart of London's Docklands, go into overdrive. How I would have loved to have been there that night. There's no greater thrill for a national newspaper journalist than when a big story breaks late at night and the paper, carefully crafted over the course of the day, is ripped up and redrawn at breakneck speed for a late-breaking story. The cry that used to go up is 'Hold the front page!'

It's approaching midnight. Night news editor Martin Newman has a quick discussion with the late-night sub-editor, Bryan McComb, who calls his immediate boss, Jon Clark, who has left the office to drive home to Hertfordshire.

'Are you absolutely positive the picture is genuine?' asks Clark, excited by the story but nervy about making major changes to the front page so late at night.

If he gets it wrong, his head will be on the block. If he does nothing, the story will no doubt be everywhere the following day and he will have missed a golden opportunity to get the paper some great exposure for breaking a sensational exclusive story.

He is told that the Panama estate agent had confirmed the story and the date is embedded in the photograph. Everything checks out.

'Right, let's go for it,' says Clark, who, as night editor, is in overall charge of production that night.

He takes the brave decision to rip up the front page and replace it with a new 'slip' edition – getting as many copies as possible printed with the dramatic picture and an exclusive story revealing that John and Anne Darwins' charade is over.

CANOE'S THIS IN PANAMA? is the eye-catching and hilarious new front-page headline, alongside the incredible photograph. A smaller sub-deck reads: *'Dead' Darwin with his wife in July 2006.*

Next day the *Mirror's* front page will be shown on all the major television networks – publicity newspapers just can't buy. Clark, who today is Editor-in-Chief of the *Daily Star*, gets big pats on the back as he arrives for work.

While the *Mirror* is making final changes to its front page, the police have been in overdrive. Cleveland detectives had alerted their colleagues hundreds of miles away in Hampshire, where Darwin is staying with his son Anthony.

Officers from Basingstoke dash to his address and at about 11.50 p.m., ring the doorbell. Anthony opens the door and is stunned to see three officers standing there. He's politely told it may be better to speak inside as there are journalists within earshot. He shows them to the lounge and is asked if his dad is in the house. Told he's upstairs in the spare room, two officers bring John down and arrest him on suspicion of fraud. Anthony can't believe what is happening.

His dad has been back from the dead just three days.

'Dad had just been on the phone to Mam in the lounge,' Anthony would later recall. 'He looked blank; I couldn't work out what was going on. They asked me to get Dad's possessions.

'I couldn't work out why they were taking him away so soon after I'd just got him back.

'We hugged and cried as they took him out. I really didn't have a clue what was going on.'

As his father is driven away, along with his few worldly belongings, Anthony calls Mark and tells him what's happening. The brothers are dumbfounded. Neither can quite believe it. Surely their lives are not about to be ripped apart once again? Are they?

The decision to arrest Darwin immediately puts the investigation under the custody time constraints of the Police and Criminal Evidence Act. He can't be held for ever: the maximum is ninety-six hours, but generally it is twenty-four. Interviews need planning, the gathering of evidence needs ramping up, the press conference needs rethinking. The inquiry has been turbo-charged. The luxury of slow burn has gone.

Hutch decides to appoint a Tier 5 Interview Advisor, at the time a relatively new specialism designed to professionalise the investigative process within the UK police. The role of such advisors is to provide advice to the SIO as to the best way an interview should be conducted, in the same way that a Firearm Tactical Advisor provides options to a Firearms Commander. Hutch is a big supporter of the idea. Earlier that year he had written an academic 'paper' describing the benefits of Tier 5 Interview Advisors, which was published in the *Homicide Journal*.

DS Iain Henderson has been appointed as the advisor. He will help prepare the interviews and be the conduit between the interviewers and the SIO. While the interview team is holed up in an office with Henderson, two detectives are dispatched south to pick up Darwin from the custody of Hampshire Police.

It's all systems go, ensuring all bases are covered. It's going to be a long night. Darwin will be back in Cleveland tomorrow and Hutch's team will get the opportunity to question him for the first time.

Hutch knows the following morning's planned press conference will now be packed to overflowing.

I I

'The Game's Up'

BACK IN PANAMA, I am totally oblivious to the development that is causing such a massive stir back home. Halfway through dinner with Anne my phone rings. It's a warm, pleasant evening; good food, good wine. I could easily be on my holidays. The stars above are shining brightly and the high-pitched chorus from the vibrating throats of thousands of tiny tree frogs fills the night air. I often say that this job beats working for a living. It's Martin Newman, from the *Mirror*, and he sounds pretty anxious. I excuse myself and move away from the patio table so as not to be in earshot.

'David, you're not going to believe this,' he says in a pretty dramatic opening statement – and he isn't wrong.

I listen open-mouthed as he explains how a reader had found the sensational photograph of John and Anne in Panama. The picture, which he says he's just emailed, proves beyond any doubt that my dinner companion is lying through her teeth and knew full well her husband was alive long before getting the late-night 'back from the dead' phone call from her son.

It is easily the most astonishing development in a story that's getting more unreal by the day. And it went a long way in explaining why Anne appeared so frightened and preoccupied. She does, indeed, have plenty of other things on her mind . . .

Now I am put in an almost impossibly tricky position. Newman is asking for reaction from Anne but insisting I don't breathe a word of the *Mirror*'s story to the *Mail*, who sent me to find her in the first place. If the *Mail* gets wind of the *Mirror*'s story, it too will quickly change its 'splash', meaning that tomorrow's *Mirror* front-page scoop will no longer be exclusive.

Faced with the task of keeping both paymasters happy, I decide the only thing to do is stall until it's too late for the *Mirror* to get any reaction from Anne in tomorrow's edition of the paper. That way, I will have had no input or involvement in the new story and the *Mail* can't accuse me of breaking my agreement to give both papers every word I filed.

It's a fairly rare situation to be working 'exclusively' for two rival giants of the tabloid newspaper world, and this is by far the stickiest moment I have yet encountered. Anne, oblivious to the drama racing through my mind, smiles as I sit back down at the dinner table. I return the smile and make a remark about the papers never giving me a moment's peace. I order an espresso while trying to work out my next move.

'One of the papers has sent me something that I need you to have a quick look at before you turn in for the night,' I say as casually as I can, not wanting to unduly alarm her.

'Okay,' she says and nods her head.

She has not the faintest idea of the Exocet missile heading her way.

By the time we get back to the room, Steve is already there, but he too has no idea of what the *Mirror* has unearthed. He quietly tells me he had shown Anne's photograph to staff at the complex we had earlier turned away from, but it hadn't rung any bells, so, for the moment, that remains a mystery. (Weeks later we discovered that the complex was, by an amazing stroke of coincidence, one that John and Anne had actually stayed at for a few days while looking for a place to buy in the area. Anne had obviously been terrified that someone would recognise her.)

Anne, a little baffled but not unduly concerned, sits down opposite me as I turn on my laptop and look for the email from the *Mirror*. Opening the attachment and seeing the dramatic picture of her and John smiling happily back at the camera, I feel the hairs on the back of my neck stand on end as the adrenalin starts to kick in. I have to warn Anne that she is in for one hell of a shock.

'I've got something to show you Anne, a picture, and I'm afraid it's not going to be very easy for you,' I say.

The colour drains from her face even before I turn the laptop towards her and she focuses on the photograph, an unforgettable image that must have leapt out from the screen in front of her and smacked her between the eyes.

'The game's up, Anne, I'm sorry,' I say. 'We know you've been lying.'

As she sits staring at the screen, transfixed by the picture, I know we have to capture the moment on camera: it is just too powerful an image not to have. The atmosphere in the room is intense. What the hell do I do? I can't ask Steve to stick his camera in Anne's face. I hastily type out a text to him on my Blackberry and press send. *Can you get any shots . . . discreetly?*

Steve gets up and walks around, mind racing but movements nonchalant.

The curtains and nets are drawn. He quietly pulls back a small section of the curtain, then slips one of his Canon camera bodies and a 70-200mm lens into his jacket pocket.

'I've left my wallet in the car,' he says. 'Just going to get it.'

I silently acknowledge Steve's speed of thought. It's doubtful, given what has just happened, that Anne even registers what he is saying, and he leaves the room unnoticed.

It is only a matter of three or four minutes before I hear the whir-ring of Steve's camera outside our balcony window as he covertly captures what will become unforgettable and award-winning images of a distraught and broken Anne Darwin holding her head in her hands, then covering her eyes, the enormity of what the Panama photograph means slowly sinking in.

The room is quiet and the noise of the rapid-firing shutter – 'spray and pray' in photographer-speak – sounds to me like a Gatling gun going off. I raise my voice to an absurd level to try and drown out the noise. Steve, shooting through a net curtain into the dimly lit hotel room, is desperately trying to get some usable images. Obviously not able to use flash and alert Anne, he has opened the camera's aperture as wide as possible, slowed the shutter speed and cranked up the ISO to make the images as light as possible. A final rat-a-tat from the camera and it all goes quiet. I can stop shouting.

It was obvious Anne would not be happy about the pictures, but this was a huge news story and *that* photograph proved she has been lying and is almost certainly guilty of some pretty serious crimes. Journalistically, it was just something that had to be done, as would be borne out by the next day's *Mirror* and *Mail*, which again wiped out their front pages to carry the pictures alongside dramatic headlines. THE GAME IS UP is the *Mirror*'s, while the *Mail* goes with THE MOMENT THE LIES HAD TO STOP.

I ask Anne if she is okay, if that really is her husband in the picture and if there is anything she wants to say. She takes a sharp intake of breath, shakes her head, then in a barely audible voice, while still staring at the screen, replies: 'Well, I guess that picture answers a lot of questions. Yes, that's John, that's my husband.'

It was the dramatic moment her fantasy life came crashing down.

After a few minutes of silence, she tearfully continues, her voice in monotone.

'My sons are never going to forgive me. It looks as if I am going to be left without a husband, a home or a family now. I'm not sure if there's much more I can say.'

To all intents and purposes, the game is up. Her lies have been undone. Quite what her role is in the bigger picture is still not clear. But she has an awful lot of explaining to do. She again insists she initially believed her husband had died after paddling out into the North Sea and claims it was 'quite some time' before she discovered he was still alive, but she can't, or won't, specify when she found out. *Why?*

Choking back tears as she contemplates a seemingly bleak future, she adds: 'Do I still love John? Yes, I do, and it's probably that what's got me in this situation. When you love someone, all you want to do is protect them.'

Asked if this is now the end of her dream of a new life in Panama, Anne says she is prepared to return to the UK to 'face the music'.

'I don't want to live my life as a fugitive,' she says. 'But I guess my life, anywhere, is going to be pretty awkward now.'

It will indeed.

The woman who just six weeks earlier had quietly left her home and family behind to begin a new life in the sun, adds: 'I will have to go back because I won't have any life here. My family will be absolutely devastated by all this. My sons knew nothing. They thought he was dead. Now they are going to hate me.'

As a father of two myself it's hard to fathom how the Darwins could have done this to their own children. Anne admits to not having slept in days because of the stress of the situation. Is it any wonder? She must have known this day was coming.

'But that's nothing,' she adds. 'My sons will be having dreadful nights for days and weeks and months to come. I will have to explain everything to them first, before anyone else. They will be devastated and probably want nothing to do with me ever again. I can't see why they would want to stick by me now.'

Neither could I if I were being honest.

She adds, somewhat poignantly: 'Maybe I just chose the wrong husband?'

Maybe indeed. But now, suddenly, everything is starting to make sense. Anne looks a broken woman. I gently press her on whether she is really this time telling the truth. She denies my accusation of being party to the disappearance from the outset. But again, she won't say exactly when she discovered her husband was alive. Why? What exactly is she hiding?

'It was years later,' is all she will say.

She refuses to tell me how much money she received in insurance payouts after her husband's 'death', only saying that it 'wasn't a fortune'. What's a fortune, Anne? How much was it?

'I suppose these are the questions police will want to ask me now,' she adds.

Indeed, they will. I tell her there are reports that the police had been investigating possible sightings of her husband in Panama for the last three months, to which she responds, in a partial confession: 'He has not been here all the time.'

She says she had no idea the police had apparently been closing in on her husband's – or her – alleged deceit. And she can offer no explanation as to the puzzling question of exactly why he had walked into a London police station, claiming he was a missing person and suffering from amnesia.

'I knew he was going back: he went back just before he turned himself in, but I didn't know he was going to the police,' she says. 'But I don't suppose the police will believe anything I tell them now. Yes, it looks pretty damning.'

It's hard to disagree. She says it's 'possible' her husband had suffered some kind of breakdown, but she couldn't be sure. 'John was under a lot of pressure,' she says.

I sit in silence, allowing her to speak without interruption. It is more a monologue than an interview. It's a form of confession with an in-built defence.

'John had grown disillusioned with teaching. It wasn't the job it used to be, the job he signed up for and the job he loved,' Anne continues.

'Then he went to the bank but he hated that. He couldn't do the things he said they wanted him to do, such as selling products to people who didn't really need them. That's why he joined the Prison Service, but whether that had anything to do with all this, I couldn't really say.'

The room falls silent.

After a minute or two I again ask whether she really believed her husband had died in the canoeing accident. I wasn't at all convinced.

'Yes I did,' she insists. 'And that was the nightmare I lived through.'

She refuses to say how or when her husband had made contact with her after his 'disappearance', but admits they had spent time together in Panama, including a number of short holidays there.

'I did nothing wrong . . . in the beginning,' she says. 'Now I don't even know how I can talk to my sons. They thought they had just got their dad back and now he's been whisked away.'

And, in a massive understatement of a story that could be straight from the pages of a novel, she adds: 'None of this seems real.'

You can say that again, Anne.

12

Sons in the Frame

THE NEXT MORNING everything becomes crystal clear for Mark and Anthony Darwin.

After another sleepless night, the brothers see the damning photograph of their parents together in Panama on the morning TV news and plastered across the front page of the *Mirror*. The date clearly shows it had been taken eighteen months earlier, meaning, once again, they have been lied to in the most cruel and heartless way imaginable. Their father has been alive and well throughout the years they've mourned his loss. Their mother has cold-heartedly lied to them, not once, but a thousand times. And not what could ever be classified as little white lies. Truly stomach-churning, unforgivable lies.

Once more, their lives have been shattered by their own parents. They feel betrayed, angry, heartbroken . . . and hatred. Hatred towards the two people in the world they are supposed to trust above all others.

And who can blame them?

When Anthony sees the picture of his parents together, he is mortified. He calls Cleveland Police, then his uncle Michael trying to make sense of what's going on. He doesn't want to believe it, convinced the picture must have been photo-shopped. But then he starts to grasp that his parents' entire story has been a series of devastating and monstrous lies going back nearly six years.

'I saw the date and knew my parents had been lying all that time,' he later recalls.

'I was really angry, I felt betrayed; knowing that my mother knew he was alive all along was hard to take.

'They were the two people in the world who I was supposed to trust and believe, and yet they had put me through hell.'

Trying to live their normal lives is impossible. Anthony is in a terrible state: angered, heartbroken, confused beyond belief. His dad's disappearance had nearly wrecked his relationship with Louise. It had ruined their planned engagement and they had been forced to postpone their wedding because it clashed with his inquest. Anthony had struggled to cope with his grief. He became withdrawn, refusing to discuss anything with anyone, including Louise, who he'd meet at an adventure camp in Pennsylvania in 1999. Three years into their relationship, they became strangers living separate lives. It had nearly driven them apart. Only Louise's love, understanding and devotion had saved it.

And now this . . .

As their worlds fall apart, Mark calls Flick, sobbing, to tell her the sickening news.

'I think we have been lied to,' he says.

He would later admit that the 'death' of their father had crushed both him and Anthony. He had lost his dad; his best friend. Now their mother had left them devastated beyond belief for a second time.

And there's another very real fear to contend with. What if the police think they were in on their parents' deception? There were things they had done at their mother's request, such as helping to transfer money abroad and being named as directors of a company she had set up. Do detectives think they knew about the vanishing act all along? *Were they in the frame?*

In truth, the police weren't entirely sure. They certainly weren't discounting it. Privately, some senior officers were convinced they were; so too were many journalists.

Questions are already being asked in the press about their possible involvement. Journalists have started looking into their backgrounds and personal circumstances. There are reports that they had planned to quit their jobs and start a new life in Panama with their parents. Does that not sound more plausible?

Papers are also reporting that when Anne left the UK for a new life in Panama she had made at least £455,000 from the sale of Nos 3 and 4 The Cliff, and had cashed in life insurance policies and made claims on John's teacher and Prison Service pension contributions. She was loaded. It was a lot more than the 'it wasn't a fortune' Anne described after she was shown that picture. It's also revealed that, as well as the flat in Panama City, Anne has bought a large parcel of land in Escobal, a rural village two hours' drive from the capital in the province of Colon, at the northern end of the Panama Canal.

Again, Anthony speaks to Cleveland Police to see what he can find out. But it is an active criminal investigation and there is little the cops can divulge. He is told detectives would like to speak to him. As a witness or a suspect? He isn't sure. He's panic-stricken.

In tears, he calls relatives, asking what he should do. He doesn't want to stay at home, because journalists are camped outside, so he checks into a Reading hotel. He goes to work, where he is employed as a service advisor brokering insurance policies for large firms such as Monsoon and Heinz. He explains to his bosses that he's finding it near impossible to work because of what is going on. They are sympathetic and tell him to go and get things straightened out.

But Anthony is struggling to cope with anything. His life has descended into a crazy blur in which nothing makes sense any more.

Mark hurriedly leaves the rented flat he moved into a month earlier in Finchley, north London, with all his belongings. He tells his flatmates to tell the press he's moved out if they come knocking. He inadvertently leaves behind a notebook for Flick with strange instructions about only using phone boxes to make calls and not telling anyone your name. The notebook is recovered by the police. Is it to protect him and Flick from the press – or the police?

While the boys feel frightened and alone, everyone else is loving the rip-roaring saga. It's captivated the country, even seeping into the top echelons of public life. During Prime Minister Gordon Brown's weekly parliamentary grilling, Conservative leader David Cameron hammers the British leader for forgetting past promises: 'He wants us to think he is like the man in the canoe – he hasn't been around for the past five years.'

Laughter erupts in the House.

Everyone is beyond sceptical of John Darwin's story. Nothing adds up.

Hutch walks onto the press conference stage in the Media Briefing Centre knowing he is live on the screens of the twenty-four-hour news channels. Flashguns fire, cameras roll, pens are poised. The media circus, national and international, is in town and Seaton Carew is about to be catapulted onto the world stage.

Hartlepool will find itself famous for something other than Andy Capp and hanging a ship's monkey, washed ashore during the Napoleonic War, which locals believed to be a hairy French spy. (Two months after John Darwin went missing, H'Angus the Monkey, Hartlepool United's mascot, became the directly elected Mayor of the town on a manifesto of giving all school children a banana every day.)

Despite having hundreds of press conferences under his belt, this is the first time Hutch has seen a TV crew from The Netherlands in Police HQ, Ladgate Lane, Middlesbrough. The story has gone global.

As he sits down behind the desk laden with microphones, the murder squad chief knows this conference is different. John Darwin hadn't died, at least not for real.

The 'Lazurus Conference' is about to start.

Typically when someone has been arrested, the police do not name them. Hutch had decided that in this case it was futile. Everybody knew who had been arrested and he had no intention of denying it was John Darwin live on TV.

Besides, everybody had seen the 'Canoe's This in Panama?' headline.

Hutch believed that identifying witnesses and uncovering information was much easier with the help of the media. He never belonged to the 'tell them nothing brigade' and always respected they had a job to do too. His honesty with the media would lead to reporters contacting him from around the world and sharing information on Darwin over the next few days.

He reads a prepared script, ending with his appeal.

'There will be people out there who'll know exactly where he has been, where he has been living and what he has been doing. My appeal today is that if there is anybody with any information whereby we can piece together what has happened over these last five years please contact us.

'Without doubt, this is an unusual case.'

A damn sight more unusual after that *photograph*, he thinks, as cameras flash and questions are fired at him from all angles. Most of the time you can plan for the questions beforehand, but occasionally a curve-ball is thrown.

Hutch isn't expecting the last one.

'Was this a Christmas miracle?'

Amid much mirth from the journalists, he chooses his words carefully. He is live. He smiles.

'I don't know. I just deal in the facts.'

And the facts are coming in quick and fast.

There is already speculation from journalists that if Darwin is charged with fraud, a conviction could earn him up to ten years in jail. Hutch says police have not spoken to Anne Darwin since the inquest into her husband's 'death', but they would now, of course, like to speak with her. He's relaxed, knowing, through Jezza at the *Mirror*, that she is on her way back to the UK with me.

That morning, police are granted a further thirty-six hours to quiz Darwin about alleged fraud involving pensions, insurance payouts and property deals.

As the realisation that they have been lied to in the cruellest way possible begins to set in, and no doubt wanting to distance themselves from their parents' alleged crimes, the Darwin boys issue a damning statement through Cleveland Police.

It reads:

Having seen the recent media speculation surrounding our parents ever since our dad was arrested, we are very much in an angry and confused state of mind. In the short space of time following our dad's appearance in London on Saturday, we have gone through a rollercoaster of emotion.

From the height of elation at finding him to be alive to the depths of despair at the recent stories of fraud and these latest pictures. And the shock of being thrust into the media spotlight. If the papers' allegations of a confession from our mam are true, then we very much feel that we have been the victims in a large scam. How could our mam continue to let us believe our dad had died when he was very much alive? We have not spoken to either of our parents since our dad's arrest and at this present time we want no further contact with them.

Cleveland Police have asked for anyone with knowledge of our dad's whereabouts over the last five years to come forward and we support this wholeheartedly. We too want to know where he has been and what he has been doing. We have been in constant contact with the police and will be helping them with their enquiries in any way we can. We hope that the public can appreciate our shock and frustration at this distressing time and again plead with the media to respect our privacy and allow us to deal with this in the best way we can.

Back in Panama, I then have to read their devastating words to Anne, who, more aware than anyone of the damage she has done, is distraught beyond belief. She holds her head in her hands as I break the news.

'What sort of mother am I?' she sobs.

Not a very good one, I think to myself. Not for the first time I wonder how any parent could do that.

Anne continues: 'Who can blame them? How can they ever forgive me for what I've done to them?

'They were overjoyed at getting their father back from the dead – then they discover he was alive the whole time.'

Her sentences are interspersed with silences. I make no effort to fill them.

'And I lied to them, my own sons. They are totally innocent.'

She cannot look me in the eye; her hands are shaking.

'They knew nothing,' she says. 'They thought their father was dead.' She loves the boys dearly and prays they'll forgive her, but she understands if they won't.

The silence is long, the headshake slow.

'I really am so sorry. Sorry to them and all my family and friends. How can anyone make sense of the foolish things I've done?'

Dazed and shell-shocked, she weeps openly. It is a pitiful sight. The pain is real.

But she and her husband are the only ones to blame. She knows that. Tears stream down her face as she shakes her head and keeps repeating: 'What have I done? What have I done?'

She falls silent for a minute, maybe longer, then continues.

'I hate lying. I am not a dishonest person.'

Sorry Anne, but many will disagree.

'For twenty-two years I worked at a doctor's surgery and I loved my job. When I left I got so many presents and people said so many kind things. And I've let them all down.'

She is a woman who had lived an honest, hard-working life, whose one previous 'offence' was a solitary parking ticket. Then she had agreed to tell one whopping lie – a lie that led to an avalanche of deceit.

I tell her Cleveland Police are continuing to quiz John. She knows it will soon be her turn. She is patently aware that both she and her husband could go to jail if they are found to have committed fraud, which now seems very likely. The prospect terrifies her. You can see it in her eyes.

'I really don't think I could cope,' she says. 'I just don't. I'm not strong enough.

'And as for John, he's a former prison officer. What would it be like for him? He'd have a terrible time.'

Anne regains her composure and admits she is now no longer sure they will spend the rest of their life together. She blames him, but of course knows she's equally culpable.

'It's difficult to say,' she says. 'I love him and he says he loves me, but there's a lot that's happened.'

I suspect there's a lot more of what happened still to be revealed.

Asked for a truthful explanation of why her husband had suddenly returned to England and walked into a police station, claiming amnesia, she responds: 'Maybe he wanted his old life back, I don't really know. I know he missed our sons tremendously.'

But is she really telling the truth? The whole truth? It seems unlikely.

She describes her sons as 'great boys', ones any mother would be proud of, adding: 'They have both done well for themselves and never given me any trouble. And I go and do this to them. How could I?

'I do blame John, yes. I should never have listened to him. I know that, but he can be very persuasive.

'But, of course, I'm to blame too. I just wish I had told the boys when I found out. I'm sure they would have talked some sense into me.'

Was that because the boys already knew? How could they not have known? That's what everyone is thinking. It's a subject I need to return to.

Anne claims one lie led to the next and soon things were totally out of control. I can't even imagine how she has pulled this off. If she is telling the truth about her boys not knowing, how could she have the coldness to tell such despicable lies to her own sons and family? Let alone the nerve to lie to the police, knowing full well she is aiding and abetting a serious crime. I ask, yet again, if she really believed her husband of twenty-eight years had died in the North Sea. But she is vague and unwilling to talk about exactly when she discovered he was still alive. I know she's hiding something.

But she does admit the decision to start a new life in the Central American state of Panama was both of theirs – not made under any duress, something which would later prove to be very significant.

'It was a joint decision,' she says. 'Well, it was John's decision but I went along with it.'

She admits her husband had been living and waiting in Panama when she arrived after selling up and leaving her home in Seaton Carew six weeks ago. I feel like I'm being drip-fed the truth. She's like the thief 'caught red-handed' hoping to admit as little as possible.

'Yes, he was there, he had been living there and was waiting for me,' she says. 'And then he said he was going back. But I had no idea of what he was about to do.'

Anne knows her husband's return from the dead is making news at home in England, but she doesn't really grasp exactly how big a story it has become. She isn't asking to see what the papers have published and, because she is now no longer in touch with anyone in the UK – if there was anyone there who would even talk to her – she isn't aware her revelations are front-page news for the third day running and have been picked up by just about every newspaper, TV and radio station going.

Although, journalistically, things could not have gone better for me and Steve, and the lies Anne had told were truly shocking, I still felt a tremendous emotional attachment to the story. Anne is in my care and I need to make sure she is okay. I am honest with her and give her what advice I can. Tell the truth, I urge her. Say how sorry you are and take whatever punishment is coming your way. You have to stay strong, Anne; there are mitigating circumstances; you can get through this. It was John's idea and you did what you were told. You didn't tell the boys because you didn't want to drag them into this sorry mess and make them accomplices to the crime. Whether she takes in what I am saying I have no idea. She just weeps.

The *Mirror* and *Mail* are, of course, delighted to be breaking such cracking news stories filling four or five pages every day. But rival papers aren't, to put it mildly, quite so happy and are desperate to catch up and spoil the show.

Each night, as soon as the first edition of either the *Mirror* or *Mail* 'drops', chapter and verse of my story is being copied, 'lifted' is the journalistic term, and fed into later editions of other papers, as often happens on such a big story. They are basically stealing it all – running a coach and horses through English copyright laws. Sadly, today it has become the norm.

Opposition news and picture desks, getting kicked by their respective editors, are putting their teams on the ground under enormous pressure to find us and end my run of exclusive revelations. My reporters in Splash's Miami bureau are even being offered thousands of pounds in kickbacks just to reveal where we are. I trusted them, of course, but such was the secrecy of the operation, I hadn't told a soul, even the papers we were working for, exactly where we were hiding out: my thinking being that if no one knows where we are, no one can spill the beans.

I still needed more from Anne, but this isn't the moment to push her any further. I am genuinely worried she might self-harm, and tell her that although her sons and family will of course be hurting a great deal, time is a great healer. Anne isn't convinced. 'I don't deserve to be forgiven,' she says. 'I've ruined everything and lied to everyone I hold dear to me.'

But that night, whatever she has done, whatever lies she has told, she is a broken woman and my heart went out to her.

13

'I Wasn't Staying with the Queen'

THE PHOTOGRAPH OF the Darwins happily posing for the camera in Panama has already exposed John Darwin to be a liar and his amnesia story to be, as Hutch quaintly put it on Sunday, 'complete bollocks'.

But the investigation is just beginning. Darwin is being held on suspicion of fraud, but evidence is still needed before charges can be brought. Most importantly, was the whole escapade a plot dreamt up by him with his wife's help so she could claim life insurance policies and pensions to escape the couple's crippling debts? It's what the police strongly suspect.

The indicators look pretty compelling. Anne has already admitted in newspaper interviews to receiving insurance payouts. Then there's her very strange – *extraordinary* – decision to up sticks and start a new life in Panama. It is now obvious that her move to Central America was so she could start a secret new life with her not-so-dead husband.

Crucially, however, she is still insisting that initially she believed her husband had died and that he only turned up on her doorstep 'a year or so' after disappearing, and by then she had already received the insurance payouts, which had been claimed in, that phrase again, 'good faith'.

Her claims are all so vague – and unbelievable. Hutch isn't buying them for a moment.

With parts of Darwin's story already collapsing around his ears, these questions and many more are churning through the minds of his team as they meet to discuss developments. It's no wonder there had always been so much doubt over the Canoe Man's 'death'. A body that was never found and at least two known sightings of him in the years after he vanished by people who knew him well.

The murder team has been liaising with the detectives who worked on the original investigation, reviewing the coroner's files and speaking with DC Gary Dolan, who was leading the Economic Crime Unit's cold case review. He has quickly been drafted onto the investigating team and is sharing the information that had already led him to believe Darwin was very much alive and kicking before his sudden reappearance, including the sophisticated means by which Anne had transferred money to Panama via offshore accounts in Jersey.

Lots of riddles to solve. Hutch is confident it's just a matter of time.

After being arrested in Hampshire, Darwin is driven north. With travel not included as detention time under the Police and Criminal Evidence Act, the 'relevant time' for him being held in custody will not start until he arrives in Cleveland. The interview team set to quiz him have studied every word of Anne's tearful confession in the morning papers. With the clock ticking, detectives are primed and waiting to get to the bottom of what he is hiding and how deep this mind-boggling crime really goes.

The interviews will be split into three stages.

1. The 'suspect agenda'. Hear what the suspect has to say; let him give his side of the story and get all his claims out into the open.
2. The 'police agenda'. Introduce the police case so that the suspect knows what he is up against.
3. The 'challenge stage'. Confront the suspect's 'lies' with the hard evidence that disproves them.

At 2.27 p.m. on Thursday 6 December, two days after his arrest, Darwin is questioned under caution for the first time. He has been pronounced fit to be interviewed by a medical practitioner.

Two highly accomplished interviewers, Cleveland Police detective constables Steve Rowland and Jim McArthur, are already seated at a table in an interview room at Kirkleatham police station, Redcar, as Darwin shuffles in. He is accompanied by Mike Fowler, one of the solicitors from the local firm representing him, Brown, Beer, Nixon and Mallon. The room, like the rest of the building, is a year old: fresh paint, pristine chairs and walls yet to be drenched in prisoners' lies and stink.

The cops have been told Darwin has a number of medical issues. The man they are convinced has fooled everyone for five years is on heart medication, desperate for an inhaler and suffering from an astonishing level of amnesia, which, with the ultimate irony, they'll soon discover is something he keeps forgetting. He also claims to be partially deaf. The trickier the question, the more acute it becomes.

But the murder team is full of wise heads and they are taking no chances. The detectives know he's having them on. But they have to play the game his way, for now, at least. They need to tread carefully. Until they can prove otherwise, they will treat Darwin with kid gloves and not present his defence team with an opportunity to make application at trial to have the interview ruled inadmissible. They treat him as a 'vulnerable adult'. They know the rules only too well. To that end, also present in an observing role as an 'appropriate adult' is Jennifer Price, from Redcar and Cleveland Social Services.

Darwin is told that the interview will be recorded on video and audio cassette tapes. He is also informed that monitoring equipment is fitted in the room and the illuminated red light indicates somebody is watching.

That someone is Detective Sergeant Iain Henderson, a highly rated member of the murder team and the officer who rang Hutch on Sunday. Iain is sat in another office staring at Darwin on a TV screen. *Let's see how smart this guy really is*, he thinks.

Darwin is asked to give his full name and date of birth.

'John Ronald Darwin. Fourteenth of August 1950.'

'And how would you like to be addressed during this interview?' the officer continues.

'John,' John replies, before being formally cautioned and warned that anything he says may be used in evidence against him.

He is advised that as the tape recordings can't pick up gestures or nods or shakes of the head, he has to speak his replies.

With the formalities taken care of, the interview begins.

'Do you understand?' DC Rowland asks.

And, of course, Darwin nods that he understands.

'We need you to speak, please,' says the officer, a ten-year veteran.

'Yes,' says Darwin, who is looking away from his interrogators. 'And, err, the reason I'm not looking at you is because I'm, err, slightly deaf in . . . well . . . I'm deaf in both ears actually.'

DS Henderson, a Scot with a dry sense of humour, has discussed with the interviewers what 'topics' to cover in the first interview. No mention will be made of the Panama photograph. That will be kept back until a later interview. Give Darwin enough rope . . .

Before the detectives get started, Darwin's solicitor interjects, revealing his client has prepared a statement, which he has been asked to read. DS Henderson grins. No surprises there then. In preparation for the interview the team had addressed the likelihood of a written 'prepared statement' being presented. And here it comes.

'Prepared statements' as they are known in law are nothing new. Type the phrase into a search engine and solicitors from all over the country are extolling their virtue. It is a tactic designed by the defence to try and take control of the interview.

Mike Fowler reads the statement: 'John Ronald DARWIN. I am the above named and this is my statement. It is my own hand and they are my words. There was never any intention to defraud anyone or any business.'

DS Henderson smiles at the TV. Get 'no intent' in quickly. For a theft to occur there has to be an 'intention to permanently deprive'. No intent, no offence. Nice try.

'The last thing,' continues the solicitor, 'that I remember, before any of this, is a holiday in Norway in the year 2000. I have hazy recollections of being in a kayak but I cannot remember the accident or anything leading up to it at all. It is therefore true to say that I do have some form of amnesia.'

DS Henderson smiles again; writes 'self-diagnosis' on his pad.

The solicitor continues: 'It was some years later (I am still not sure when) that I turned up at the family home, though I don't know how I got there, and my wife was understandably shocked, given that she thought I was dead.'

DS Henderson is grinning now. What sort of amnesia reminds you where you live when you'd only moved there *after* the holiday you're claiming is the last thing you remember?

'I soon realised the monies had been paid out on the basis that I was dead. By consideration of my mortgage agreement, I knew that if I now alerted the relevant financial institutions to the fact of my still being alive, I would be made bankrupt and still left with a huge amount of debt. I am very sorry for all the mess that this has caused by me not alerting the authorities sooner, but I was trying to protect my family.'

DS Henderson sits back in his chair, erupting sarcasm. He shakes his head as the solicitor continues. Basic error; his wife has already revealed the monies had not yet been paid out when he first reappeared. Again, that was *after* the holiday in 2000, which he claims is when his amnesia kicked in. The interviewers show no expression.

'There is every intention of paying back whatever is owed and that is why I recently returned to London to make those arrangements.'

Does John Darwin really think it's as simple as that? Pay back the obviously fraudulently obtained money and that's the end of the matter?

DS Henderson laughs. *Arrangements? You thought you were missing. You couldn't understand why the Christmas decorations were up; you couldn't remember anything after Norway. But you remembered you owed money? Which is it?*

The statement continues: 'I would also like to add that my wife acted under extreme duress. My sons and the rest of the family knew nothing about the things which occurred after my memory returned. To stress again, I have limited memory of what occurred between 2000 and the year I regained my memory, which is still unclear. I have read back the above and can confirm that it is true.'

The statement is signed and dated.

The detectives terminate the interview, which has lasted exactly ten minutes. They want to study the prepared statement in more detail.

Hutch is brought up to date. Darwin is performing exactly as expected. They could have handed him a script. He is desperately trying to protect his wife and sons. Were they *all* in on it from the start?

Just over an hour later, at 3.40 p.m., the second interview starts.

Darwin is again cautioned and warned anything he says can be used in evidence. DC McArthur tells him he will be questioned about his actions and movements 'before, during and after March 21, 2002', and that this is his opportunity to give his version of events.

'Your recollections, your memories, if you like,' he says.

DS Henderson, watching remotely, smiles. Let's see what memories you've got John.

DC Rowland starts by asking Darwin to recall the events of 1 December, five days earlier, when he had walked into the West End Central police station in London.

'In your own words, in your own time John, can you tell me what happened on that day?' he asks.

Silence.

'If you just say, "No comment",' says Darwin's solicitor.

'No comment,' Darwin obliges.

DC Rowland explains he is simply asking Darwin to tell them about the circumstances that led to him attending the police station.

'No comment,' comes the reply.

'Tell me what you said to the police officer at the police station, John,' asks DC Rowland.

Another 'No comment'.

The non-compliance does not faze the detectives. They have been here numerous times before.

Prisoners saying 'No comment' or not replying is nothing new to them. In the event of a 'Not Guilty trial', when every question is read out by the prosecuting barrister and every 'no comment' from the accused spoken by a detective in the witness box, members of the jury will form their own view. In criminal proceedings, the burden of proof falls on the prosecution – they must convince a jury that the defendant committed the alleged offence beyond all reasonable doubt. The problem with a sustained 'no comment' approach can be that silence fuels doubt and uncertainty while allowing the other side of the story to hold the floor uninterrupted. This becomes the dominant narrative.

And so it continues, with 'no comment' to the next eighty-six questions, as Darwin declines to explain how he had got to the police station, where he had been living beforehand, or whether he had spoken to his wife.

At 4 p.m., he indicates to his solicitor that he wants to talk in private. It's agreed they can take a short break.

Eight minutes later, the group reconvene. But if the officers are hoping for Darwin to be a little more forthcoming, they are disappointed. Over the next forty-one minutes, their questions are met with a further 103 'no comments' as he refuses to talk about where he lived; his work as a prison officer; his relationship with Anne; whether there had been problems within their marriage; how much in debt he had been at the time of his disappearance; or about the actual day he went missing.

'You say you have hazy recollections about being in a kayak,' he is asked. 'Can you tell me about that?'

'Could you repeat the question?' Darwin responds.

Finally – is this the long-awaited breakthrough?

'You say you have a hazy recollection about being in a kayak. Can you tell me about that?'

Maybe not, think the detectives as he pauses.

'No comment,' he says with a smirk.

His arrogance doesn't rile DC Rowland, a down-to-earth detective with a good investigative brain. Steve was brought up in Wingate, a mining village near Darwin's Blackhall, and has not lost his colliery accent.

He remains calm and composed throughout. He advises Darwin to think 'very carefully' about what they will be discussing in their next interview. He reminds the prisoner of the huge media interest in the inquiry and how new information is coming to light all the time – indicating to him and his lawyer that Anne has been talking freely about what had happened in interviews that have appeared in the papers and been widely reported elsewhere.

Asked if there is anything he wants to say before the interview is terminated, Darwin replies, somewhat predictably, with his two new favourite words.

Just under three hours later, at 7.25 p.m., it's time for the third session of the day. DC McArthur asks Darwin to identity himself with his full name and date of birth.

'Who, me?' he replies cockily.

Many people in that moment would describe Darwin as having the type of face your arms would not get tired of punching.

Jim McArthur doesn't flinch.

'Yes, please,' he says patiently, and Darwin duly complies.

And they're off again . . . but getting nowhere fast.

There are a further ninety-eight 'no comments', but each question closes the 'if you do not mention something you later rely on in court' door.

The police are giving Darwin an opportunity to put forward his version of events, but they don't need an admission. There will be plenty of other evidence.

Then Darwin starts to open up a little. Or is he trying to save his own skin?

He seems at pains to stress that none of the money paid out by the insurance companies following his 'death' went directly to him.

'If they were paid out, they were paid out to Anne,' he says.

DS Henderson shakes his head. *Are you now shifting all this onto your wife?*

Darwin also says he hasn't had a chance to alert any of the financial institutions and insurers who had made payments to Anne that he wasn't actually dead and therefore the money had been paid in error.

Just how busy were you at your son's house? thinks DS Henderson.

And then Darwin has a mini-rant about the lenders, which he blames for his predicament in the first place.

'I am not getting into the workings of mortgage companies and banks and how they act if people owe money,' he says, but, such is his contempt for them, he can't help himself.

'If you need to know that, then all you have to do is pick up a newspaper and it tells you about bank repossessions immediately: repossessing immediately means you get turfed out; the banks then sell everything in a thirty-day sale. It does happen in this country. It happens a lot but apart from that . . . no comment.'

The detectives, like all good interviewers, wait for the silence to be filled. They don't wait long.

After a brief pause, Darwin adds: 'When you're bankrupt, you've got nothing. When you've got a lot of debt, you owe money, so if you've got nothing and owe a lot of debt, it follows that you are bank-rupt and still in debt.'

Darwin is saying very little but actually giving a huge indication that his financial woes, as they strongly suspect, played a very impor-tant role in his disappearance. He is inadvertently digging a rather large hole for himself. He also again seems to be forgetting he has amnesia, by revealing he has an excellent grasp of his financial situa-tion in 2002 – two years after the holiday that he claims is the last thing he remembers.

Maybe sensing this, Darwin's solicitor asks for a break and spends ten minutes alone with his client before the interview resumes.

Now, suddenly, Darwin is far more open, saying there are matters he wants to clarify from his earlier statement; in particular, that he realises he should have alerted the financial institutions to the fact that he wasn't actually dead.

He maintains he hadn't orchestrated his disappearance, that the canoeing accident had been genuine and he really only has hazy recollections after the year 2000. *Hazy when you choose them to be*, think the detectives.

Asked what he has been doing in the years after his disappearance – one of the key unanswered questions – he replies: 'I don't honestly know. I don't seem to have long fingers. I seem to have fat ones. Probably have been doing manual work or something. I don't know. I don't have a lot of fat on me.'

DS Henderson shuffles in his seat, moves closer to the screen. He could sell tickets to this performance. Darwin lets slip that had he alerted the financial institutions when he first came back from the dead, 'it would have been exactly the same as at the beginning'. All the properties would have been repossessed and sold in a 'fire sale' for much less than they were worth, and although the financial institu-tions would recover their money, he and Anne would be left with nothing and declared bankrupt.

The detectives, of course, know he is still claiming he remembers absolutely nothing about that stage of his life. To them it is a clear admission that he is well aware he was about to lose everything when he disappeared in his red canoe with the banks and credit card compa-nies beating at his door. Darwin is proving to be a pretty inept liar.

He goes on to tell the officers that he only felt it safe to publicly come back from the dead when the Seaton Carew houses had been sold and he had enough money to repay what Anne had received from the insurance companies. But if he has been suffering from amnesia since 2000, how does he remember any of these rather important details?

He feels that once he had the money to repay what was owed, it was then just a case of figuring out how to return to the land of the living.

He claims he wanted to avoid hurting his sons' feelings through revealing he had secretly been hidden away with their mother for a 'year or two', so came up with the idea of walking into a police station in London, hoping everyone – the boys, the police, his friends and family – would believe he'd had a miraculous resurrection.

'When I returned to the family home, I, me, John Ronald Darwin, decided not to inform any financial institution, because I knew I would be made bankrupt/we would be made bankrupt,' he says.

'Because I knew what would happen, I delayed informing any financial institutions until I could properly, officially, return from the dead, which happened to be this Saturday just gone. However, because of press coverage and one thing or another, I have not been able to do that.'

He insists no one else had a clue that he had actually come back into Anne's life several years earlier. 'Just Anne knew, right?' asked DC McArthur. 'So no other family members knew?'

'Oh God no,' Darwin says.

'And the answer to why I said "God no" is because at the moment, err, at Basingstoke police station, my son left a message that he would not speak to me. Neither son will speak to me; they, all of the family, won't have anything to do with me.

'My wife – sorry, it should be my ex-wife, because she won't have anything to do with me now because I created all this mess – so nobody had anything . . . I've lost everything.'

The investigators still want to know where Darwin has been during his missing five years and ask him outright. He claims that after coming back from the dead he had lived locally, but won't specify where, other than admitting to spending some of the time at The Cliff after turning up on Anne's doorstep a year later.

'Where were you, John?' he is asked directly by DC McArthur.

'No comment to that,' he responds.

But then he gets cocky again.

'But you don't know where I was last month: if I had a million dollars, a million pounds, a million yen, or whatever, I bet you don't know, and the point I'm making is I came back for a specific reason. I didn't have to. The only reason I came back, which is on the statement, is to repay; there was never any intention of defrauding anybody.'

Again, he is asked where he has been.

'If you want us to believe you, tell us.'

He cracks, a little.

'Locally,' is the response.

'How local are we talking, Hartlepool?'

'Not a million miles away.'

'Seaton Carew?'

'No comment' is the reply and he accuses the detective of asking leading questions.

'How is it a leading question to ask, "Where have you been?"?'

'Because I used to do maths and I know a flow chart when I see one,' is the bizarre response.

Darwin has already let slip far more than he intended, but he hopes the main part of his lie is intact: Anne is innocent. Keep lying, he has decided; these buffoons haven't got a clue.

There is a ten-minute break while the officers change the tapes.

Hutch pops his head into the monitoring office in response to the detective sergeant's quick update. 'If the intention was to come back and pay back, why the pantomime in the London police station?' he asks. 'He's had all this time to plan his comeback and this is the best he can come up with? Tosser.'

The interview is about to resume. Hutch is convinced that John the-big-I-am Darwin believes he'll soon be walking away. No chance, Hutch mutters, scrolling through emails on his Blackberry as he heads back to his office. It's 9.12 p.m. and what will be the last session of the day is underway.

Darwin says that after his return he had instructed Anne to sell the two Seaton Carew houses.

'That was the whole point,' he says.

He insists it had been his idea to put both houses into his son Mark's name, while Anne was trying to sell them, because it was possible she would be out of the country, planning her new life abroad, and it would be far simpler for Mark to carry out a sale transaction.

It's important to remember that at this stage the detectives still believe it is entirely possible the boys had been in on the plot, so they ask Darwin if he had spent some of the time hiding out at the home of either Mark or Anthony, who both live just outside the capital.

'Were they involved, John?'

Darwin chuckles.

'Well, the Queen lives in London too, but I haven't been staying at Buckingham Palace,' he tells them.

He can't help himself. He may be under arrest and facing jail, but he is still confident the detectives will never discover exactly why he had ended his adventure and walked into a police station nearly six years after he was presumed to have drowned.

He is convinced he has all bases covered. It's all part of the Darwin master plan – and these guys will never figure it out, he reassures himself. I'm much smarter than them.

'Have you had any contact with them [the boys] at all?' he is asked.

'No,' he responds.

'None whatsoever?'

'I can categorically say that that is correct and I will tell you why. The gunpowder plot failed because too many people knew about it. Myself and my wife knew that I wasn't informing the relevant authorities and that was all. There were two people involved therefore. Two people. Nobody else. Therefore, it could be kept quiet. More than two people and it certainly wouldn't. That's my explanation.'

It's DS Henderson's turn to chuckle. *Guido Darwin*.

Addressing both officers, Darwin says: 'As I mentioned before, both of you didn't know where I was last month. Therefore, if I wasn't going to come back to do this, why the hell did I come back?'

Darwin seems convinced they will buy his explanation and

confident the real reason for his return will remain his secret. Of course, the police already know his entire story is lie after lie, but there's still no concrete proof that his wife was in on it from the beginning.

The walls are closing in, but there's still work to be done.

14

'The Ugly One's Me'

DETECTIVE CONSTABLES ROWLAND and McArthur have spent the day asking question after question, listening to 'no comment' answers for most of it, but the moment they have waited for has finally arrived.

It's time for the introduction of the damning photograph that has blown apart his and Anne's concocted story.

'I'm going to show you a photograph, John,' says DC McArthur, 'and you may well have seen this before because, in fairness, it has been in the press. I'm showing you a photograph of three people.'

The picture from Panama is placed in front of him.

'Can you identify those three people?' he's asked.

'Well, the ugly one's me,' Darwin replies.

'And which one would you say the ugly one is?' the officer asks.

'The little one. Little fat fella on the left.'

In the remote monitoring room DS Henderson bursts out laughing. This is comedy gold.

Darwin is asked to describe himself.

'An old man, balding, blue eyes.'

'Physical build?' asks the officer.

'Slight.'

'Anything distinctive about you, would you say?' McArthur continues.

'Not really, no.'

'The person in the middle?'

'Person in the middle's my wife.'

'And the gentleman in the striped shirt?'

'Er, Mario Vilar, from Move to Panama.'

Asked if he would like to explain the photograph, there's a predictable 'No comment'.

Told it was taken on 14 July 2006, John replies: 'I've no idea when it was taken.'

He admits he had been planning to move to Panama 'sometime in the future', but is vague about timings.

McArthur continues.

'During the time that you were . . . I'll say "in hiding", because that's in essence what you were: hiding from the authorities . . . did you ever disguise yourself?'

'No comment,' says John.

'Did you ever change your appearance?'

'No comment.'

'How would you describe your lifestyle before you went missing?'

'Private. Private family man. Now I'm a private ex-family man.'

He's asked about the discrepancies over his alleged amnesia and the fact that he remembers things that happened in the years during which he claims to have no memory. He's on the back foot, saying he remembers 'some things, not all'.

Right . . .

He's questioned about his private life.

'Did you go to the pub and stuff like that?' asks McArthur.

'No,' says John. 'I read a lot.'

No doubt books on amnesia, thinks DS Henderson.

'Did you go out for walks, go to the beach? You know, things like that?'

'No comment,' says John.

'Have you been out of the country recently?'

'No comment.'

The detective continues.

'During the course of these interviews, you started off by saying that you had amnesia and couldn't remember things.

'We've now established you do have some recollections and we've gone over those and spoken about them . . . for example, turning up back at your wife's and then having a conscious decision about what you were going to do and the course of action that you were going to conduct over the next period of time, shall I say.'

Darwin interjects: 'That is quite different from having recollections of *all* periods of time throughout my life.'

The questioning turns to Anne, but as the detective begins to ask a question Darwin interrupts.

'I would like to state that my wife acted under extreme duress.'

Explain, he's asked. 'What's extreme duress?'

'No comment.'

'Is it a threat of violence?'

Another 'No comment.'

Then: 'I explained earlier, in another interview, that the decision for any course of action after I turned up at The Cliff, having been presumed dead, was mine and mine alone.'

He insists that under 'extreme duress' he had persuaded Anne not to alert the authorities. And then to sell the houses. 'She had no choice,' he says.

'So your wife always does what you tell her?' he's asked.

'Ninety-nine per cent of the time, yes.'

It's getting late, almost 10 p.m., so McArthur tells John that, since he has given them a lot of information and plenty to think about, he is ending interviewing for the day.

It had indeed been a long day, but John still believes he has the upper hand.

The officers, though, are happy with the day's developments and now more convinced than ever that the whole amnesia story is just another of John's lies and that he had faked his death in 2002 to escape his crippling debt.

But they still have to prove it.

Hutch later reveals that each time detectives had finished interviewing John they felt like they needed a shower.

'He was just a thoroughly objectionable, dishonest and arrogant little man,' he says.

While Darwin was being quizzed, Detective Inspector Andy Greenwood had called a press conference.

He tells the large gathering of journalists that the investigation into alleged fraud is 'ongoing' and that it appears John Darwin has started to regain his memory by giving 'an account' of his activities since his disappearance in March 2002.

'It is fair to say he is putting forward some form of explanation,' says DI Greenwood.

He turns his attention to Anne, saying the police have not been in contact with her but are very keen to speak to her.

'I want Mrs Darwin to come and see me,' he says. 'I will speak to her. If she doesn't come, then I will seek her out and speak to her in my time. But I am certainly not going to be chasing Mrs Darwin around the world – the public purse does not stretch to flying to Panama.'

DI Greenwood says it would be remiss of him to say whether he considered her as a witness or suspect in the case, but adds: 'I am aware of the rumours and speculation in the media. My latest information is that she may be accompanied by two men in Panama.'

No prizes for guessing who they are . . .

He says the investigation had become a 'global inquiry' with leads coming from North and South America, mainland Europe . . . 'all over the world'. The detective inspector also reveals that Darwin had not asked to contact his family or friends, saying: 'He did not take up the opportunity to speak to anyone.

'It is a complicated and protracted inquiry and it will go on for some considerable time.'

Regarding the intriguing question as to whether police considered Mark and Anthony to be part of the investigation, he says: 'I am in contact with their sons.

'I spoke to them yesterday.

'They are keeping their heads down at the moment because of the publicity and the trauma they have been through.

'They have been affected by the publicity, but time is a great healer.'

Asked outright if they were witnesses or suspects, DI Greenwood concludes: 'That's for me to decide at a later date, but at the moment they are witnesses.'

15

'Fancy Seeing You Here'

WHILE JOHN IS feeling the heat in Cleveland, back in Panama I'm still working on a plan to get Anne home to face the music. But not too quickly. My job is not yet done. I want her full story.

For two days, she has been growing increasingly restless, desperately trying to contact her immigration lawyer in Panama City, Beth Ann Gray. On Wednesday afternoon, she tracks her down and makes an appointment for the following morning. I'm conscious that she seems more concerned about seeing her lawyer than she does about getting back to see her husband, but, for me, that's fine.

Exactly what is going on in Anne's mind only she knows. But, with the world – and most importantly, her sons – now knowing she has told some unforgivable lies, she is in turmoil.

'What on earth is going to happen?' she keeps asking. 'How am I going to sort this all out?'

Her lack of sleep is reflected in her face: heavy eyes; crimson nose; pale and blotchy skin. She knows Cleveland Police have been kept abreast of her movements and detectives want to speak to her on her return. It's evident she has done some pretty bad things, but, for me, it is still impossible not to feel some sympathy towards her. Watching someone's life fall so dramatically apart is not easy. Readying herself to go home and face the music must have been daunting beyond belief. Whatever her fate, it wasn't going to be easy.

Steve and I are exceptionally nervous about taking Anne back into the lions' den – the city where all our journalistic rivals are on the ground looking for us. But it would be totally irresponsible not to get Anne to her lawyer. She was, after all, in the mire right up to her neck.

We rise early, load our bags in the boot of the rental car and head off. There's nowhere to grab a coffee so Steve says he'll pull over when he spots somewhere en route to the capital an hour or so away.

It's a glorious sunny morning and with Steve at the wheel we sit back and enjoy the scenery, pondering what lies ahead. There is little in the way of conversation. Traffic is light at first but gets much heavier as we reach the outskirts of the city.

It's the first time Steve and I have seen the capital in daylight; it was dusk when we arrived on our flight from Miami three days earlier and pitch black when we fled with Anne.

We pass the slum tenements of El Chorillo before hitting the dense clusters of steel skyscrapers, high-rise condos, offices and shiny new hotels of the crowded inner city, which is noisy, colourful and vibrant. Framed by the pristine sandy beaches of the Atlantic Ocean and lush tropical rainforests, Panama City is home to 1.5 million people.

Sadly, there's no time for sightseeing, or visiting the four-centuries-old historical quarter, the Casco Viejo, an ornate mix of Spanish, French and Caribbean architecture and cobbled streets, with pastel-coloured buildings, for which the hippest part of town is famed.

The closer we get to our destination, the more apprehensive we become. There are some top newspaper operators on the ground from rival papers – both dailies and Sundays – and any one of them will jump through flaming hoops to spoil our party.

We are craning our necks in all directions as we approach the offices of Gray & Co. on a street called Calle Eusebio A. Morales in the leafy district of El Cangrejo. Sweat is pumping out of my body and, just like when I was waiting for Anthony Harwood to give me Anne's address, it has nothing to do with the heat and humidity.

We find the building, drive past and circle twice. On the third recce, we pull up on the side of the road thirty metres away. Steve uses his binoculars, a vital piece of equipment for all photographers, to see if he can spot anyone lurking with a camera in a nearby window or doorway. When you do this for a living, you know how industrious colleagues can be. He can't see anything but . . . anybody on that street could be the paid eyes and ears of one of our rivals. Two white men and a white woman aren't a difficult spot. We move the car and pull up outside.

Our nervousness isn't lost on Anne, who remarks that she feels like a character out of a spy movie.

'What on earth are you expecting to happen?' she asks.

'I just don't want anyone else getting to you,' I respond, though, admittedly, as much for our good as hers.

Clutching her document folder, Anne gets out of the car. She has a mobile phone and my number is programmed into it. I lean out of the window.

'Call me if you need anything and let me know as soon as you're finished. We'll meet you back here.'

Anne walks the few feet to the steps and disappears into the lawyer's office. My heart races. I'm nervous. This is the first time since I met Anne that I do not feel in control.

Steve and I decide not to wait outside in case we are spotted, so we park in a nearby underground garage and find an Internet cafe where we grab a coffee and go online to see if there are any updates on the story. *It is a terrible, terrible mistake.*

After an hour, we have still heard nothing and assume (something I've been taught never to do) that Anne must have an awful lot of matters she needs to discuss with her lawyer. We are reading the British papers online when my mobile rings. It's Anne and she sounds absolutely frantic. My heart rate surges.

'Where are you?' she says. 'I've been trying to get through to you for ages.'

My hand tightens around the phone and I press it hard against my ear. What the hell has happened?

'Some journalists have been here and barged in while I was with my lawyer.'

Shit, shit, shit.

'They were trying to take pictures. There was a terrible commotion and they were thrown out.

'I couldn't get through to you so I rang the British Consul.'

My heart stops. You did *what*? Not only had other journalists busted the story, but Anne has rung the British Consul and someone there is bound to have told her to have nothing more to do with any journalists, meaning the show for us is almost certainly over. It's worse than a nightmare. I knew the mobile phone reception was weak in the area, but I was furious with myself for not having checked there was a signal at all times. I should never have let the lawyer's office out of my sight. What an idiotic mistake.

Steve and I dash around the corner on foot, only to have our worst fears realised. We are greeted by the sight of a smiling colleague from a rival newspaper standing right outside the lawyer's office with a photographer.

'Well, fancy seeing you here,' the reporter says with a smile.

My forced smile probably does little to mask my abject horror. I knew if one paper was on to us, others wouldn't be far behind. A pack mentality often kicks in when journalistic rivals are hunting their prey. Every journalist working the story has spent days looking for us. Now they've found us. I am absolutely gutted. Being told they are there is one thing, but seeing them in the flesh is shattering.

We exchange pleasantries, mine through gritted teeth, then Steve and I walk up the iron stairs to the lawyer's office and ring the bell, fully expecting the worst.

'It's David Leigh,' I say to the receptionist who answers the buzzer. 'I'm a friend of Anne Darwin's.'

Silence for a few seconds, and then I hear the girl talking to someone in Spanish. I am fully expecting to be told to get lost, but am amazed when she says, 'Okay, you can come in,' and pushes a buzzer, releasing the catch on the door.

Inside, I am warmly greeted by Beth Ann, who shakes my hand and says, 'Ah, so you're David; we've been trying to get hold of you. Where have you been?'

I shake my head.

'I'm so sorry,' I say. 'I didn't realise the reception around here was quite so bad. What's been going on?'

The lawyer leads me through to a small, glass-fronted conference room where Anne is sitting shell-shocked on a chair in the left-hand corner, looking like a frightened mouse.

'We had some visitors, didn't we Anne?' the lawyer says with a smile. Anne bites her lip, nods, but says nothing.

Beth Ann, in her late thirties, with long flowing blonde hair and what looks like swirling, henna tattoos on her hands is an incredibly jolly character, upbeat and smiling and totally unfazed by the whole episode: there is nothing very lawyer-like about her.

Her accent is unusual, distinctly English in some ways but Hispanic in others, and she explains her father was Panamanian and her mother English, and that while growing up she spent at least one holiday a year visiting relatives in East Sussex. She explains how two journalists had barged in and tried to take photographs before her staff had managed to wrestle them out. She had rung the local police and, unable to contact me, had also called the British Embassy to see if they had any advice, but got the distinct impression that they didn't really want to get involved, which was music to my ears. They were, however, making checks to see if there was an international arrest warrant out for Anne and had offered with help in making travel arrangements for her to return to England. I have to stop that from happening at all costs.

The news isn't great but it could have been far worse and I know, thank God, we are once more back in the game. Not that life is going to be particularly easy from now on. Peeking through the conference room's slatted blinds, I see several other journalists have joined the reporter outside. I know the 'pack' – now working together and with Anne firmly in their sights – will grow as time wears on.

Getting away from everyone is going to be nigh impossible. Some of the journalists have already driven their cars up to the entrance of the lawyer's office; there are photographers walking about with their cameras slung over their shoulders and even one guy with a TV camera. Among others, I recognise reporters from the *Telegraph*, the *Express* and the *Sun*. Everyone sitting and waiting for us to make our move. Fuck!

For hours, Anne remains seated on a chair in the corner, no doubt contemplating her future. Her mind is thousands of miles away in England, worrying about what she is going back to, whether her beloved sons will ever forgive her and, perhaps first and foremost, if she is headed to jail.

Steve and I chat on a terrace at the rear of the building discussing possible escape options. None seem particularly good. The predicament in which Anne now finds herself really is the least of her concerns: that's our problem. Anne says she had discussed the visa issues she needed to address with Beth Ann, and they are also making arrangements for the lawyer to be allowed to sign for her shipment of goods from England when it arrives any day now.

Anne explains that she still hadn't actually formally applied for a visa allowing her to live in Panama and is adamant she must do that before she returns to the UK. The significance of that isn't yet fully apparent to me.

I bring Beth Ann up to speed on what's been happening and explain that Anne is in for a pretty rough ride when she gets back home. I ask if there is anything preventing her from returning to Panama if, worst-case scenario, she is convicted of a crime and serves time in jail. Amazingly, there's not. As long as she declares the crime on the immigration form, she will be welcomed back with open arms. That's Panama for you.

Anne seems pleased to hear the news. The previous evening, we had talked late into the night about exactly what the future now held for her. She knew she had betrayed everyone close to her and felt there was no one left to turn to.

And there was the theme that she kept returning to: 'Why did I listen to John?'

I again try to reassure her that her family and true friends will, in time, forgive her for what has happened. But Anne isn't convinced. She has no idea where she will go after the police have finished talking to her . . . if she's granted bail, which seems unlikely. She has told a lot of lies and betrayed those nearest and dearest to her. Her future looks grim and she is a very frightened woman with seemingly no one in the world to turn to.

I genuinely feel very sorry her. She isn't some crazed killer and is certainly no danger to anyone. She is actually quite good company, with, at times a very dry sense of humour. But I know she is in big trouble once she returns to the UK and have already asked the *Mail* to help find her a good lawyer. Such was her dazed state of mind it was something she hadn't even thought about.

I have been working hard on trying to persuade her to open up and tell me the whole story, so the more time I have with her the better. But at this precise moment, I have far more pressing matters to contend with. Pacing around the lawyer's office, my immediate concern is how the hell can I get Anne away from the pack of journalists outside?

After three days of filing exclusive stories that were making headlines across the UK, the situation I now found myself in was a disaster and shaking off the 'enemy' was not going to be at all easy.

16

'Ladies, Start Your Engines'

Anne peers over the top of her frameless specs, affording a half-smile and a puzzled look that appears to be questioning my sanity.

'I assume you are joking?' she asks.

To be fair, I have just asked how she feels about being dangled from a second-storey balcony by her wrists, dropping onto a rusty corrugated tin roof, climbing down a ladder with most of the rungs missing, then hopping into the boot of a waiting car that will shoot off at high speed through the bustling streets of Panama City at rush hour. And, oh yes, there will probably be three or four other cars in hot pursuit. All very James Bond – and totally unrealistic.

There's a bit of a silence, so I stroke my chin, lamely trying to give the appearance of someone who knows what they are talking about, having methodically considered all options.

'Well, um, yea, that was kind of Plan A,' I respond eventually, knowing full well my cunning 'escape' plan will undoubtedly end up more Frank Spencer than Freddy Forsyth.

'I know it's not ideal . . . But, err, what do you think?'

I laugh, a little too nervously for my own good. Anne looks down at the ground 20 feet below, then straight back at me and shakes her head.

'And what the hell is Plan B?' she says.

It seems a fair enough question under the circumstances.

'Not quite sure,' I respond honestly. 'Still working on that one!'

To my astonishment, and what can only be attributed to Anne's slightly dazed and confused state of mind having hardly slept in days, she says she is willing to give the absurd escape plan a go. But she isn't the only one with misgivings and I begin pondering the headlines that will almost certainly follow when my ridiculous scheme ends in catastrophe, with death or serious injury a high probability.

'Think I'll give Plan B a little more consideration,' I say, somewhat forlornly.

Truth is, it would have been hard to pick a more unlikely person for such a daring getaway. Anne is a small woman with intense brown eyes: she is free of make-up and would not have looked out of place standing outside a supermarket wearing a Salvation Army bonnet and uniform, rattling a collection box.

Just a fortnight before Christmas, she should be at home with family or friends, not thinking about whether or not to launch herself off a balcony in the middle of Central America. She turns away, shaking her head and no doubt asking herself how on earth she had wound up in this mess. She's not the only one . . .

'Shame,' says Steve as Anne walks out of earshot. Always one for a spot of adventure, he's grinning again. 'Would have been fun to give it a go.'

Outside on the street are a steadily growing number of journalist 'friends'. To say it's a nightmare is an understatement.

I still haven't figured out exactly why Ann had agreed to pack a suitcase and disappear into the night with me and Steve, two people she had never even met before: not that I am complaining. By agreeing to do so, she had given me a series of incredible scoops on a news story that is making headlines throughout the UK. From the BBC to Sky News, from *The Times* to the *Sun*, her astonishing revelations in the *Mirror* and the *Mail* are being followed up by just about every news organisation going, and up until that moment, everything had gone like a dream.

Now, I thought to myself, we're fucked.

Having decided dropping Anne over the balcony isn't really a sensible option, I have to come up with another plan. I briefly go outside to talk to my rivals and see if there is any way I can work out a deal with them in exchange for a photograph of Anne, but it was never really going to happen.

They are hungry to gatecrash the party and I'm determined they get nothing.

I walk around to check out the car park at the back of the lawyer's office, but quickly see there is no other escape route. It is surrounded by walls or fences on all sides, all too high to climb. There is only one door out of Beth Ann's office and one driveway by which to leave, and my colleagues now have it comfortably covered, waiting for our departure, with several cars ready to follow wherever we go. It's one heck of a dilemma.

Fortunately, Beth Anne is amazingly helpful and says if we need her or her staff to assist in any way we only have to ask. I consider staying inside the building until after her staff have gone home, then trying to slip out under cover of darkness. But I know only too well how these guys operate; they'll never leave their positions or be fooled that easily.

I tell Beth Anne we are just going to have to make a run for it and she suggests enlisting the help of local police to move the journalists on. But I know the chances of losing everyone are beyond slim. One of the main problems is that it is impossible to get Anne to the car park without being seen. My mood isn't helped by knowing that they are probably laughing and backslapping each other, congratulating themselves on their tracking and trapping skills.

We needed something a little more cunning. Eventually, I decide to take up Beth Ann's offer of help and use most of her staff. 'Plan B' is on.

We wait until 4.30 p.m., the start of rush hour. Will my great escape plan work? Or will it end as badly as it did for Steve McQueen?

Like the buildings of the city, the traffic is an odd mixture of old and new. Gleaming luxury new cars jostle for road positioning with huge, battered old trucks spewing clouds of deadly fumes. And there are former American school buses, brightly painted in psychedelic colours, resembling something from the flower-power days of the 1960s. Apparently, the yellow vehicles were shipped from the States when they went out of service, splashed with bucket-loads of paint, then put to use as public transport.

Meanwhile, noisy phut-phut motorbikes and mopeds with wire cages precariously strapped to the back, carrying chickens to sell at street corner markets, weave in and out of the cars, buses and lorries, their riders doing their best to avoid running down the vendors, who risk life and limb as they stand in the middle of the road peddling strange-looking fruit, bottles of water and gum. Throw in the incessant horns and it all added up to traffic chaos. And for my plan to work, it's exactly what we need.

With the help of about ten smartly dressed secretaries and legal assistants, we all huddle closely together around Anne and inch down the black wrought-iron staircase, carefully keeping her out of sight from the prying camera lenses.

We must have looked quite ridiculous, like something out of a Monty Python sketch, as we slowly made our descent with Anne hidden in our midst. Naturally, as soon as the waiting journalists see the huddle of bodies, they know we are about to make our move, and while some jump in their cars and start their engines, ready to follow, others wait on either side of the automatic driveway gates – the only way out – with cameras ready. Everyone is desperate for new photographs of Anne.

Our huddle heads back into the car park and moves to where we are just about out of sight. I tell each of the women assisting to get in their cars, line up and wait for my order to go. The phrase, 'Ladies, start your engines', sprang to mind.

'Ready? . . . GO!' I yell, and with a piercing screech of tyres – these women were good – the convoy roars down the drive and out into the capital's rush-hour traffic. Crouched down on the floor in the back of the last of the six vehicles, Anne looks petrified.

'Keep your head down!' I shout from my hiding place alongside her – and Anne's nose instinctively moves to within an inch of a rubber floor mat.

From my low vantage point, I can just about make out the look of horror on the faces of some of the journalists outside, as they helplessly try to peer into the blacked-out windows of the cars racing past them and out onto the busy one-way circular system.

Bedlam ensues: brakes squeal, horns shriek at jet-engine deafening decibels, locals scream – not speaking Spanish is a definite bonus – but it's too early to celebrate.

They had almost certainly been expecting one, maybe two, vehicles, but now they were in a blind panic about which of the six to follow. They are trying to take photographs while frantically dashing for their own cars. To make matters even worse for them, each driver in the getaway convoy has been instructed to starburst in different directions as soon as they possibly can, making the ensuing pack's task of picking the right car a nightmare.

'Just stay down,' I repeat to Anne, who by this time is crouched up in a ball.

We both stay glued to the floor of the car as we race along the traffic-choked streets, weaving in and out of vehicles, while our driver, Joe, a burly black guy who looked like he'd go ten rounds with the best of them, runs a seemingly endless stream of red lights – his horn constantly blaring. It may not have been much fun in the back, but up front, judging from the insane grin on his face, he is having a ball.

There's a sudden thud as the car swerves violently to the right and I glance out of the window to see we have mounted the pavement to steer around a stationary bus, whose disembarking passengers are running for their lives as Joe roars by, furiously yelling and gesticulating at them to get out of his way.

Obviously delighted with his latest manoeuvre and, without taking his foot off the gas, he turns around and gives a beaming gold-toothed smile, convincing me that he really is mad. His teeth remind me of Goldie in 007's *The World is Not Enough*. I'm seeing James bloody Bond everywhere. I give him the thumbs-up, then turn to look at my fellow passenger, who now appears to be praying.

'Don't worry, he's bonkers,' I mouth, twirling my finger next to my head, in case she hasn't grasped what I am saying.

Anne looks horrified and says nothing. What on earth had she got herself into with this crazy cat-and-mouse escapade?

I have been on some pretty hairy car rides during my time on the road as a reporter, including one I recalled in the Middle East, wearing a bulletproof jacket as I was driven at high speed though Gaza with the rat-a-tat sound of machine-gun fire ringing in my ears. But, believe you me, Joe's own one-man Panamanian Grand Prix isn't far behind in the shit-your-pants stakes.

My phone rings.

'Come on Dave, which one are you in?'

It's my mate Lee Brown, one of my pursuers and a reporter from my own news agency working on assignment for the *Daily Express*.

'Tell me it's the Merc?'

I laugh. *Full marks for trying Browner but I'm not about to give the game away.*

'Sorry mate, this line is terrible,' I respond. 'I think I'm losing you . . .' Click.

It wasn't the Mercedes, or one of the three smart black BMWs in the convoy, that I had chosen as our getaway car. I had picked the least likely of the cars available to me – a battered old heap, which I hoped the journalists would dismiss as too unlikely an option. Fortunately, I had been right.

Now out on the open freeway and with Joe doing his best to break the land speed record, while driving with one arm dangling out of his open window, I decide to pop my head over the parapet, and look back to see if we are in the clear. My opposition journalists have obviously chosen to follow the luxury cars, whose drivers, with Beth Ann's blessing, have instructions to circle the city centre for the next hour, which, I hope, will give us just enough time to make our getaway.

Initially, we had been heading directly away from the airport – the most obvious destination. Now I instruct our driver to double back and get there as quickly as possible. Joe repeatedly nods his head and grins but says nothing, jerking the steering wheel violently to the right to make the latest in a series of highly illegal turns. 'Quickly' equated to supersonic in Joe's world.

Ahead, Steve is already at Tocumen International Airport, fifteen miles to the east of Panama City, having stayed behind and made his way there after we had made our getaway. He had waited until the pack had left in hot pursuit, collected our rental car from the underground garage, with bags in the boot, and, once he was 100 per cent sure he wasn't being followed, made his way to the airport. I message, asking if there's any sign of photographers with prying lenses. I couldn't have asked for a better lookout man.

The response is a simple text: *coast is clear.*

I had checked possible 'escape flights' before setting off and the best bet was a Copa Airlines flight to Miami leaving in just over an hour's time. Joe stands on the brakes and screeches to a halt outside the terminal and Anne and I jump out. Joe is still smiling but says nothing as I thrust a wad of crumpled notes into his enormous palm and shake his hand. He just keeps on grinning. We dash inside and meet Steve.

Seeing there is no unwanted welcoming party, we quickly check in and go through security to an airside lounge, where we huddle tightly together in the corner. My mobile almost makes a hole in my pocket as I constantly check it for the time. I'm convinced my watch has stopped. We expect to be caught any moment. Finally, the flight is called. We go to the gate, board the plane and take our seats. We hold our breath, wait for the doors to close, scrutinising every passenger. Steve and I let out a huge sigh of relief as the Miami-bound Copa 737 takes to the skies.

Game on.

17

John Knows Best

SHATTERED AND BEWILDERED, Anne flakes back on the sofa in our suite at the Conrad Hotel in the Brickell business district of Miami and accepts the offer of a brandy. She doesn't really know if she is coming or going any more.

It's a fancy suite with two bedrooms, a kitchen, a dining area and a living room with comfortable armchairs and sofas. Outside, the view across Biscayne Bay from the thirtieth floor is ablaze with what looks like a million sparkling lights. But Anne is oblivious to her surroundings. Never could she have imagined that her first stay in the United States would be under such extraordinary circumstances.

'I suppose I just didn't think things through properly,' she says as she reflects on the latest calamitous chapter in her life.

It's hard to disagree.

'I told John no one would believe his ridiculous story about amnesia, but, as usual, he wouldn't listen to me.'

She's right about that, too.

'We'd been on holiday in Costa Rica for a week and John had seemed fine and very relaxed. It was the first time he'd really been himself in years.'

I suppose it's difficult being yourself when you're dead, I thought to myself.

'We'd spent time horse riding, walking and lying by the pool.' (It was John who had taken the photograph Anne sent Anthony after his reappearance.)

'We had a lot of fun . . . a bit like the old times. Then we got back to Panama and he said, "I'm going back", and that was that.'

I have no idea whether to believe Anne or not. Perhaps she no longer has any reason to lie, but on the other hand . . .

'He came up with the amnesia plan and convinced himself he'd get away with it. I thought he was crazy and told him no one would believe him.'

She shakes her head. John always knows best, she says. *Is she practising her defence again?* She says the amnesia story was particularly ironic because her husband prided himself on his memory – making a mockery of his ridiculous charade.

'I told him he was a bloody fool,' she says. 'He's got such a good memory and was always very good with dates, which is one of the things that made him such a good teacher. Anyone who knows John knows what a good memory he's got.'

That very telling quote will be among many picked up the following day by the Cleveland detectives who are busy trying to extract the truth from Mr Amnesia. Anne is providing all the evidence that her husband is trying very badly to conceal. The cops will scrutinise every word of the interview.

On the one hand, Anne seems a little in awe of her husband and comes across as a proud and very much devoted wife, someone who would do anything to stand up for him and fight his corner. But on the other hand, she is barely able to contain her fury, firmly blaming him for getting them into 'this whole bloody mess' in the first place.

The brandy is gone and she accepts the offer of a second glass. She shrugs her shoulders.

'Why not?' she says. 'I don't normally drink more than one glass of anything. But I suppose it will help me get some sleep. I could certainly do with it.'

Anne and I are alone in the suite. My home is fifteen minutes away, but I've learnt my lesson and am not letting Anne out of my sight again. My wife has dropped a bag of fresh clothes at the hotel for me, but Steve has opted for a night in his own bed at his South Beach condo. He'll be back bright and early in the morning.

Anne's mind and emotions are in chaos. While angry at her husband, she is also furious and ashamed at herself, and very aware that she could and should have, if she'd had an ounce of sense in her body, walked away from the whole absurd scheme at the very start.

'Why didn't I just tell the boys at the very beginning?' she asks. 'I wanted to and kept telling myself, "Talk to the boys, Anne", "Stop being so stupid", but, of course, I didn't.

'They would have talked me out of it and put an end to all this foolishness there and then.

'They're both very sensible – certainly more sensible than their parents, it would seem.'

She isn't wrong. Maybe it was because she knew what they would say, or maybe it was because she didn't want to risk implicating them in what she knew to be a pretty serious crime? Whatever the reason, she had kept mum and very soon now she would have to pay the price, likely a very heavy price indeed, for her unconscionable lies.

Once Anne had started lying, she felt she was almost immediately in too deep to go back and, by her own admission, didn't have the guts to undo the considerable damage she had already done. One lie immediately led to another and another, and everything quickly escalated from there. She admits to having no idea of how quickly things would spiral out of control after making that initial phone call to the police saying her husband was missing. Within days, she was lying to every single person she knew and loved.

Yet one telephone call could have ended it. Yes, there would have been public humiliation and shame and John would have been incandescent. But it would have been over and the consequences not a fraction as serious as they had now become. She was in it right up to her neck and knew there was a very real chance of going to jail. The thought has been playing on her mind constantly. She says it's the most frightening possibility imaginable. The fear of the unknown is haunting her.

'There's also the humiliation, the indignation and the humiliation for my sons that both their parents might end up behind bars,' she says.

There's very little 'might' I'm afraid, Anne.

'I feel I have been living a kind of prison sentence for the last five years, but that's been my own private sentence and the public one will now follow.

'It's John's fault, but I know I have to accept my share of the blame too. He's a very clever man, very well read. He was a very good teacher and well respected.

'The problem is he was never satisfied with what he had. He always had ideas above his station. He wanted to be grander than he was. He wanted people to look up to him, but I wasn't interested in all that and never really cared what other people thought.

'All I ever wanted was a nice, quiet life.'

***

John already owned his own home, 187 Durham Road, Leadgate, and that was where married life for the blissfully happy young couple began. To be married and living in her own home was everything Anne had ever dreamt of, and she and John excitedly talked about having children to make their family complete. John had bought the house a few years earlier and Anne loved it, but he already had ambitions on a bigger, grander home.

While Anne was perfectly content, she would quickly discover that her husband was never quite satisfied with his lot. They were both earning a fair wage, but money was still tight and Anne repeatedly told John not to be so foolish when he told her he wanted her to have the best of everything.

To her, it really didn't matter if they didn't have the latest model of fridge or television – but it mattered to John. And as Anne was very quickly learning, what John wanted, he usually got.

It was still early days in their marriage when he dropped a bombshell, the prospect of which terrified his young wife. Why didn't they up sticks and emigrate to Australia, he suggested?

'It wasn't something I had ever given any thought to prior to that, and at that time I was still finding my feet within the relationship because we had never lived together before we were married and I was reluctant to move and lose contact with my parents,' she says.

Then, in early 1975, she got the news she had been praying for when she learnt she was pregnant. John was genuinely pleased and dutifully told his parents, though by then his relationship with his father had strained somewhat. No one could quite put their finger on what had happened to cause the fallout, but it was a matter never to be resolved.

In November 1975 Mark was born, but the birth was not the joyous event it should have been for Anne. Although John had been with her throughout the labour, he suddenly decided to leave at the very last minute when nurses told him they would have to perform an emergency caesarean section.

'I was devastated,' Anne recalls. 'He just said he wasn't staying and he left me. It was very upsetting.'

She went home with her newborn and very soon her sadness at being left alone for the birth disappeared as she lovingly cradled her baby in her arms and pondered the rosy future ahead. Now they really were a family, she thought to herself. As was the done thing at the time, she gave up her job to stay at home and be a full-time mother.

When, three years later, she fell pregnant again, she couldn't be happier. She delivered a healthy baby boy, who was christened Anthony. But although she now wanted for nothing, her family complete, John was becoming increasingly restless. He was growing disillusioned with the teaching profession, muttering about declining standards and lack of discipline in the classroom.

It was the era when schools were being closed because of a lack of pupils, and teachers were getting moved around to different schools. With that and an increasing amount of paperwork, John grew disenchanted.

The years after Anthony's birth were not happy ones in the Darwin household. John seemed to have little time for the boys and hated the fact that Anne constantly nagged him about smoking around them in the house. They began to argue more and more, and Anne felt her views were always overlooked.

'He wouldn't shout,' says Anne. 'Through his teacher training he had learnt how to control disruptive pupils and that's how he pretty much made me feel at times – like a second-year pupil in one of his classes.

'I would just be talked down to. Superficially we would discuss things, but my thoughts never seemed to carry any weight.

'Whatever John wanted to do he did in the end.'

She reached the stage where she felt it was pointless even arguing with him. And then, with their relationship at rock bottom, Anne discovered he was having an affair. Worse still, it was with a woman Anthony was working for part-time who ran a door-to-door catalogue company. Anne was furious and heartbroken in equal measures, but the prospect of being a single mother with two young boys to bring up alone terrified her: it was something she just couldn't face. There were tearful confrontations, during which she asked him how he could have betrayed her in such a cruel way.

'What about the boys, your sons?' she screamed at him. 'Don't you care about them?'

John sheepishly apologised, assuring her the affair was over, and slowly they picked up the pieces of their marriage. But it was a clear warning of the sort of man John was and it would take Anne years to recover from the deception.

'I did consider leaving him, but I just couldn't see a life without him,' she says.

The boys, of course, were much too young to know anything about the affair that shook their parents' marriage or the unhappiness it brought their mother.

Mark and Anthony had a happy family life and enjoyed family camping holidays in Scotland and Wales, progressing to the Normandy area of France as they grew older. They would play on the beach as their mam looked on, while John would usually be sat in a deckchair, his nose buried in a book.

Back home, John would take any opportunity he could to go canoeing, having been reintroduced to the childhood sport he loved so much by a fellow teacher. He frequently paddled down the River Wear or in the sea.

His other great passion was computers – he was well ahead of his time. He added more RAM to his beloved ZX Spectrum and taught himself how to write programs to help the boys improve at maths and other subjects. He wrote programs to test his theories about the risks and rewards of investing in 'penny shares' after scouring the *Financial Times* for investment ideas. He would play the stock market during lunch breaks. Like his dad, Mark soon became a computer whizz, to such an extent that his teachers would frequently ask him to explain things to his class.

Anthony was seven when Anne decided to return to work, at least on a part-time basis, and John was only too happy at the prospect of his wife once again earning some extra money. After ten years being a full-time mother, she found a job, first as a sales assistant at Marks & Spencer and then at Boots.

Being out of the house was a breath of fresh air for Anne. John, on the other hand, was miserable at work and told Anne he couldn't go on much longer. Finally, in 1990, like thousands of other teachers around that time, he decided to quit.

When a letter arrived one morning, offering him a job as a financial advisor at Barclays Bank, in Newcastle upon Tyne, he took the plunge. After eighteen years, John's days of teaching were over.

It would take no time at all to discover that the grass isn't always greener on the other side.

'I think John thought a change of career would make everything better – but it didn't,' says Anne.

'He just didn't take to the bank. He felt he was being asked to sell products to people who didn't need them or couldn't really afford them and he wasn't prepared to do that.

'He stuck it out for a year but he was pretty unhappy the whole time he was there. He started looking for other jobs and totally surprised me one day when he said he had decided to join the Prison Service. But it was his decision and I was happy for him. As long as he was happy, I was happy.'

So in 1998, at the age of forty-eight, John embarked on another complete change of career. After finishing his training, he started work at HMP Holme House in Stockton-on-Tees.

'At first he seemed happy,' says Anne. 'But, of course, like any job, it could be stressful at times. It's bound to be stressful working in a prison, but John never brought his work home with him. He never talked about it.'

John did not endear himself to other prison officers. He gave out the impression of being intellectually superior to his colleagues and annoyed them by constantly bragging about his supposed wealth, claiming he had made thousands buying stocks and shares. His colleagues, mainly former miners or servicemen, weren't interested. Worse still, he was a 'scab' who had crossed picket lines when the union went on strike. For that, he was hated.

'John was always very materialistic,' says Anne. 'He bought an old Jag we didn't need and certainly couldn't afford. And at one stage, he bought a sporty little kit car, the sort of car a normal person might drive on a Sunday afternoon – but, not John; he'd drive it in the snow with the roof off if there was a chance of someone seeing him.'

Returning to his disappearance, Anne says there were times when she became a nervous wreck, terrified of going out, or going home.

'One lie led to another and all of a sudden it was way out of control and I was past the point of no return,' she says.

'I know now there has to be no more lying. And that's why I have decided to put my hands up and admit I have done wrong. And I accept I will have to suffer the consequences of my deception.'

It was, indeed, the time for the lying to stop. But is Anne now really telling the truth about what had happened? It doesn't feel that way. Whose skin is she trying to save? Just hers, or also the boys? Something is still very wrong.

It's gone midnight and the end of another long, extraordinary day in the life of the very ordinary Anne Darwin.

She had fled Panama in a scene straight out of an action movie and now here she is, a 'good' Catholic girl from a little pit village in the north-east of England, sitting in a swish hotel in Miami drinking expensive brandy and reflecting on a life in which just about everything has gone wrong. She's in no hurry to go to bed and, although tired, seems almost grateful to be able to talk to someone openly for the first time in years.

Perhaps relaxed by the drink, she opens up a little about the couple's finances and reveals how she and John had set up a company, Jaguar Property Corporation – named after her husband's favourite car – as a vehicle for controlling their assets and buying property.

She says they had more than £200,000 in various bank accounts, adding, incredibly grudgingly in the circumstances: 'I'm sure everyone will want their money back with interest. I know I'll probably end up ruined – with nothing.'

With the lies she's told and having done what she's done, isn't that what both she and John deserve?

Although full of self-pity, she appears genuinely distraught about the damage she has done to the boys, insisting they had been unwittingly dragged into the deception by being named as shareholders of the property company. The boys' role in all this is weighing heavily on my mind. *Surely they must have known?*

'I knew we should never have done that, but John wanted to include them,' she says.

'No doubt that will all come out and then everyone will think they're involved in some way, but they're not, they really aren't.'

I think of *Hamlet*, of Queen Gertrude: 'The lady doth protest too much, methinks.'

'We've dragged them into this mess and they are going to be furious with us and probably hate us for ever.'

That's certainly not out of the question. The boys' statement has revealed how bitterly angry and distressed they are at both their parents. Do Anne and her husband even deserve to be forgiven? Many would argue not.

Anne's arrival into Miami International Airport three hours earlier had, unlike the mad scramble out of Panama, been undramatic, with none of the expected newsmen waiting for her. The night air was hot and humid as she walked through the virtually deserted airport with Steve and I either side of her, forever on the lookout for unwanted rivals.

After collecting our luggage from baggage reclaim, we took a yellow cab for the twenty-minute journey to the hotel. Reservations had been made in false names and when I checked in, I instructed the receptionist that absolutely no calls were to be put through to our suite. I'd had enough close shaves in Panama to leave anything else to chance.

Steve and I also decided to turn off our American mobile phones to prevent other journalists – who were still calling us at all hours of the day and night, fishing for information – from being able to hear the change in dialling tone now that we had left Panama. Somehow, we had managed to slip out of the country unnoticed and although reporters would know that my base in Miami was a possible stop-over destination on the way back to the UK, no one could know for sure where we were.

Early the next morning on his way to the hotel, Steve bought two pay-as-you-go phones – untraceable 'burners' as drug dealers call them – and I emailed the numbers as a way of communication to the select few executives who had been running the story on the *Mail* and the *Mirror*. No one else had a clue where we were – Steve had triple-checked he wasn't followed to the hotel – but speculation was rife.

I receive an email from my close friend, Paul Henderson, one of the best reporters of his generation, who has flown to Panama City from London for the *Mail on Sunday*. Hendo is desperate for a good exclusive line to keep his bosses happy. I tip him off about the Darwin brothers being directors of Jaguar Holdings, through which their parents bought the apartment in Panama City and the huge parcel of land in Escobal. It's a strong story but I already have more than enough new angles to keep the daily papers happy. Despite the highly competitive nature of the business, it's not unusual for reporters to help close colleagues who are up against it. What goes around comes around.

That morning, I turned on my laptop and, for the first time in a week, signed into Instant Messenger meaning work colleagues could see I was online. Message bubbles instantly started popping up on my screen from people wanting to know how we were getting on . . . and where the hell we were.

'*There you are!!!*' wrote Samantha Lawton, one of my staff reporters in Miami.

'*Papers have been offering us money to tell them. So come on, where are you? I could do with a few quid!*'

'*Brazil,*' I quickly respond, '*but don't tell anyone.*'

'*Get lost!*' responds Sam, who hails from Stoke. '*Are you really?*'

Of course, I wasn't about to tell anyone where we were, not even my own trusted reporters. And what Sam didn't know was that we were in a hotel suite less that 50 feet from where she was sitting in the Splash offices in the next building on Brickell Avenue.

Sometimes it really is best to hide in plain sight.

18

'Don't Tell Me He Was Hiding in the Garden Shed'

GETTING WHAT JOURNALISTS call the 'full sit-down' interview with Anne remained my primary objective.

There remained so many unanswered questions. Where had John really been all that time? What had he been up to? The now infamous photograph revealed he had spent some of his time in Panama, but where was he before that? It hadn't even crossed my mind to ask how he'd managed to travel abroad on his John Darwin passport when he was supposedly dead. And how much did Anne really know? It was certainly a lot more than she would have people believe.

I had been joined in Miami by one of the *Daily Mail*'s feature writers, Natalie Clarke, from London. Senior executives at the paper decided they wanted their own staffer on the ground to help out, so we hooked up at the Conrad. I understood the reasoning but wasn't overly thrilled at the writer's impending arrival, and was worried that a new face on the scene at this delicate stage of negotiating for an interview with Anne might scupper my chances.

When Natalie arrived, I explained how close I was to getting the interview the papers were crying out for and, a consummate professional, she agreed to do whatever she could to assist. She also took on a role as Anne's shopping companion. Anne had left Panama with just a few items of clothing and was running out of toiletries and other essentials. Steve drove them to the Village of Merrick Park shopping centre in the upmarket residential area of nearby Coral Gables.

Natalie had expected Anne, who she had only just met, to be distracted or flustered, but was astonished how particular and fussy she was as they went from store to store. No, she didn't like that neckline, or that shape of trouser; she didn't like yellow, she liked blues and simple tailoring.

'I was amazed that she wanted to try everything on, not just grab a bundle of whatever she first saw and dash back to the hotel to sob and shake with emotion,' she said.

'The really strange thing about her was that she seemed so normal. How could she be discussing hems and necklines at a time like this?'

Back at the hotel, Anne tells me she's feeling a little better. She is wearing a new outfit – lilac polo shirt and khaki trousers – and looks refreshed and relaxed. We order room service sandwiches for lunch. As we finish, without fanfare or warning comes an announcement I wasn't expecting.

'Well, I guess we should get on with this interview then.'

Excuse me?

My pulse soars. It's Friday, it's 3 p.m. and I want to cheer as I did as a kid when *Crackerjack* came on the TV. I had been working towards this from the moment I knocked on the door of her apartment in Panama City four – very long – days ago. I had chipped away and already extracted some amazing revelations, but Anne's 'full and frank' was what I and everyone else wanted to hear.

It's 8 p.m. in London, and finally, without any prompting, she is volunteering to grant the interview she knows I am desperate for. Quite why didn't really matter. Patience has paid off. Of course, I want to get on with it straight away, but Natalie has gone to the airport to try and retrieve some lost luggage, which is a massive headache. I can't start without her. Neither she nor the *Mail* would ever forgive me. I call and tell her to get back to the hotel asap.

★★★

Anne, Natalie and myself are seated in a semi-circle in the hotel suite, sipping sparkling mineral water. Steve is moving around the room taking photographs of Anne from different angles, which she has agreed to. There is an air of nervous anticipation. *Are we finally about to learn the truth?*

I turn on my tape recorder and place it on the rectangular glass table in front of her.

'Well, what do you want to know then?' asks Anne in her very matter-of-fact manner.

Still finding it hard to believe she is opening herself up to a full-on interrogation, I take a deep breath and tell her that the first question is easy.

'Where the hell was John all this time? And please don't tell me he was hiding in the garden shed!'

Nothing could have prepared us for the answer that followed or the staggering 'confession' that poured out of Anne's mouth over the course of the following four hours.

Initially, there is a long pause as she stares down at the ground, carefully considering her words as usual. She clasps her hands so tightly together that her knuckles go white. She then looks directly at me with her intense hazel eyes.

'Well . . . almost,' she replies and my eyes widen.

'For three years, while virtually everyone close to us believed he was missing, presumed dead, John was actually at home with me.'

My jaw drops open: she has *got* to be kidding me! Anne can see from the look on my face how shocked I am.

'Yes, I know it seems too incredible to be true: but it is,' she adds.

'We were living as man and wife, although it was far from a conventional life we were leading.'

No shit Sherlock. Tinseltown couldn't make this up.

For many of those missing years, while her family and friends mourned her husband's death and her distraught sons tried to pick up the pieces of their lives, John Darwin was in windy old Seaton Carew, living under everyone's noses and sharing his 'widow's' bed. And here was me thinking I had done well hiding near the office in Miami.

How was such an astonishing deception even possible? It was mind-boggling; the audacity breathtaking. And this was just the tip of the iceberg. This was going to be huge.

Anne took us back to the winter of 2000 and explained how John's dream move to Seaton Carew had been the real cause of their perhaps inevitable downfall.

For her husband, the move to No. 3 The Cliff summed up his life's achievements. She had not wanted to change their comfortable exist-ence in the smart, three-bedroom house in the County Durham village of Witton Gilbert. Money was tight but manageable and the stress of moving to a new, much bigger home with a heftier mortgage was the last thing she wanted. But for John, the tedium of village life in what he considered a modest home was never going to be enough. As ever, he wanted more. He'd been obsessed by money all in his life: it made his world go round.

For years, he had dabbled in various, peculiar to say the least, side-lines, but he knew they would never make him a wealthy man. He'd made a few quid messing about in penny stocks and shares and then invested in something that certainly wasn't your everyday road to riches: garden gnomes.

He bought rubber moulds and enlisted the boys to help mix and fill them with cement in the garage. They were then painted, mainly in red, blue and green, and sold at Durham's indoor market. When that novelty faded out, he decided to try his hand at something even stranger, breeding snails, having read an article about how you could make a tidy side income in doing so.

Needless to say, he made no money and soon decided his snail venture was going nowhere fast.

He needed a better plan and remembered his father telling him you couldn't go wrong investing in bricks and mortar. It was time to turn his attention to building a mini-property empire. It was the mid-1990s and his latest get-rich-quick scheme would be 'the one'. As usual, he drew up spreadsheets on his computer, highlighting income and cash flow, which he produced when asking the bank for a loan.

Within the space of a year, using money handed out without the most basic of checks by greedy lenders, he had bought twelve houses in the poor former mining villages around their then home in Witton Gilbert. He used that address when in July 1997 he set up a company called Eagle Enterprises UK Ltd, with John being listed as a director and Anne as a director and secretary.

He bought five houses that were among the cheapest homes in the village of Easington, where pit owners had been notorious for provid-ing the most basic housing they could get away with. John boasted he bought one on a credit card for £6,000. John told Anne it was like playing a real-life game of *Monopoly*. But this was no Mayfair or Park Lane. They were simple 'two up, two down' brick-built properties in long, uniform terraces. There was a sitting room at the front of the house, with a small kitchen at the back and two bedrooms upstairs. Some were built with outdoor toilets in the back yard, others with shared toilet blocks at intervals along the terrace.

The outside toilets, 'Nettys' as they were known, were freezing and usually had squares of cut-up newspaper hanging from a nail on the wall. A tin bath would have hung outside the rear door of each house, to be dragged in front of the fire and filled with hot water from the stove when the miners arrived home covered from head to toe in coal dust.

Darwin had invested in Easington for one reason: it had nothing to do with an appreciation of history and everything to do with the legacy of pit closures. The houses were as cheap as chips. Easington had been devastated by the demise of an industry that in 1951 employed 81,000 people in the county of Durham alone. Those jobs had simply vanished, leaving appalling levels of economic, social and environmental deprivation and rising crime rates. Virtually all the tenants were on the dole. And this was the exact area in which John believed his rental homes would make him a millionaire. It was sheer lunacy.

But if Darwin believed that stretching himself financially by expanding his portfolio of rental properties was the right thing to do, he was not alone. In the late 1990s, thousands of people saw the burgeoning buy-to-let market as the ideal way to make money. Small, part-time private landlords were being encouraged to borrow at favourable rates and, for the first time, potential rental income was taken into account when the lender decided how much to hand over. The race to buy up properties and let them out under the new tenancy rules was like a modern-day gold rush.

John was an easy target for the seductive get-rich-quick message coming from every side. If the greedy-as-ever banks would lend on prospective rental income at a time of rising property prices, this was surely his opportunity to make the kind of real money he had long craved. The chance to live a life of leisure was being handed to him on a plate. What his father had started – dabbling in property, building himself up from a council labourer to the owner of a detached house – John could now finish in style. A life of leisure, something he was convinced was rightly his, was within his grasp.

The move now to Seaton Carew offered endless possibilities and the chance to show everyone that John Ronald Darwin had made it. He would be able to realise his long-held boast about becoming a millionaire. The north-east's very own Del Boy.

The move to the big house on Seaton's sea front was not just about a fancy new home. The adjoining property was also for sale, meaning he could buy two grand four-storey town houses, side by side behind a private driveway with magnificent views over the sea. The very thought horrified Anne and she tried to talk him out of it. Her pleas, as ever, fell on deaf ears. *What John wanted . . .*

After protracted negotiation, he agreed to buy both 3 & 4 The Cliff from the owner, Robert Meggs, for £170,000. No. 5 was on the market for £350,000, so it did seem a bargain. Now it was just the small matter of securing a mortgage, which John claimed involved a little 'creative accounting'.

With Anne at his side, he went to the Yorkshire Bank and set out his stall. House prices were rising steadily, their twelve existing properties, some of which had cost less than ten thousand pounds to buy, were now worth much more, *on paper at least*. The idea of a 'global mortgage' was discussed; bundling their twelve former colliery houses together with Nos 3 and 4 The Cliff, into one loan. Instead of a messy range of borrowing that would be complicated to control, they would have just one lump sum to pay every month.

John was confident they could easily afford it. The Darwins' combined salaries came to a little over £2,000 a month after tax. John was bringing home around £1,300 a month from his job at the prison and on top of that there was plenty of overtime on offer; colleagues knew that money-obsessed Darwin was the man to call if they needed a pair of hands to cover for them. Anne was earning almost £750 from her part-time job at the doctors' surgery. And then there was £2,950 in rental income.

Their property portfolio clearly had the potential to create a healthy revenue stream, and the relatively new rules allowing prospective rental income to be taken into account for calculating mortgages was a big factor in the Darwins' favour. What bank could fail to be impressed with the income from No. 4 The Cliff, plus a dozen other houses, each capable of bringing in hundreds of pounds a month?

The sums all added up, John was convinced, and the bottom line showed he and Anne were going to be rich.

The reality, of course, was somewhat different. Their salaries were their only reliable income, giving them roughly a third more than the average UK family. Yet every month their interest-only mortgage was going to cost them five times as much as the average household was paying for both interest and capital.

Worse than that, the bank was lending to an amateur private landlord who – unbeknown to them – was secretly struggling to cope with personal debts, incapable of managing the properties he already owned (several of the rental properties were usually unoccupied) and with the repayments on his luxury Range Rover swallowing half his take-home pay. John was visibly living beyond his means. This latest property venture would sort everything out, he told Anne. Of course, he knew if it didn't, they would face ruin. He pushed such thoughts to the back of his mind.

When John signed on the dotted line, he must have felt as though he had been handed an open cheque. The Bank of England base rate at the time was 6 per cent and the mortgages were available at 7 per cent or less. With house prices rising steeply and interest rates expected to fall, the bank agreed to an interest-only loan of £245,000, with repayments of £1,700 a month. The initial twelve-month interest-free period was to tide them over to the following summer, by which time they expected to have sold their house in Witton Gilbert, which they had initially rented out when a buyer couldn't be found.

Everything was coming nicely together, John reassured Anne. She was far from convinced.

19

Numbers 3 & 4 The Cliff

A T THE CENTRE of a Victorian terrace of five majestic properties, Nos 3 and 4 The Cliff had been built in the 1890s, so local legend had it, for the five daughters of a wealthy industrialist. Next door, but set just far enough apart to block out the noise from departing guests, was the town's best-known hotel, The Staincliffe, built in the same gothic style by the same wealthy pillar of the community.

No. 4 had been converted into bedsits some years back. Branching off the once-grand staircase were thirteen low-rent rooms, spread over four levels, one partially across the top floor of No. 3 by a so-called 'flying freehold'. The two houses had been joined together more than sixty years earlier when low, narrow connecting doorways were cut in a coffin-shape into the walls beside the central chimney breast on every floor. The doorways were a throwback to 1970s safety regulations, a means of escape for tenants in the event of fire in the days when the rooms were full of itinerant workers building Hartlepool's nuclear power station. The houses were a warren of rooms, corridors and connecting doors.

John could never have imagined just how useful those doors would be in the years to come.

The fortunes of a very neglected No. 4 had declined in the intervening decades; the rooms were draughty, the decoration fading, the wiring far from ideal and good rental income not easy to make. But at the time of purchase, all he could think about was the goldmine in which he had invested. The rental income would give him and Anne the lifestyle he had always longed for. He had moved his family from a nondescript house in a former mining village to the splendour of a seaside resort. Parked outside and looking suitably expensive was his pride and joy, a gleaming charcoal grey Range Rover with plush leather interior and the cherished number plate, B9 JRD, for John Ronald

Darwin. He was a cut above the rest – he had finally arrived. At least in his mind. To others, he was just a 'Ten Bob' millionaire: a boring and dull man with an air of superiority without the financial substance.

'To be honest, I was not happy buying the house in the first place, because I did not want to be living with all those tenants,' Anne continues.

'I tried everything I could to persuade him otherwise, but John thought it was a great investment. He loved buying houses and saw it as a great way of making us money.'

He made plans to retire on the profits he would make, imagining the look on the faces of the other prison officers when he drove his Range Rover out of the car park of Holme House prison for the last time. If the previous owner could make money out of it, he certainly could. After all, he was an experienced landlord with another twelve properties. He would double the number of tenants he had at a stroke and the rent coming in would pay their new mortgage and more.

What's more, living at The Cliff would show the world he had made a success of his life. The boy from a poor pit village had climbed the property ladder right up to the Victorian splendour of his favourite seaside resort. Everyone would see that his new properties were majestic, imposing and expensive. The big front doors, the stone-mullioned windows, the imposing balconies and the private parking for his beloved car added up to the perfect image.

It all sounded so nice and simple. To the surprise of no one, John's venture quickly ran into trouble. And opting for a global mortgage would prove, in a relatively short space of time, to be a disaster. The Darwins quickly started running up debt because of the rental properties. Tenants left, or didn't pay their rent, things broke – everything that could go wrong did go wrong.

'We did try to address it,' Anne says. 'There were lots of things in the press and on the radio about debt advice and I actually persuaded him to make some enquiries on one of his credit cards to see how it went.

'They seemed to be very understanding and accepted lower monthly repayments. We were struggling to make payments, we had money owed to us as well that was slow in forthcoming, but what crippled us were the late fees and bank charges.

'We tried desperately to keep our head above water, but it got increasingly difficult. People were slow in paying us and that was causing our problems, and when we moved to Seaton Carew in December 2000 it just became too much trying to look after all the properties and both of us trying to keep full-time jobs going as well. I had another part-time job.'

Of course, John didn't let the increasing number of calls from debt-collecting agencies get in his way. He was not paying off the money he owed on a growing number of credit cards, but who cared? Their properties were rocketing in value, he told himself, and the figures showed that their tenants would pay more than twice as much into the Darwins' account than the two of them were paying back to the bank. Their new financial freedom would soon settle the debt and give them money to spare for renovations at Nos 3 and 4 The Cliff.

John could see a comfortable future ahead of them.

If only things had been that simple. He knew that he hadn't been quite as honest with the bank in securing the mortgage as he should have been. There were a number of what other people might describe as rather important details he had neglected to mention, such as his rapidly increasing credit card debt. But he knew that if he had confessed to any financial woes, he would have been asked lots of awkward questions and there was, he decided, the distinct possibility that he would have been shown the door.

He had instead said nothing, got the loan and the new houses . . . and everyone was happy. Everything would sort itself out eventually. It was surely worth a little harmless deception.

With Christmas just five days away, John and Anne moved into No. 3 and began their new roles as landlords to sitting tenants who lived next door and, quite literally, on top of them.

The tenants' front door was right next to theirs. For the first time in their short careers as landlords, they were up close and personal with the people who were paying them rent. They shared a common parking area, a driveway and effectively, a house. It didn't take long for John, never the best at getting along with people, to start complaining. The Darwins, unknown to perhaps everyone but themselves, were hopeless landlords.

Finding tenants dependent on benefits was not too hard, but proper contracts were not put in place, checks were not carried out, vague promises were accepted at face value and they were ripped off by some tenants who knew how to play the game far better than they did.

The other rental houses John had bought were at the bottom of the pile to start with and they soon slipped into further disrepair. Even maintaining the houses stretched John's limited capabilities – and finances – to breaking point: with stuttering rental income there was no money to pay to have repairs carried out by qualified people. He tried to do what he could himself, but he was the original Mr Bodge-it.

Rent trickled in from a handful of houses – the rest were leaking cash like a sieve. Anne would often take 'Tom', the odd-job man, along to try and fix things when tenants reported problems. Kay Graham, a tenant who reported a broken toilet, watched in disbelief as 'Tom' tried to fix it by tying a plastic bag from the flush to the ballcock. Her son said the scruffy man reminded him of a comedy character in fancy dress from *The Benny Hill Show*. Needless to say, as soon as the Darwins left, the toilet again stopped working.

John and Anne got such a name for themselves as bad payers that some tradesmen refused to work for them unless they paid in cash up front. They quickly got into the habit of ignoring problems and, on more than one occasion, the local council had to force them to bring properties up to a habitable standard under threat of court action.

But if it was difficult managing properties ten miles away, it was even worse looking after ones, quite literally, on their doorstep. John found that when problems arose at The Cliff he couldn't ignore them and he couldn't easily solve them either. Minor niggles rapidly grew out of hand and soon he made the fatal mistake of falling out with the people who were supposed to be paying his mortgage. In Seaton Carew, the talk was of how the surly and argumentative Darwin could start a fight in an empty pub. His were not the qualities required of a landlord.

Darwin's shortcomings as a private landlord, and his problems finding and keeping tenants in his increasingly dilapidated ex-colliery houses, was one of the things he had not mentioned to the bank.

The mortgage 'experts' he had spoken to were impressed with the figures he had on paper and there was no doubt that twelve houses had the potential to bring in a healthy amount of rental income.

Before John and Anne moved to Seaton, they had room for manoeuvre, but now they had taken on an even bigger loan and even bigger responsibilities. It was the 'shit or bust' scenario; a gamble based on deception. His bank would not have lent money on an interest-only basis had the Darwins been honest about their worse than shaky finances.

Having taken on the new loan and the extra tenants, it was not long before the vicious circle of debt repayments and poorly managed rental properties began to spiral out of control. With the new global mortgage to pay, bedsits left empty after aggrieved tenants moved out, and extra bills to meet for repair and maintenance, John and Anne were completely out of their depth.

In hindsight, it's hard to imagine how even a casual observer of John Darwin's inept business abilities could have failed to see the tidal wave that was fast approaching. It was a financial tsunami.

The chances of John and Anne ever being able to claw their way out of the mountain of debt that had engulfed them by the start of 2002 were remote at best. They were so broke they were having to buy tins of food for their dogs with credit cards, John holding his breath each time a card was swiped in case it was declined. They frequently were.

John had been reckless with his money and his property investments had been a disaster, but there is no doubt that lenders, too, deserved their share of the blame for a willingness to hand out credit cards like confetti. It never ceased to amaze John how easy it was to add another one to his collection: it never ceased to terrify Anne.

By early March, John owed £64,000 on thirteen different cards, with a minimum monthly payment of £1,700, and various other high-interest loans. He had been struggling for months to juggle his perilous finances, but in the end, it was the relatively small amount of £5,000 on two American Express cards that would prove to be the final nail in the coffin.

From the start of the year, the company had begun threatening court action over non-payment and John had nowhere else to turn.

He had exhausted all his financial escape routes: no one would lend him another bean. Anne had tried to help and had successfully negotiated reduced monthly payments with some of the other lenders. But American Express had had enough.

John decided on one last throw of the dice, asking the Yorkshire Bank for a further £20,000 to be added to the global mortgage on their thirteen properties. But even before it was declined, the bank – unhappy at his poor payment history – sealed his fate by refusing another, earlier, request to extend by a further six months the length of the interest-only period on the mortgage.

Now he would have to start repaying the capital too, meaning his monthly payments would shoot up from £1,740 a month to £2,500. Add to this the monthly repayment of £639 to Range Rover finance, for a luxury car he drove out of sheer vanity and couldn't afford, and it was obvious the numbers simply didn't add up. Talk about fur coat and no knickers. Even with their combined take-home pay and income from the rental properties of about £5,000 a month, their monthly deficit, with minimum payments on his credit cards, was close to two thousand pounds. And that was before the imminent rise in his mortgage repayment with the interest-only period coming to an end.

He simply couldn't cope, and knew the bank's refusal to extend the interest-only period on his mortgage marked the end of any prospect of being able to keep the American Express bailiffs at bay.

John was cornered, with seemingly no way out. He was convinced if he was taken to court and faced bankruptcy, the Yorkshire Bank would foreclose on the £220,000 global mortgage, meaning all his properties would be sold off in a 'fire sale' at prices far short of their real value. The banks would realise enough money to settle his debt – but John would be left penniless, homeless and asset-less.

The global mortgage he had so readily accepted when he switched to the Yorkshire Bank two years earlier, enabling him to buy the two adjoining houses in Seaton Carew, had proved to be an unmitigated disaster.

If he could have sold one or two of his rental properties he could have settled his debts and would have had cash left over. It actually seemed incredibly harsh; John had property worth hundreds of thousands of pounds, but, under the terms of the 'catch-all' global mortgage, he wasn't allowed to dispose of them individually.

He had convinced himself the Yorkshire Bank would be his salvation: it was not to be. He pleaded for a loan increase, saying he had updated and upgraded many of the rental properties, thus increasing their values. The bank didn't want to know.

As the first year of the new millennium drew to a close, what should have been the beginning of a golden chapter in the lives of John and Anne Darwin was, in reality, a lurch towards their inevitable train crash into financial disaster. With hindsight, the bank's decision to lend almost a quarter of a million pounds on an interest-only basis to enable John and Anne to double the size of their empire was a catastrophic error.

As they teetered on the brink of financial ruin in early 2002, the by then deeply suspicious bank sent a personal representative round to The Cliff to meet them and discuss their request for a loan increase. They sat chatting in the lounge, John, trying to sound as upbeat as possible, explaining that an initial £5,000 was all he needed to tide him over what he described as an 'unfortunate little cash flow problem'.

Predictably, the bank said no.

John looked at every other possible way to alleviate his financial fix. He even telephoned Range Rover to see if he could refinance his cherished vehicle, but it was a wasted call. He contacted the teachers' union about claiming a lump sum of his pension, but was told it was out of the question. American Express was not interested in any pleas to negotiate a reduction in monthly payments.

It was at this point that a beyond-desperate John began dreaming up a hair-brained scheme to end their woes.

Significantly, on 6 December 2001, he took out a £50,000 fatal accident policy in joint names with the American International Group, a US multinational finance and insurance corporation.

20

The Tunnel of Love

'I'VE BEEN THINKING, love, I could sort of . . . disappear . . . fake my own death.'

Anne looked at her husband in stunned silence. It was not your everyday conversation opener.

John had been putting off telling her for days, knowing full well what she would say, but eventually he had plucked up the courage to tell her. Sitting in the drawing room of their home one evening in front of the blazing flames shooting out from the magnificent oak fireplace that dominated the room, he stuttered as he began telling her that he had been giving an awful lot of thought to a way out of their dire financial straits and the clasp of the debt collectors.

If they opted for bankruptcy they would lose everything, including a place to live. So too would the twenty-seven tenants they had scattered about in their various rental properties, and he would hate to see those people out on the streets. In truth, he couldn't have cared less about them. It was nothing but emotional blackmail.

There was one another option, he told her. He could take a leaf out of Reggie Perrin's book and disappear. The banks and financial institutions had deserted him and thrown him to the wolves. He could vanish, then come back after Anne received the life insurance and pension payments that would enable her to straighten out their finances.

'Don't be ridiculous,' Anne scoffed, assuming he was joking, or had taken leave of his senses. 'That's the most stupid thing I've ever heard.

'What about the boys?' she said. 'And the police? You'll be found out and locked up; we both will.

'For God's sake, John, you'll have to think of something else, but you can't just disappear.'

He was joking . . . wasn't he? He was not.

'Well it's either that or I do it for real,' he replied.

Another sprinkling of emotional blackmail. He didn't have the balls for that. Faking his death was so much easier: no drama, no danger, no derring-do. With Anne starting to realise he was deadly serious about the latter, the argument quickly escalated until eventually she stormed out of the room in floods of tears and locked herself in the bathroom. *What on earth is he thinking?*

John knocked on the door but she was having none of it.

'Go away,' she yelled. 'You're mad!'

'Okay, well I'll do it for real then,' John told her, 'and then you'll be free of me and the debts.'

I imagined him stamping his feet like a toddler. When she had calmed down, Anne unlocked the door and approached her husband.

'Tell me you won't do it, you won't just disappear,' she demanded, looking directly into his eyes. 'You can't possibly be so stupid.'

'Okay love, I promise,' John said. But only to appease her. He was deadly serious.

They argued about it for days.

'We had a lot of debt – in the tens of thousands – and he told me this was the only way out,' says Anne, taking up the story once again.

'I tried desperately to get him to change his mind, but he said there was only one way out of the situation and that was to fake his death. I pleaded with him and said it was the wrong thing to do and I could not go along with it, but he badgered away at it.'

Eventually John went quiet on the subject and Anne said she was sure he had put the mad-cap idea out of his mind. He had not.

She recalled the night of 22 March 2002, coming home from work, seeing his car on the drive, finding the canoe missing and calling 999. And then the full-scale search-and-rescue operation springing into operation.

'I *honestly* didn't know a thing that night when I came home and he was missing,' Anne assures me. 'Whether people believe me or not, I *genuinely* thought John had had an accident at sea and drowned.'

All of a sudden, Anne is using the words 'honestly' and 'genuinely'. I'd been around long enough to know the use of such words often meant precisely the opposite.

'I guess it was in the back of my mind, but I just didn't think it was possible that he might have done that,' says Anne. 'I suppose I didn't want to believe he would do that, but he did.

'Where he went initially I do not know.'

Anne is now in full flow, still speaking carefully as if she had rehearsed what she was going to say many times in her head, insisting it was nearly a year before she even found out he was still alive. It was February of the following year when John first turned up on her doorstep, or so Anne claims. Was I really expected to believe this after she admitted knowing what was on his mind at the time he disappeared?

'There had been no contact in all the time he had been missing,' says Anne, perhaps sensing my doubts.

'I really thought he was dead, I really did, especially when they found the canoe and because of the state it was in.

'Now there he was, standing in front of me – and I was then terrified of the implications.

'He was an absolute mess, all dishevelled. I didn't even recognise him at first. He had a beard and looked dirty – as though he had been living rough. He looked like a tramp.

'He was so thin and he smelt dreadful. He hair looked like he had probably cut it himself with scissors. I was shocked, but I could not leave him standing there on the doorstep.

'Although I was pleased he was still alive, I think deep down a part of me was always angry. To think of what he put us all through.

'He had basically come back expecting me to forgive him.'

There's a long pause. Anne rubs her hands together, twisting her wedding band as she does so. By the time John came back from the dead, she continues, he assumed all the life insurance would have been paid and he was surprised, irritated, that it hadn't. It appeared he had then turned on the theatricals and wept, saying how sorry he was for all the anguish he had caused.

But when she said they needed to go to the police, he turned angry saying there was no way they could do that or he'd be locked up. He'd tell them she was part and parcel to his vanishing act and she would be locked up too. The fourth example of emotional blackmail in this one conversation. According to Anne.

'I was trapped,' she says.

John claimed he wasn't exactly sure where he had been living, but none of that mattered as he was now safely back home. Was John lying to Anne or, more likely, Anne lying to us. Either way, it was obviously untrue.

'He had a bath and put some clean clothes on and I fed him – all his clothes were where they had been when he left,' Anne recalls. 'I hadn't been able to bring myself to part with his clothes.'

Natalie and I are frequently exchanging astonished glances. What's coming out of Anne's mouth is like something from a movie script. John's audacity was breathtaking. Her cover-up lies astonishing.

'I know I should have been happy, but basically we argued because I was so annoyed, upset and angry,' she says.

'He said there was no alternative and he had had to do it. That was the way he felt. He said he had done it for us so that we didn't lose everything, which I know seems rather ironic now.

'I was just so glad that he was alive.

'He told me to go along with the story and not to tell anyone he was back. It was just so hard not to tell the boys, but he was adamant I mustn't tell them. He didn't want the boys to know anything.'

Natalie and I both wonder if this is really true. How could Anne not have told her own sons that their father was alive? We can't exactly call her an outright liar so we let her continue.

'He said the alternative would have been to lose everything we had worked for. We had always both worked very hard. There were times when John had actually done two jobs because we needed the money. I do not know the exact figure we owed but it was tens of thousands and it was nothing to do with me.

'I guess it had been building up for some time; he kept applying for credit cards and he used to always get me to co-sign the applications, but I never ever used the cards. I had one of my own and I only ever had one. I still have it today and I always managed to keep on top of it.'

Anne claimed John had stayed for a couple of days and after that he was always coming and going but he never told her where. *And she didn't insist on knowing?*

et. Supt. Tony Hutchinson reveals the
ng, shaggy-bearded passport photo that
hn Darwin used to resurrect himself as
ohn Jones', at a packed Cleveland Police
ress conference.

A clean-shaven John
Darwin's arrest mugshot.

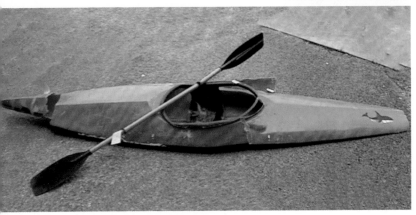

John's battered red canoe, *Orca*, after it was washed ashore six
weeks after he vanished.

The picture of John Darwin that Anthony sent to his mother in Panama when he miraculously came back from the dead five years after disappearing.

Anne Darwin in Panama before it was revealed she had been party to John's mind-boggling fraud.

PANAMA CANAL TRANSIT

Saturday, July 22 th of 2006

Let it be known to all Ditch Diggers, Mosquito Swatters and Adventure Lovers, that I have transited the Panama Canal aboard the good ship M/V Pacific Queen.

**Been There.....
Done That!**

South - Bound Canal Transit

Anne pictured visiting the Panama Canal in 2006.

When asked why she had moved to Panama, she said it had been a life-long dream to visit the famous canal. The 48-mile-long shipping route is considered one of the Seven Wonders of the Modern World.

The Darwin's top-floor apartment in Panama City.

John and Anne's wedding at St Joseph's Catholic Church in Blackhall Colliery, on 22 December 1973.

And with her parents Harry and Catherine

John posing with the Jaguar car bearing the private number plate –
B9 JRD, for John Ronald Darwin.

The astonishing photograph that brought ↑ end to the Darwin's lies. John and ↑nne with real estate agent Mario Vilar ↑ 2006 – date-marked 18 months before ↑e came back from the dead.

A smiling Anne while claiming to be overjoyed at her husband's return.

Then distraught after confessing to the couple's outrageous lies and begging her sons for forgiveness.

Nos. 3 & 4 The Cliff, Seaton Carew.

John Duffield, who bought No. 3 The Cliff, exposing the bricked-up secret doorways that linked the Darwins' two imposing sea-front houses in Seaton Carew.

This is the Seaton Carew road sign that a prankster changed after John Darwin's lies were exposed.

Anne Darwin on her long flight home to Manchester, where she was arrested onboard by heavily armed officers.

John Darwin at a benefits office in Durham after his release from prison.

Mark and Anthony Darwin photographed after their parents were each jailed for more than six years. The hearing exposed the full extent of their parents' cruel and heartless lies.

Anne Darwin at a beach in Yorkshire, from where husband John staged his now infamous disappearing act.

'He would often come when I was at work,' she continues. 'I always knew if he had been because I would find food missing, and if I had left any money around, he would take that too.'

You were stone broke but left money lying around? Really?

She says John had his own key for No. 3, so he could come and go as he pleased. She claimed to have had no idea where else he was living; he didn't want her to know. But why?

'He must have had shelter but I don't know if he had any transport of his own. As far as I know he didn't as he would always arrive on foot.

'My biggest mistake was trying to protect him.'

We take a short break and order more water from room service. Natalie and I have a brief conversation, excited and astonished at our sensational scoop. What's coming next we both wonder?

It didn't seem possible – but it was about to get even more incredible.

Anne then explains their living arrangements. It was like something out of a black comedy.

'John was around for a few months and then he came back on a more permanent basis,' she says.

'But because he was officially missing he rarely went out.

'He lived at the house with me for three years.

'We lived as man and wife.'

With a twist.

No. 4 had originally been a small hotel, then a guest house and then finally converted into £40-a-week bedsits with shared bathroom facilities. Room 12 on the top floor was officially part of No. 3. Next to the door of Room 12 was a locked door that opened, via a short, hidden corridor and a cupboard with a false back, into the hallway at the top of the stairs of No. 3.

Astonishingly, that hidden passageway – 'the tunnel of love' as it was later dubbed – was one of John's secret escape routes to next door, where he occupied a bedsit whenever the need arose.

Unbelievable! John was secretly living under the same roof as his 'grieving widow' and flitting between adjoining houses through secret passageways when Anne had visitors – including the sons mourning his death. They would probably have heard him creaking about, assuming it was simply one of their mother's tenants: callous beyond belief.

'It wasn't at all easy for him,' Anne says. 'He was used to being outdoors and was going stir-crazy trapped inside all the time.'

But this was far from the end of the deception.

He needed, as Baldrick might have told Blackadder, 'a cunning disguise'. If you could call it that.

He kept his hair and beard long and unkempt – and shuffled about with a stoop and an exaggerated limp and used a cane. When it was cold, he put on a woolly hat and pulled his collar up. That was the full extent of his disguise. Amazingly, it seemed to have fooled everyone.

During the summer months, he could barely get out. Seaton Carew was very busy at that time of the year and there were always lots of people about.

'There were a few hairy moments and I lived in fear of being found out,' Anne continues.

A few? It must have been like walking on eggshells most of the time. How she kept her nerve God only knows.

'Most of the time I used to be frightened to even open the door,' she says. 'I was frightened that someone would see him.'

Anne says by far the worst thing about the almost unbelievable situation was deceiving the family.

'I said to John many times, "You know I can't lie, I hate to lie", and I so wish I hadn't because I would not have got myself into the mess I did,' she continues.

In truth, she had become an exceptional liar. How else could she have deceived so many close friends and relatives for so long?

'I absolutely hate myself for having done it. There were many times I was tempted to come clean; many times.'

I'm sorry Anne but I just don't believe you.

'The boys missed their dad and I know deep down he missed them as well and he always wanted to find a way back so he could be reunited with them.

'I am sure both boys did believe he was dead. But there was never a body. I do not know how long it took for them to come to terms with the fact that he might be dead and not just missing, which was very difficult for them. They used to look at newspapers and the Internet and scour the reports of missing persons and reports of bodies that were found. They were tortured. And yes, it was hard to keep up the front.'

I blink, picture the boys in front of a laptop or iPad searching for a body that is, unbeknown to them, alive and well. It is a heart-wrenching image.

'Over the course of time, John and I managed to get things back together and thus our lives went on, mine, on the surface at least, as normal.

'The boys would ring up wanting to talk about all manner of things and they would say, "If only Dad was here to advise us."'

'Sometimes John was sitting there next to me and I would put the telephone onto loudspeaker so that he could hear them.

'If I did not have an answer to one of their questions, John used to write it down.'

Anne explains that they had few friends and weren't ones for socialising or going to the pub. They kept themselves to themselves and enjoyed a glass of wine together in the evening. She would often visit her parents who lived close by.

I ask how she coped when visitors were being sympathetic to her as she played the grieving widow.

'As time went on it sort of got easier because I suppose they thought I was putting things behind me and getting on with my life,' Anne explains. 'But most of the time I just used to be terrified. I think John probably was too.

'I sometimes used to dread coming home, worrying myself sick that John might have been seen, or maybe even that the police would be there, that he had fallen and broken a leg, or even that he had actually died. Then, what should I do?

'Our house overlooked the sea and the curtains were never drawn open during the day. Often John was a prisoner at our home.'

It's something I suppose. A tiny piece of poetic justice.

'Being inside was not easy for him, but he was an avid reader,' she says. 'Mainly fiction, I think he read all sorts, anything really to keep himself occupied.

'As time went by, he used to do odd jobs around the house to try and keep occupied. Sometimes he would watch daytime TV, but he also had the Internet so he would spend a lot of time on his computer.'

Little did I know that many of us would be doing exactly the same thing when Covid hit in 2019. No, it wasn't much fun, but our enforced incarceration was not down to having committed an outrageous fraud.

'After John's disappearance, I had been pushing for an inquest – long before he turned up again – because I couldn't cope with it any longer. I needed to be able to get on with my life,' says Anne.

'It was making me ill. I had managed, after a long time trying, to get the debt frozen, because as the time went by there was more and more interest being added onto it.

'I just could not afford to pay everything. John said if we got the money from the insurance payouts and cleared our debt, we could find a way back, then we could start over again.'

When the interview was finally over, Anne seemingly having got a lot of things off her chest, I sat back and considered where to start. My head was spinning. There were still lots of unanswered questions, but the fact that John had returned to the marital home and resumed living with Anne as husband and wife, under everyone's noses, was mind blowing.

I'd filled both sides of a whole A4 notebook with thousands upon thousands of words and now I had to turn it into a story for the following day's paper. It actually wasn't that difficult; it was so good it almost wrote itself. Natalie returned to her room and I shook my head in wonder as I opened my laptop and sat down to write. Like many reporters I am not a trained typist and began frantically tapping away with two or three fingers.

I sense Anne staring at me.

'You know I can touch-type,' she says after a few minutes.

I turn around and look at her, flabbergasted by the offer I presume she is making.

'Are you saying what I think you're saying?' I ask.

'Yes,' she responds. 'It will give me something to do.'

And so, for the next hour and a half, Anne took over my role and typed as I created and dictated a story from the extraordinary revelations that filled my notebook. That had to be a first in any reporter's book.

It was gone midnight when Anne said she was turning in, but I still had a long way to go to finish my story. By 3 a.m., I was literally falling asleep at the keys, so I decided to get an hour's kip, setting my alarm for 4 a.m. (9 a.m. in London), so I could complete the story well in time for Friday's traditionally early newspaper deadlines.

I filed the thousands of words I had already written and put a note at the top of the copy for the *Mirror* and the *Mail* saying I would be finishing off first thing in the morning.

By 7 a.m., Anne is up and walks into the room where I am still beavering away.

'Surely you haven't been there all night?' she asks.

'Not quite,' I say, stifling a yawn, 'but almost.'

She walks over.

'Move over,' she says. 'I'll finish it off for you.'

And with that, she sat down, read what I'd already written, then rattled off the last few hundred words of the story, adding quotes and expanding her thoughts as she went – greatly improving my account. Another astonishing twist.

'I understand his motivation in going back,' she wrote.

'He could have stayed in Panama, but then he would never have got to see the boys again.

'All I can say to them at this stage is that I am really, really sorry, and I hope one day they will realise that what I did was not easy.'

I rubbed my eyes. Astonishing stories equate to astonishing hours. And, speaking directly to her sons, she added: 'Boys, please believe your mam when I say I am truly very sorry and I still love you and hope you can find it in your hearts to one day forgive me.'

It was a moving moment and Anne appeared genuinely grief-stricken and sorry for the pain she had caused her family. Although I still felt she wasn't telling the entire truth, for the moment that didn't matter. I had an amazing story and the papers for which I was working would be delighted.

I read the copy through one last time, made one final spell check, then hit the send button on my email.

The *Mirror* and the *Mail* each cleared seven pages of the following day's papers to run every word of Anne Darwin's 'confession'. The *Mail*'s front-page headline read: I CONFESS, with sub-decks revealing how John had faked his death to escape crippling debts and moved back into the family home within a year. The *Mirror*'s front page read: WHY WE DID IT – *Canoe wife tells her extraordinary story*.

It was indeed an extraordinary story. If she was to be believed, John had told her he planned to fake his death and disappear, but she didn't believe he would ever go through with it and so assumed he must genuinely have had an accident in his canoe and drowned at sea.

But she never mentioned his thoughts to anyone – her sons, family, or the police. And for over a year, until he turned up a dishevelled mess on her doorstep, she genuinely believed he was dead. Then she kept his reincarnation a secret for the next four years.

It sounded almost too incredible to be true . . .

21

'A Nice Dream While it Lasted'

A NNE SHRUGS HER shoulders and gives a wry smile.

'Well, it was a nice dream while it lasted,' she says.

For much of the seven-hour flight home to England she had appeared lost in thought, occasionally flicking through a magazine or closing her eyes and trying, largely unsuccessfully, to snatch some sleep. While chatting, she had given me an incredible insight into what was going to have been the Darwins' new start, a fresh beginning, thousands of miles away in the ever-sunny Central American Republic of Panama. It was so far-fetched as to be totally unbelievable. But as I'd discovered over the past week, they were quite good at conjuring up things others would think impossible.

They planned a new life on a secret tropical estate – a newly acquired parcel of unspoiled countryside on the other side of the world on which she and the man thought to be dead would develop and run an eco-friendly tourist resort. They would live in a log cabin and eat freshly caught fish, and fruit from the mango, plum, fig and kiwi fruit trees growing in the forests.

The land they had bought, known locally as 'Finca no. 1031', bordered the shores of Lake Gatun, in Escobal, a rural town two hours' drive from the capital at the northern end of the Panama Canal, on the country's central, north coast. It was partly jungle and there were steep ravines, swamps, wide-open spaces, and some of the land bordered the shores of the lake, meaning it would be ideal for boating. There was also a tremendous variety of trees, birds, insects and other wildlife – howler monkeys, sloths, parrots, tapirs and toucans.

No matter that it covered 481 acres, had no running water, no electricity and the only access road was rutted with potholes; *John Darwin wasn't about to let reality get in the way of his dreams*. Once he heard there were plans afoot to build an international airport at Colon and another bridge over the canal, making the area far more accessible, his mind was made up. It would mean real-estate prices would soar, he had told Anne. The land would soon be worth millions, he bragged, and 'we'll be laughing all the way to the bank'. He said it would be worth 'monopoly money in excess of $2million'. He even told locals he planned to build a cable car from the main property through the trees to the beach.

I could hear the howler monkeys singing 'Daydream Believer'.

Darwin also loved the fact that Colon, a province that Sir Francis Drake called 'the treasure trove of the world', was steeped in history. He rather liked the idea that he would be following in the footsteps of some of his more famous countrymen. At this stage, he obviously had no idea quite how *infamous* he himself would soon become.

But in reality, the very idea of buying land and trying to establish an eco-resort in a remote and lawless part of a country they knew nothing about was, to put it bluntly, insane. The Darwins had no experience in the tourism industry, had already proved themselves inept at running a business, were not exactly in the prime of their lives and didn't even speak the native language. Mowing the grass and pruning the roses was about as far as their gardening skills went, so quite how they planned to cope with looking after hundreds of acres of a tropical jungle infested with dangerous snakes and poisonous spiders is anyone's guess. Ludicrously, John envisaged himself as a kind of Indiana Jones character, clad in a khaki jungle outfit and clutching a machete.

Perhaps he would have been better off following the example of Christopher Columbus, who decided to steer well clear of Colon after seeing what he described as a 'pestilential swamp filled with mosquitos, snakes and caimans', a large reptile related to the crocodile. The English historian James Foude put it even more bluntly, writing in 1886: 'In all the world there is not, perhaps, now concentrated in a single spot so much swindling and villainy.'

Just over a hundred years later, little appeared to have changed: John and Anne were choosing a crime-ridden area of extreme poverty and unemployment. In most guidebooks, tourists were advised to avoid the region or risk being mugged at knifepoint. But, of course, the delusional Darwins paid no attention to such warnings.

Anne dismissed the suggestion they would have canoes, as various newspaper articles had suggested.

'I suppose that was someone coming up with a bit of poetic licence,' she smiled – but, yes, they had planned to get a boat of some kind.

But now, with the plane taxiing across the tarmac at Manchester International Airport at just after 9 a.m. on a bleak Sunday morning, her lips quiver and she fights back tears as she looks out at the grey skies and light drizzle welcoming her back to reality.

Her journey home had begun the previous day. After checking out of the Conrad Hotel, we had taken a cab to Fort Lauderdale-Hollywood International Airport, a forty-five-minute drive away. The press pack was still desperately trying to find us and I considered nearby Miami airport too obvious and risky. From Fort Lauderdale, we had flown to Atlanta, Georgia, and then boarded a connecting flight, Delta Flight 64, to Manchester – where we now found ourselves after a seven-hour flight across the Atlantic.

'I'm feeling sick to my stomach,' Anne admits.

But, at the same time, relief is written all over her face. Relief that nearly six years of, by her own admission, 'living a lie, watching over my shoulder and dreading every knock on the door' is now over.

'Yes, I'm frightened,' she says. 'But at least it will be over.'

It is possible, though, even as Anne flew home to face the music, that she may have been thinking not quite all was lost. Yes, she knew she could well be joining her husband in jail for fleecing insurance companies out of hundreds of thousands of pounds and hoodwinking everyone, including, most cruelly, her two sons, that their father was dead. But after nearly six years of enjoying the fruits of the couple's breathtakingly audacious crime, their by now very considerable assets were safely tucked away in the tax haven of Panama – and that was surely the reason they had chosen to start a new life there in the first place.

Anne was also aware that, even if she was convicted of fraud, returning to her new life in the sun would not be a problem after she had served her time. Her Panamanian immigration lawyer had already told her that the country happily opened its arms to convicted criminals, with the one ultra-ironic proviso that you simply had to honestly admit your dishonesty by declaring the crime you had committed. You couldn't make it up.

So perhaps even as Anne boarded the flight to Manchester she had in mind that she would one day be able to pick up the pieces of her life, maybe even with her husband and her sons, once 'all the fuss' had died down. There were still secrets she was holding back on, I was sure.

They had oodles of cash swirling around in different bank accounts. The money, largely from the sale of Nos 3 and 4 The Cliff, had cleverly wound its way to Panama through accounts in the Channel Islands. There was also the odd thousand here and there. Asset recovery detectives were still trying to piece together the extent of the couple's ill-gotten gains.

Had the Darwins been forced to sell their properties and cars at the time John vanished, they would have barely had enough to pay off their debts. As it was, they had doubled their money and ended up sitting on a tidy little package worth about £679,000. Not bad for a couple teetering on the brink of bankruptcy as their world crumbled around them in 2002.

Once we had landed, Anne knew what was coming, at least to a degree. She had been warned that police would be waiting for her and she would be arrested and driven back to Hartlepool police station in Cleveland, from where the investigation into the couple's incredible deception was being spearheaded.

She didn't have long to wait. Within minutes of the packed 767 arriving at its gate at Terminal 2, the aircraft doors swung open and it quickly became clear that this was going to be no ordinary arrival. A towering Greater Manchester police sergeant, uniformed and armed, like the five officers behind him, was the first on board.

'We would like to speak to a Mrs Anne Darwin,' he tells the clearly startled flight attendant.

Passengers already reaching for their bags from the overhead lockers are told over the Tannoy to return to their seats. There is a buzz of confusion and then people suddenly begin to twig that they have shared their flight home with the now infamous 'canoe widow'. All eyes are now on the ashen-faced and totally panic-stricken, bespectacled woman with grey hair slowly making her way the few steps forward from seat 1A to make herself known to police.

I jump up and try to speak to the sergeant. This isn't how it was supposed to happen, I protest. I had been assured that once we had arrived at the gate Anne would quietly be asked to stay in her seat until all the other passengers had left. Then, a plain-clothed Cleveland detective would board the plane and escort her back to Hartlepool. It was all to be very low key. It wasn't as if she was a terrorist threat or a danger to anyone. She had returned to the UK of her own accord.

But the sergeant made it clear that he wasn't in the least bit interested in what I had to say. Shut up, sit down and mind my own business, I was told. So was Steve, who had jumped up and was now taking photographs of the dramatic scene unfolding on the packed jet. Steve yelled at me to grab my video camera and record what was happening – something I should have been doing anyway, had I not been so caught up in the drama. At least someone was thinking clearly.

Anne, wearing black trousers, a bright red zip-up raincoat and with her brown leather handbag slung over her shoulder, said nothing, nodding to confirm that she was indeed Anne Darwin. She was read her rights and told she was being arrested on suspicion of fraud. Surrounded by her welcoming party of burly policeman, some armed with Heckler & Koch submachine-guns, she was led along the air-bridge to a lift, her head bowed down to the floor as the doors slowly closed.

Steve and I ignored repeated requests from the police to return to our seats and continued filming.

'Are you okay, Anne?' I ask, but her face is crumpled and she says nothing as, dwarfed by the surrounding officers, the lift doors close. It's doubtful she even heard my words.

The scene was all so ridiculously over-the-top.

From the air-bridge, Anne was taken to the nearby Manchester Airport police station, where she would spend the next three hours. She was in a terrible state and seen by a doctor, who said she had suffered a panic attack. That she was 'very distressed' was obvious to anyone.

Shortly after midday, having been declared fit to travel, her broken figure emerged from the station, and after being frogmarched across the car park by sergeant plod, obviously very much enjoying his five minutes of fame, she was driven to Cleveland in an unmarked police car escorted by two marked vehicles.

'There were blue light and sirens when I reached Hartlepool,' she later told me. 'You'd have thought I was a gangster's moll.'

Detectives from Cleveland later privately apologised for what had happened at the airport. They were grateful to us for having brought Anne back home and were embarrassed there had been such a commotion on the plane, having given an assurance it would all be handled without any fuss. Hutch was incandescent.

It transpired that jobsworths at Greater Manchester Police had insisted on making the arrest when their Cleveland colleagues informed them that Anne would be on the plane. It was their jurisdiction and they would do 'the business', thank you very much. They must have been very proud of their day's work. A very satisfactory arrest indeed.

The fact that Anne had been arrested was made known within minutes. The *Mail* decided to put a one-line 'snap' on its website, reporting she was being held at Manchester Airport police station – amounting to an open invitation for every photographer and journalist in town to get there as soon as they possibly could.

To me and Steve, it was a horrible decision. Having kept Anne hidden away from the world for more than a week, thus protecting the *Mail* and *Mirror*'s exclusivity, the *Mail*'s website was now letting all its rivals know exactly where she was. They could easily have kept the story and pictures exclusive for another day. It was the very early days of the *Mail Online*, now the most read news website in the world, and was a very early sign of how the digital revolution of news reporting would change the industry.

Sure enough, more than a dozen photographers and several TV crews were there waiting to take pictures and video images as Anne was led out to the police car that would transport her to Hartlepool. Executives at the *Mirror* were furious at the *Mail*'s decision, taken without any consultation, and there was a brief inter-paper slanging match, but it quickly blew over. But it was a terrible anticlimax for me and Steve. The front pages of the following day's papers all carried their own photographers' images of Anne – not ours. When you're in this business, you like to win.

Until then, we had been the only ones with pictures and video of her. It was an incredibly disappointing way for our run of exclusives to end. That evening we headed out for a curry (you just can't get a proper one in Florida), washed down with a couple of ice-cold Kingfishers, and caught the highlights of the day's football on *Match of the Day 2* on the TV. Our moods quickly lifted. We'd had a pretty successful week and life didn't seem quite so bad after all. And it's always nice to be *home*.

On the flight back, Anne had picked at her chicken dinner and then managed a bowl of cornflakes for breakfast, an hour before the 767 would touch down. But from time to time during the journey, she opened up about the couple's now shattered dreams. She said living as a widow had become a way of life for her.

'It was very difficult, though, and I was always terrified that we would be found out,' she said. 'I was always on eggshells.'

After her husband's arrest, there had been an awful lot of finger-pointing at the Darwins' sons, with many refusing to believe that they didn't know anything about the scam, and Anne knew that she and John had made matters worse by making the boys they had deceived shareholders of the Panama property company: they had implicated them right up to their necks.

She was relieved that everything, according to her, was now out in the open (although it most certainly wasn't), but nervous about the future. Because John was now behind bars, there had been no contact with him since his arrest five days earlier, and she had heard nothing from any of her family, her parents, her brother and sister.

'Our house is sold and I have nowhere to live and no one to go to,' she said.

'Even if they agreed to put me up, my parents don't have the resources or room to. I just don't know what I'm going to do.'

Incredibly begrudgingly, considering what she'd done, Anne added: 'I'm sure I am going to have to give the money back that I got from John's death, so I will have no money.

'I have paid a very high price for my own stupidity. And, of course, I'll regret what I've done to my dying day.'

Anne had opened up a great deal during the time we spent together, but I couldn't help feeling she was still holding back and lying about a number of key points. I stressed to her a number of times that it was now vitally important if she was ever to have any hope of being reconciled with her sons that she tell the police the entire truth. It didn't matter, I told her, if she had lied to me, but there was nothing whatsoever to be gained by lying to the police – or her sons.

Before the plane had taken off from Atlanta, one of the stewards had jokingly announced over the Tannoy: 'Welcome on board this flight to Honolulu', which had brought a wry smile to Anne's face.

'I wish!' she said.

22

Introducing John Jones

IT'S A HECTIC Monday morning for Hutch's team. John Darwin is due before Hartlepool magistrates and his wife will be interviewed by detectives for the first time.

Before John is led to the dock, a court usher asks three times if there are any relatives present. Deafening silence. No one is there to support him. But there are a handful of Cleveland detectives and thirty or so journalists crammed into the press benches to get their first sight of the now infamous 'Canoe Man'.

John's widower father Ronnie, ninety, and wheelchair-bound after a stroke, is still in shock at the arrest.

'I don't know why they wanted a big house like David Beckham's in Panama City,' he tells reporters. (The modest flat in Panama most definitely did not compare to any of Beckham's multi-million-pound homes.) 'They never used to have anything like that before.'

His sister Margaret Burns revealed the extent of Ronnie's pain. 'He was very distressed when he heard the news and when it finally sunk in he cried. He has been through hell. We've no idea why John has done all this.'

John, clad in the same maroon tracksuit top and t-shirt he was wearing when arrested at Anthony's house, trudges into the courtroom looking a little dazed and confused. He confirms his name and date of birth and is then told he is accused of dishonestly obtaining £25,000 from NUAT Direct Insurance on 16 May 2003, by falsely claiming he had been killed in an accident. Prosecutor Sue Jacobs says the charge relates to the fatal accident policy he took out in December 2001, just three months before he vanished.

He is also accused of making an untrue statement to procure a passport on 8 October 2003.

The prosecutor tells the court she opposes bail. It's obvious to anyone that the chances of Seaton Carew's very own Harry Houdini being released at this stage are slim to zero.

'This man has already shown he can disappear for a considerable period of time, and shown, if granted bail, he would fail to surrender,' she says.

But no application is made and Darwin heads off back to the cells before returning to Durham Prison, where he will be held on remand.

With the hearing over, his solicitor John Nixon tells the press that his client is desperate to be reunited with his wife Anne for their thirty-fourth wedding anniversary the following week.

He issues a statement that reads: 'John is desperate to see his wife, to be reunited with her. He is anxious to know about her well-being. It is their wedding anniversary in 10 days. They are going to spend their wedding day apart. He is anxious for everything to be resolved. He is in good shape, bearing up. He has not spoken to me about any plans for the future.'

If the lawyer was expecting any sympathy for his client it was not forthcoming. The papers all cover the court appearance and the following day have a field day with Darwin's plea to be reunited with his wife. HOW ABOUT A CANOODLE? is the *Mirror*'s headline. The papers can't get enough of the story. Seeing John is actually the last thing Anne wants right now. She is already far from sure she sees a future for them together. Incredibly, the last letter she received from him asked if she'd mind if he corresponded with a woman who had written to him in prison. Is he mad?

★★★

The photograph of the Darwins in Panama has raised another intriguing issue.

How did John Darwin travel abroad when he was dead? Checks with the Passport Office confirmed his passport had expired in 2003. Admittedly, as I mentioned earlier, it wasn't something that crossed my mind. I was too busy with Anne to consider John's documentation.

Hutch knew he must have used a fake identity. One of his team is instructed to speak with the Panama real-estate agent Mario Vilar.

Mr Vilar has some very interesting information. He's never heard of John Darwin. The man he's pictured alongside in the now infamous photograph is known to him as John Jones. The same name that was on a number of the letters that John Duffield had put aside with the mail that arrived for Anne Darwin.

In Hutch's office among others are Detective Inspector Andy Greenwood and DS Iain Henderson.

'How does John Darwin get a false passport?' Hutch asks. 'How does he get a birth certificate? How does he become John Jones?

'He's a prisoner officer, ex-bank employee, ex-teacher. As much as he likes to think he's a clever shit . . .'

Hutch stands up, looks out of the first-floor window. He sees a smoker having a crafty cigarette. Smoking is now banned anywhere in the grounds, even outside. He makes a mental note to bollock the detective for being visible and potentially dropping himself in it with the goody-two-shoes brigade.

Hutch continues: 'Even if he knew where to go, someone he met in prison perhaps, they would grass him as soon as.

'Do you think he's done a *Day of the Jackal*?'

An avid reader, Hutch explains how in Frederick Forsyth's best-selling novel, later turned into a movie starring Edward Fox, the book's protagonist had trawled graveyards looking for the headstone of a baby boy who, had he not died, would have been about the same age as the assassin.

Having found what he was looking for, the Jackal used the details of the late Alexander James Quentin Duggan to buy a copy of the deceased's birth certificate – all the proof needed to successfully apply for a passport and create a fake new identity. In the book it was a key part of the plot to assassinate General de Gaulle.

'Let's see if John Jones is our Jackal,' says Hutch. 'Search for deaths of John Jones with a date of birth two years either side of Darwin. Start the searches within a fifteen-mile radius of Hartlepool.'

The search does not take long.

Within hours, detectives discover a John Jones born in 1950, the same year as Darwin, who died aged just five weeks old at the city's Hospital for Infectious Diseases. Like Darwin, he was also born in Sunderland. The Christian name is spot on and the surname, Jones, one of the commonest names going, could not have been better.

Jackpot thinks Hutch. Another nail . . .

Unlike the Jackal, John Darwin would not even have had to dirty his shoes by trudging through graveyards in the dead of night. He only had to trawl through microfiche files in the local council's genealogy and archives department for a name that fitted and then travel to Sunderland and apply for a birth certificate at the office of births, deaths and marriages. The cost was just £11.

Detectives contact the local Passport Office to see if one had been issued in the name of a John Jones, born on the date that corresponded with the birth certificate Darwin had obtained.

There had.

And attached to the application form is a black-and-white photograph of a man the detectives recognise instantly as a comically disguised John Darwin. Same man but with a long shaggy beard and unkempt hair. The home address given on the application form and the one to which the passport was mailed: No. 4 The Cliff.

Astonishingly, John Jones, mark two, had been born as simply as that. And he appeared to be living next door to his 'widow'.

There could be no faulting Darwin for his ingenuity.

Detectives can see from the paperwork that the John Jones' passport photograph has been verified by a librarian, Susan Garrington. Next stop – Hartlepool Library.

Shown the photograph, Mrs Garrington confirms that the man she recognises instantly as John Jones was a regular visitor and would spend hours crouched over one of the library's publicly available computers.

Records indicate he joined the library on 22 April 2002 – just one month and a day after the man he used to be disappeared. This is explosive evidence. Library records reveals 'John Jones' had joined using two acceptable forms of identity: the birth certificate he had obtained four days earlier and, tellingly once again, a tenancy agreement for No. 4 The Cliff.

Because he was such a regular visitor, the librarian had happily signed the back of the photograph needed for the passport application that October, verifying he was indeed John Jones, of 4 The Cliff,

Seaton Carew. The former schoolteacher had done his homework and discovered librarians were public figures able to vouch for identities on passport applications. The detectives then discover that a driver's licence was issued to the same John Jones in August of the following year. He was nothing if not resourceful.

It is now as clear as day that he has been living locally the entire time. The library is a ten-minute bus ride from his old home. Was he really brazenly sheltering in a bedsit in the house next door to his wife from the moment he vanished? It certainly looked that way. If so, was Anne Darwin in on the plot from the start? She had to be. But proof is still needed.

Tony Hutchinson turns his thoughts to the relatives of John Jones.

'I do not want any living relatives finding out from the media that Darwin used John's identity,' he says to the staff in the Major Incident Room. They quickly identify a brother. John Jones died before any other siblings were born. His parents are dead, but he has family who are very much alive.

Time for another chat with Darwin. He's back in the hot seat at Kirkleatham police station.

His wife's confessions are continuing to make a mockery of his story. She has admitted he faked his death to escape their crippling debts, there was no canoe accident and no amnesia. He had made the whole thing up to avoid the shame of bankruptcy.

Furthermore, the detectives also know the truth about the not-so-mysterious John Jones.

At 2.50 p.m., DCs Rowland and McArthur sit across the table from Darwin and his solicitor. He is again cautioned.

Stage 3 of the interviews, the challenge stage, is about to begin. This is going to be interesting.

'John, I want you to listen very carefully to what I've got to say,' says McArthur.

'You've been interviewed now over the past three days.

'Your account has been recorded on tape.

'We've listened to it and we've considered what you've told us so far.

'I now want to put some facts to you that conflict with your views.'

McArthur tells him that Anne has been quoted in the papers as saying 'we were being crippled by bank charges and late payment fees' and 'John said there was only one way out of the situation and that was to fake his death'. Pseudocide – the act of faking your own death to avoid serious personal, financial, or legal problems and start a new life – is the official name for it.

Added to that, the detective says the police's own financial investigation had shown that on 1 December 2001, just three months before he vanished, John had taken out a fatal accident insurance plan and, not to beat about the bush, everything pointed towards him having disappeared to save his skin.

'Were you planning your disappearance in 2001?' McArthur asks John directly.

No prizes for guessing his response. As the question swirls around John's brain, the policeman reminds him that in his initial prepared statement, he had claimed it was only 'some years later', when he had turned up at the family home, that he realised monies had been paid out to Anne on the basis that he was dead.

But there's a big problem with that, says McArthur: Anne has now revealed he turned up in February 2003, just under a year after his disappearance, meaning the policies had not yet been paid out as he still hadn't officially been declared dead. It's a lie, John. A big fat lie.

Darwin is also told that when his computer was removed from his house after his wife had first reported him missing, police discovered a research document on the hard drive entitled: 'Police Response to Missing Persons'.

'Can you explain that?' says McArthur, knowing Darwin had obviously been researching what steps the police would take as part of their investigation.

'No comment.'

He is quizzed about mortgage and endowment policies, pension funds, property deals and the life cover associated with his global mortgage.

'Tell us about these policies that you say you have come back to repay. What steps have you taken to repay that money?'

'No comment'.

He's asked about his teacher and Prison Service pensions. How much he owed on credit cards, other loans and his total debt when he disappeared.

Police believe the overall fraud could total more than a million pounds.

'When you were declared dead, John, what happened to that debt? Did the debt die with you? Is that the reason you disappeared?'

An immediate 'No comment', but surely he must know he's backed into a corner with no way out?

The detectives have decided it's now time to see what John Darwin has to say about John Jones. Rowland picks up the interview.

Darwin is told that on 5 June 2004, two years after he vanished, a fellow prison officer had seen him outside his old home.

'He describes you as having longer hair and a greyish-brown full beard,' says Rowland. 'He describes that man as not dissimilar to Saddam Hussein when he was captured. But he says he is 100 per cent certain it was you. This was part of your deception, wasn't it, John?'

'No comment'.

'Can you describe why you've disguised yourself?'

'No comment'.

The photograph of the man that's obviously him is placed on the table in front of him.

Darwin's eyes dart back and forth between the interviewer and the black-and-white photograph. He definitely had not seen this one coming.

He is told that police have spoken to Mario Vilar from the Move to Panama corporation.

'Would it surprise you that Mr Vilar has been in touch with the incident room?' he's told. 'Because he has.'

No response.

'Mr Vilar knows the man in the photograph as John Jones. Is John Jones the name you've adopted while missing?

'That's right John, isn't it? Were you John and Anne Jones?'

Darwin's mind is racing. But the police aren't done.

He's told they have also obtained a Hartlepool Library card in the name of John Jones, issued on 22 April 2002.

'The date is significant. This is only one month after you've alleg-edly gone missing in the North Sea.'

The librarian had confirmed that 'Mr Jones' was a regular customer and that she had co-signed a passport application form for him, which police had obtained from the Passport Office in Durham. Attached was the photograph he's now trying hard not to look at.

It shows John Jones is very obviously John Darwin with a foot-long shaggy beard.

'I can clearly see that it's you with a beard, John,' says DC Rowland.

What's more, the home address given on the application form and the one to which the passport was mailed is No. 4 The Cliff. And there were further applications for a driving licence and credit cards all mailed to John Jones of that same address.

The police know he must have returned home almost straight away and it seems inconceivable that Anne wasn't in on the plot from the outset.

'You've refused to answer any questions about you assuming a different identity,' he's told.

'You were asked about passport, driving licence, credit card applications in the name of John Jones and you refused to answer any of these questions. Is that because you've assumed a false identity, namely that of John Jones?'

Darwin replies with a 'No comment', but he can't help but know his highly unbelievable story is crumbling around his ears.

Back to McArthur who tells him that the account he has given them over the course of his interviews is falling apart. Asked to explain why, his response goes without saying. The detective then spells out what the police believe has actually happened.

'The evidence so far indicates to me that you've got no issues in relation to your memory or your recall of events,' he says. 'You haven't lost your memory John. It's a story.

'It's a story that's unravelled before your very eyes. That you've had to change on the hoof and you've forgotten things that you've said to people.

'From the evidence, it's clear to me that you're not suffering from amnesia.

'Your wife has spoken to the press and allegedly said, "John hatched a plan to return to the UK and hand himself in, saying he thought he was a missing person", which is what you did.

'It's clear to me that you've discussed this with your wife. You've discussed exactly what you were going to do and what you were going to say when you arrived in London. How else could your wife know these facts? Can you explain that?'

There's a predictable 'No comment' from John.

McArthur tells Darwin the evidence against him is compelling, to say the least. He has attempted to portray himself as a man who has lost his memory; a man who, because of an accident, has been placed in a situation where in order to protect his family, he's been forced into a course of action that would appear 'dramatic', to put it mildly. The reality of the situation is somewhat different, the officer says.

'Your account is unravelling by the hour,' says McArthur.

'Some time in 2000 or 2001, you were in considerable debt. You, together with your wife, hatched a plan to defraud the insurance companies by claiming life cover and fatal accident benefit by faking your death.

'You've assumed a false identity and you've lived off the proceeds of the funds that you've illegally obtained.

'Your downfall really was the media: the media attention the case has generated. You planned to maintain a story, your story of amnesia, but you've been forced to change it and alter your position, as various pieces of evidence have been put to you.

'What I will say to you John is that this investigation is still a live inquiry.

'And it'll continue after today. We will be interviewing your wife and your sons to establish their knowledge of the events.

'And I have no doubt that if further evidence come to light, I will be interviewing you again.

'Is there anything at all you want to tell me about the events before the 22nd March 2002 and the present time?'

Darwin is told it is his final opportunity to comment and is asked if he has anything to say.

'No,' he responds.

He is told the interview is being terminated and he should think 'long and hard' about the questions he's been asked about. His wife and sons will now be interviewed and perhaps he should consider the consequences of that.

'We have a raft of things to do now,' he's told. 'But we will be coming back to interview you again John. Be sure of that.'

Darwin must know there is no point in continuing to lie. The evidence is stacked against him and, putting him under further pressure to come clean, the detectives have told him that his wife and sons, his presumably innocent sons, will now be the ones under the police spotlight.

He is in a right old pickle for sure. For the time being, he is saying nothing. But he does have plenty to think about.

23

'Wet Footprints Going Up the Stairs'

THE FOLLOWING DAY, the *Mirror* breaks the story about Darwin's alter ego with the headline: DAY OF THE KAYAKAL.

Reporter Armstrong tells how Darwin distastefully stole the identity of a dead month-old baby to obtain a fake passport. His story is accompanied by quotes from John Jones's sister Frieda Woods, who lives close to the cemetery where her brother is buried.

'How low can you get?' she is quoted as saying. 'It makes me shake to think of it.

'It's terrible to think that this man may have used my brother's name in his scheme. I feel terrible, it's such a shock. My parents always used to speak about John and told us he'd died barely a month after being born. He was premature and underweight.

'This is terrible. The family is disgusted.'

That same morning Hutch prepares to discuss the existence of John Darwin's truly comical fake identity to a packed press conference.

He has three points he wants to get across:

- Show the passport photograph of John.
- Update them on the arrest of Anne.
- Thank the media for their help.

As always, he tries to second-guess any questions. Planning is essential, especially when the conference may be broadcast live on the news channels.

Hutch enters centre stage and there is widespread mirth when he holds up the photograph Darwin has used to obtain his John Jones passport. No one can believe that the only thing he had done to disguise himself was grow a big bushy beard.

'I have this photo of John, showing him with a beard, and many people may have seen him when he looked like this,' says Hutch.

'It's Uncle Albert from *Only Fools*,' whispers a reporter. 'Worse than Mrs Doubtfire,' jokes another. Seasoned reporters are shaking their heads in disbelief. Really? That's the best he could do?

Hutch gives it a few seconds for the chatter to settle down.

'We need to know where Mr and Mrs Darwin have been, both in Europe and in North and South America,' he says.

'We need to know what they have been saying. We need to know if anyone has seen John Darwin in the UK after his apparent death.

'They may have known him as John Jones.

'We need to know who they have been with and what they have been doing.'

Turning his attention to Anne, Hutch reveals she is about to be charged with dishonestly obtaining £25,000 and £137,000 by money transfer and will appear in court later that day.

He describes her as looking 'pale, drawn and very quiet' throughout the journey from Manchester Airport to Teesside after flying back to the UK to be arrested on Sunday.

'As she expected, police were waiting and officers based at the airport boarded the plane and arrested her on suspicion of fraud,' he says.

'She was then taken to the airport police station within the airport complex.

'Mrs Darwin underwent a medical examination to ensure she was fit and well for the 136-mile journey to Hartlepool police station. Cleveland police officers then escorted her back to Cleveland.

'The weather in the UK was cold and wet and a far cry from what she has been used to over the past few months,' he adds.

'Mrs Darwin did not speak at all in the car. On her arrival at Hartlepool, she was again seen by a police doctor before she was taken to a cell. I don't think she slept through the night. The doctor said she needed some sleep and a meal as she had travelled through various time zones.'

Hutch had been asked about John's clothes in an earlier press conference, so, somewhat tongue-in-cheek, he decided to describe Anne's at the time of her arrest. After he described her floral dress, Ian

Hislop asked in that week's *Have I Got News for You*, 'since when did the police start writing for Mills & Boon?' His team had a good laugh at the boss's expense. Hutch took it with good humour.

There is also rare praise for the media. The fact that we had found Anne, kept Hutch and his team fully abreast of our movements, and bought her home without the need for an extradition that may not have even been possible, had made his life a lot easier. There was also the small matter of her confession, albeit only partial.

'I would like to pay tribute to the media and say how grateful we have been for the help and information they have given to us during this inquiry,' says Hutch.

'Cleveland Police, over a number of high-profile investigations, have promoted a relationship of transparency and trust with journalists. That relationship has certainly borne fruit during this inquiry and for that I thank you.

'We are well aware of the stories that have appeared in the newspapers over the weekend and, in particular, will be discussing with Mrs Darwin the version of events over the past five years that have been attributed to her.

'Although our force has dealt with many wide-ranging and complex investigations, this is the first that has been on such a global scale. It has stretched from the Mediterranean to the Caribbean and beyond.

'Media interest in these events has been literally worldwide and the couple's photographs have appeared in newspapers on every continent. That has resulted in countless calls to us with information. We have had emails from Spain and the Caribbean.

'To get to the full truth of matters, I would like that information to continue.'

Hutch says Anne is insistent that her sons knew nothing of the alleged deception and tells the press conference he believes her. Police had initially thought it highly likely they had known about their parents' skulduggery but are now confident they are nothing more than innocent victims duped in a 'disgraceful fashion'.

Not that Hutch relied on Anne's word. Mark and Anthony had been interviewed at length and various communication streams were examined, but there was nothing to suggest the brothers were involved.

Even the media, so quick to report that they could have been sworn in as Special Constables, had not uncovered anything. There was absolutely nothing pointing to Mark and Anthony's involvement.

'For five years they thought their father was dead, then he walks back into their lives with apparent amnesia,' says Hutch.

'Then there is a huge inquiry by the media and a police investigation . . . then they find out their mother is involved.

'If they were going to be nothing other than victims, then our heart really does go out to them. It must have been a tremendous shock.

'I feel really sorry for them. There was just no reason that they could think of for them to do this.'

Seeing the 'John Jones' photograph on the TV news that night, former tenant Kay Graham, who was visited by odd-job man 'Tom', turns to her son and starts laughing. 'That's him who couldn't fix me toilet!' she says.

★★★

Detectives begin formally interviewing Anne at Hartlepool police station. The two officers assigned to quiz her are detective constables Terry Waterfield and Chris Marchant, both specially trained suspect interviewers.

Anne is accompanied by her lawyer, Nicola Finnerty, and as her husband had been just over a week earlier, she is cautioned and warned that anything she says can be used in evidence against her.

Anne starts by sticking to the story, which the police are convinced the couple concocted, insisting she initially made the insurance claims when she 'truly and honestly' believed her husband had died.

'It was becoming difficult for me to cope and I did start the process of making claims that I thought I was duly entitled to,' she says.

She admits that John had eventually come back, as far as she was concerned, from the dead, yet still she had continued claiming the money she knew she wasn't entitled to.

'He did come back and he'd expected everything to be over and sorted,' Anne offers by way of an explanation.

'I said, "You have to tell people that you are back," but he wouldn't let me do that.'

She says John told her she had to press ahead in claiming the money because they had debt in the tens of thousands, and he was convinced it wouldn't take much longer before the insurance companies paid out and then they could straighten everything out.

'I said I couldn't, I didn't like to lie, and he said if I didn't, then he would say I'd known all along that he was planning to fake his death,' says Anne.

In other words, she is claiming her husband was blackmailing her into going along with his deceit. It is a recurring theme. The detectives aren't buying it. Sounds like yet another lie and all part of the couple's prearranged cover story to lay all the blame on John's shoulders.

Anne says she can see, with hindsight, that it would have been better to have come clean, but instead she had simply 'learnt to live with it'. She has already admitted in newspaper interviews that her husband had talked about faking his death, but is now telling her interrogators there was nothing in his actions that had led her to believe he was planning to disappear. Another lie.

Anne recites the same story that had appeared in the *Mail* and *Mirror* about the day of his disappearance, the massive sea-and-air search for him, and having to break the terrible news to her family. John had always loved the sea, she says, and had long-held ambitions to own a boat and sail the seas.

Asked if it was a shared ambition, Anne replies: 'No, I don't like the sea. I don't swim.'

She also insists it was only much later that she discovered the extent of their debt in loans and on more than ten different credit cards, as John had kept it hidden from her.

'I knew there was some debt, but I hadn't realised the scale of it,' she says.

She can't stop lying.

Asked about her interviews with me in Panama, which had pretty much condemned both her and her husband, Anne starts to break down as she says: 'I was feeling very much alone and I accepted the offer of help.

'They asked if I'd make a statement and I said I would; well, once it started it all just came tumbling out and I said a lot more than I'd intended to say. I was just so relieved that everything was coming out in the open. I wanted it all to come to an end.'

That much was undoubtedly true. But Anne is still being devious in covering up about the timing of her husband's return from the dead: with very good reason.

Far from her being as contrite as she would have the police believe, John had told her that if they could convince the authorities that the money had all been originally claimed in 'good faith' – the phrase she used very early on in our interviews – when she believed he was dead, there was a very good chance they would not have to pay it all back. And Anne quite liked that idea.

She tells the detectives the financial burden only began to ease when a death certificate was issued for John after an inquest was held in April of the following year. Given the insurance payouts and being able to start selling their twelve rental properties, with the terms of the global mortgage relaxed because of the circumstances, Anne was able to pay off the outstanding £130,000 mortgage on Nos 3 and 4 The Cliff.

When, in 2007, she and John had decided to sell them, she received £160,000 for No. 4 and a few months later £295,000 for No. 3. They were sitting on a tidy lump sum of £455,000.

Anne says all that money is now in Panama. Safely stashed away, she thinks to herself – though she doesn't mention that.

The bulk of it is in two accounts, solely in her name: $365,000 in one and another $220,000 in a timed deposit account, one of the requirements for being able to buy property in Panama. Another account had been set up in the name of Jaguar Properties Corporation, but Anne says no money had ever been transferred into it.

Asked why she had opened the account solely in her name, Anne replies: 'Because John, as John Darwin, didn't exist.

'We couldn't be on as co-signatories and he'd always hoped that he would be able to go back to Panama as John Darwin.'

A return was indeed very much part of John's master plan – but the huge significance of that wasn't yet known and, at the time, the officers didn't press Anne any further on the matter. She claims that, in addition to the money in her accounts, she had bought an apartment in Panama City for $97,000 and a parcel of land in Colon for $360,000.

These were paid for with the proceeds of the sale of No. 4 The Cliff, which had been placed in a Jersey-based, offshore account with the HSBC that Anne had opened the previous summer. In total, Anne and John had been sitting on cash and assets in Panama worth just over $1 million.

The detectives then turn their attention to why both Nos 3 and 4 The Cliff had been transferred into her son Mark's name before they were sold. There is still a very strong suspicion that the boys must have known about their parents' deception: they were listed as shareholders of Jaguar Properties, Mark was named as the owner of the Seaton Carew houses when they were sold, and, as detectives were discovering, the Darwins' elder son had transferred money to his mother in both Panama and an offshore account in Jersey. Anne had told her sons that forming a corporation for her belongings would protect them from inheritance tax if anything happened to her.

Anne is asked to explain transferring the ownership of the houses to Mark.

'It was something that John had asked me to do and he said that as we were going to be looking for somewhere in Panama, I may not be here in the country to deal with the sales of the houses and if we transferred them into Mark's name, then he would be here to deal with everything – so I bitterly regret having done that now as I know it looks as if he was involved, which he wasn't.'

As Anne sobs, DC Waterfield tells her that, at the present time, the police are not suggesting that Mark was involved in any criminality. But he does say Mark will be spoken to at a later date.

'I'm not going to try and pull the wool over your eyes and say we'll just ignore it because you say he was wasn't involved, but I'm not looking at that at this time, all right?' he says.

Anne is horrified the police seem to think Mark, maybe Anthony too, are involved. Perhaps she should have given that more thought before she dragged them into the deception.

She says the transfer of the deeds for the two houses into Mark's name was an 'actual purchase' because John felt it would look better that way and he'd told her they would avoid inheritance taxes. She says both Mark and Anthony were given £30,000 from the sale of rental properties to buy Premium Bonds on her behalf. She had asked Mark to cash in his £30,000 to purchase the houses.

To the outside world, it would appear she had sold Mark two houses, together worth nearly half a million pounds, for just £30,000. But she insists Mark had not profited from the purchase in any way. They were his in name only and he hadn't made a penny.

When the houses were sold, the proceeds went briefly into his bank but were then immediately transferred into her accounts. The proceeds from No. 3 went into a bank in Panama, while the proceeds from No. 4 went into her HSBC offshore account in Jersey. She said Mark had obviously been aware she had bank accounts in those two places, but insists her son had no idea his father was still alive.

Turning to the property she had purchased in Panama, the police tell Anne that it appears she was the sole owner. But she quickly corrects them, proving she was very *au fait* with her husband's scheming.

'On the face of it, they belong to Jaguar Properties,' she says.

Right Anne, so you think they're outside our grasp?

DC Dolan, from the Economic Crime Unit, is already working with High Court-appointed Receivers and the Crown Prosecution Service to chase down all the fraudulently obtained money and assets in Panama. He will soon be paying Anne a visit.

She says the order to set up the corporation, which was 'John's idea', meant that Panamanian residents had to be named as directors. She said her lawyers in Panama City, Gray & Co, had found the three directors required, but she had no clue who they were and had no reason to as all they received was a small annual fee for their services.

She says John was not named as anything to do with the corporation and therefore has no legal claim on it, but she was a shareholder, as were Mark and Anthony.

The people listed as the officers of the company were Juan Montes, Ruben Barnett and Francisco Espino, all simply 'flunkies' used by the law firm to comply with the corporation's statutory obligation to have three Panamanian directors.

(In 2016, an unprecedented leak of 11.5 million files, commonly known as the Panama Papers, revealed how law firms regularly used just about anyone they could find – the guy who washed the cars in the parking lot, their girlfriend's aunt, or a delivery driver – to fulfil the roles of company directors to help the rich exploit secretive offshore tax regimes. John wasn't exactly in the same league as the billionaires and corrupt world leaders who used Panama to shield their fortunes from the taxman, but the methods used were identical.)

Anne is asked about her apartment in Panama City and why she had purchased a 400-acre plot of land in the countryside.

'The land might have been one of John's ambitions, to have some land that may become a spa or some sort of eco-tourism, because it was the "in thing" to do in Panama,' she says.

She claims that before John's disappearance, she had resisted his suggestions that they move abroad.

'I didn't want to leave my family,' she says, adding that matters had changed after he came back from the dead 'because there was a chance that we could have a life together without living in secret'.

The detectives grill Anne in detail about the claims she had made and she responds by saying that the process was started 'in all honesty' and it was only when John reappeared that 'it then became deception'.

'I wanted to ring everybody and tell them, but he wouldn't let me do it,' Anne insists.

The detectives don't believe her.

'He said he'd expected all the insurance policies to have been paid out by then; all the debts to have been cleared.

'If I said anything, he would say I was in on the plan from the beginning; I just got too frightened. I said I couldn't do it; I hated to lie and he knew that.

'We had talked about telling the boys because I knew how much they were suffering, but we couldn't, we couldn't do it. We didn't want to implicate them in any way.'

That much, at least, did ring true. If they had told Mark and Anthony what they had done, it would have been up to the boys to decide whether to say nothing and help cover up some pretty serious crimes, making them accessories, or go to the police knowing that both their parents would be arrested.

John and Anne's decision not to tell them, in the circumstances, is plausible.

Anne tells the officers John had persuaded her that he just needed to sort out the debt, and she was under so much stress and strain that she just went along with it, as it was 'somehow easier than telling the truth'.

'I just reached a point where it had all got out of hand and I found myself leading a double life,' she says.

The detectives finally question Anne about the crucial piece of evidence the police are sure will ultimately expose John – and her lies – concerning when he had really reappeared on her doorstep: John's Hartlepool library membership. Taken out in the name of John Jones, just a month after he vanished.

'Can you see what's happening, Anne?' DC Waterfield asks.

'I can see what you think is happening,' Anne responds.

'Well, he hasn't disappeared, has he?' says the detective, adding it is obvious John had been in the area the whole time.

'Well, not that I'm aware of,' says Anne, lying, but not very convincingly.

'He's giving your address all the time; he's giving the address where he's living on official documents,' adds DC Waterfield. 'What has happened here is that this has all been planned.'

'Not by me,' Anne quickly responds.

And then, just as officers had done with John, the detective sums up what police believed had really happened in the incredible case of the Canoe Man who came back from the dead.

'It's all been planned to enable massive debts to be paid off,' says DC Waterfield.

'We have passport, library membership, driving licence all in false names, a false name that you're aware of, a false identity that you have travelled with and with which you went on to deceive other people into believing that John Darwin was dead.

'I believe in the coming weeks we will uncover more evidence that will lead us to exactly where John was.

'I also believe that evidence will implicate you in the plan that was devised to make John Darwin disappear, so that insurance monies could be claimed to clear your massive debts.'

The detective pauses to gather his thoughts.

'Having been involved in this investigation and having listened to the interviews with John, and having been involved in this interview, and having looked at the evidence that's coming to light and has come to light, I'm surprised that when you called the police on the 21st March 2002, and the police attended, that the first officer who arrived at your house didn't see wet footsteps going up the stairs . . .'

DC Waterfield's nice little touch of irony to conclude the interview warrants a smile.

Anne is taken back to her cell and learns that John is being kept in the same police station. An officer says he's asked to talk to her. She's still smarting over his request to have a woman pen-pal but, assuming it will just be a brief word through the hatch, Anne agrees. She is shocked when the officer opens her cell door and John walks straight in and tries to hug and kiss her. Anne is appalled and tells him to get off and leave. He's quickly led away. The next day, she refuses John's request to speak to her again.

24

John Planned it All

Aᶠᵗᵉʳ ᵃ ᵇˡᵉᵃᵏ Christmas in which the Darwins celebrated their thirty-fourth wedding anniversary in prisons four miles apart, it's no surprise that it's Anne who finally cracks and gives police precisely what they have been waiting for. DC Waterfield was spot on.

The strain of continuing to lie has become too much. She has heard the evidence and knows her fiction is only making matters worse. *Finally*, she has seen sense. She is ready to confess.

After yet another sleepless night, she comes clean and tells her lawyer what everyone had long suspected.

She had been part and parcel of her husband's plot from the outset.

On 8 January 2008, in a sparse police interview room, the now fifty-seven-year-old admits her husband had been with her virtually from the moment he touched dry land after staging his death at sea on 21 March 2002.

In a taped confession, the interview room silent save for the whirring of the tape machine and her steady, monotone voice, she tells the detectives: 'I have had time to reflect and I'm ashamed to say that in my original interview I didn't give the whole truth.

'I knew the day that John had gone missing that he had gone missing and that he had planned it.

'I got a telephone call from him at work saying he was going out in the canoe, and he wanted me to get home by 7 p.m. and pick him up in the car park at North Gare and to help him make his getaway.'

'He went out in his canoe in Seaton Carew, and I waited for him on the shore in the car.

'He waited until after darkness fell out at sea, then came back in and I picked him up. He came towards the car and said he had everything with him that he needed.

'I drove him to Durham railway station. I had no idea where he was going. And then I went home.'

Durham station with its two platforms is much smaller than its bigger neighbour Newcastle, but trains travelling between London King's Cross and Scotland on the East Coast Line do stop there.

'He spent most of his time living next door in house No. 4 and I lived in house No. 3.

'I've nothing more to add other than I'm very sorry I didn't mention this in the first place.'

For Anne, the confession brings a dramatic end to five years and 295 days of living a lie. And an extraordinary globe-trotting adventure that has gripped millions around the world.

Anne is asked what she had thought of his idea to disappear.

'I didn't like the idea at all and I told him on numerous occasions it was a ridiculous idea,' she replies. 'Far better to go down the route of bankruptcy rather than trying to fake a death.

'But he just wouldn't hear of it. He said we'd both worked really hard all our lives and he didn't want to lose everything.'

Was John violent or threatening, she's asked?

'No, but he could be very manipulative,' she says. 'Whatever we discussed he would always end up getting his own way.

'He had a habit of making me feel quite small and inadequate. In fact, at times I would tell him that he treated me like a second-year pupil.'

Tony Hutchinson, Andy Greenwood and Iain Henderson would discuss later that day how the 'confession with caveat' could be paving the way for a Not Guilty plea.

'When he came back I tried and tried to dissuade him from continuing, to come clean, but he wouldn't and said he would say I was in on it from the beginning, when previously he'd always said he'd try and keep me out of it.

'He said if he was rumbled I'd be fine and it would be him that paid the price.

'I mean, I know it was stupid but once I'd set out along the road it was difficult to turn back.'

'And the boys, Anne, tell us about them?'

'Yes, that is extremely painful. Always has been.'

Anne's confession would appear to mean her husband has little choice but to end his ridiculous tale of amnesia. But the custody sergeant who goes to the cell to bring John to be interviewed is greeted by a sight for sore eyes. Darwin is walking around the cell in circles – in just his Y-fronts.

He's asked to put his clothes back on. John acts disorientated and confused.

'Who, me?' he asks.

'Yes, you please,' he's told and obliges.

Hutch is briefed. Ah, the old insanity card, he thinks. With his amnesia story shot to smithereens maybe it's all John has left. Is there nothing this man won't do to avoid paying for his crimes?

Told about his wife's confession, Darwin, thankfully now clothed, replies: 'I was suicidal, my wife was suicidal . . . we were non-*compos mentis*.

'We were one stage off the loony bin. We weren't thinking straight.

'I had to go missing because all we wanted was the insurance money. To be quite honest (*as ever, he wasn't*), I just wished I'd killed myself back then.'

There's a break and John chats to his solicitor. He seems to sense no one is buying his 'crazy man' story. Miraculously, he recovers his memory and his full and frank confession quickly follows.

'Yes, I planned it,' he finally admits. 'I disappeared because I wanted to claim the insurance money to tide us over.

'I took the canoe out and paddled out to sea. Paddled south to North Gare. Such was my state of mind that I didn't know whether to do it for real or not.'

But, of course, that wasn't true. He already knew he would paddle safely back to shore.

'We'd just heard from the Yorkshire Bank that we couldn't have an extension on the loan and we were going to be taken to court by American Express, who wouldn't accept reduced payments or anything,' he says.

'They wanted the full lot back and were going to take us to court, which would then cause a domino effect. Everything else had been tried.'

He's asked how Anne had taken his decision to vanish.

'Very, very badly,' he says. 'She was under an extreme amount of stress and so was I. She was basically hysterical, crying and saying there had to be another way.

'She had even threatened to throw herself in the sea.'

The interview concludes. The detectives have what they need. Job's a good 'un.

***

Hutch addresses journalists at a press conference later that day.

'Anne told us everything, and I would imagine that was something of a relief for her after all that time,' he says. 'Her husband then had little option but to do the same.'

Hutch, just weeks away from retirement, shakes his head and congratulates his team on a job well done. He knows he will be retired before they appear at Crown Court. He is due to walk out of the door for the last time on Maundy Thursday 20 March. It's fair to say he has grown to despise the man behind whose almost comical story of disappearance lay a calculated plan to defraud insurance companies of hundreds of thousands of pounds, while showing a callous disregard for the torment of close relatives who had grieved for him for years.

There's embarrassment for the Prison Service when it's discovered John and Anne were allowed to talk to each other by phone on their wedding anniversary, before the confessions, without the call being monitored. Someone had screwed up rather badly in letting two people facing serious fraud charges talk to each other without a prison official listening in. Was that when they agreed it was time for the lies to end? They knew all was not yet lost, far from it. All their assets were in untouchable Panama. Was their mindset to serve a bit of time then return to their Central American treasure trove?

Whatever was said, the reality of exactly what they have done finally starts to hit home, particularly for Anne. Neither son has been in touch. Her family and friends have disowned her. Her only contact with her husband is now through their legal teams.

Locked away in a prison cell, she has nothing but time to reflect on the madness of what she has done. She is facing a very lonely existence. She knows they will without doubt both be sentenced to further time behind bars. Quite how long remains to be seen. John will come out of prison a laughing stock, one of the most notorious fraudsters in the country. For Anne, there will be nothing but shame and remorse.

And for what? They could so easily have taken the sensible option and declared themselves bankrupt. None of this need ever have happened. John's sheer bloody-minded vanity in refusing to file for bankruptcy and admit to his incompetence as a businessman will cost him and his wife more than they could ever have imagined.

Hutch tells detectives to prepare for Anne Darwin pleading Not Guilty.

'The world's media have followed this,' he says.

'She has lied from day one. Did she look manipulated when she was sat in the sun being interviewed by David Leigh? I think she may try to use coercion to form her defence.'

He wasn't alone in his thinking.

The true story behind the Darwins' comically tragic and personally destructive road to ruin is still a long way from being known in its entirety.

25

Truth is Stranger than Fiction

IT'S SAID THAT truth is often stranger than fiction. The mind-numb-
ing truth behind the Darwins' brilliantly absurd story is testament
to that. You really would be hard pushed to make it up.

To fully understand where the wheels started to come off the
tracks for the seemingly most ordinary of couples from a seaside town
in the north-east of England you have to turn back the clock to the
weeks running up to Christmas in 2001.

A year after the Darwins moved into The Cliff, their financial
woes were spiralling out of control – as was John's state of mind. He
blamed his downfall on one of the credit card companies sending bills
and reminders to their old home, then threatening to send in the
bailiffs within days for non-payment. A county court judgment and
being declared bankrupt, he feared, would jeopardise his job at the
prison, other lenders would want their money back and everything
would quickly spiral out of control, meaning he and Anne would be
thrown out on the street.

There can be little doubt he had already started concocting the
foundations of his barmy ideas when around the time of his move he
took out a fatal accident policy with AIG. He also had a £145,000 life
insurance policy with the Norwich Union and was definitely worth
more 'dead' than alive. He was massively overstretching his already
perilous finances with the move to the house of his dreams. One last
roll of the dice was needed; a chance to become the millionaire he
always boasted he'd become. It was a hopeless, reckless gamble.

As he lay restlessly awake in bed at nights, he began to think more
and more about the possibility of disappearing. How would he do it?
Being 'lost at sea' was the most obvious choice as he was an experienced canoeist who had paddled along the coast and explored the
caves in the area many times in the past. Going out to sea wouldn't be

viewed as the least bit suspicious. But, could he get away with faking his death?

He knew it couldn't look as if he had committed suicide as that would invalidate his life insurance policies. If he could just vanish for a while, Anne could claim the insurance money, pay off the debts, he could come back to life and everything would once again be hunky-dory. He knew he'd have some explaining to do, maybe some money to repay, and would need to come up with a story for where he had been. He just had to work out how, when and where. All tricky questions, but not impossible. John used to write computer programs and liked a good puzzle. He carefully went through the pros and cons of each possibility in intricate detail.

A credible vanishing act was what he needed.

He could paddle south, past the abandoned piers that jutted out into Tees Bay and next to the busy shipping lanes for Tees Port. Here, some two miles down the coast, very few people ventured and there was little chance of being seen. Anne could secretly pick him up and then he could make his onward journey to wherever it was he decided to go.

But where would that be? What about the south coast? He worried his northern accent would quickly distinguish him, and it would be expensive, and, literally without a pot to piss in, he told himself, that was definitely going to be a major problem. He ruled out the east coast as being too close to home, and began thinking about the west coast, and the villages around the Victorian seaside resort of Silloth, a port town on the banks of the River Forth in Cumbria, where he had spent many happy times in his younger days. He could keep it cheap by camping out, as he had often done many times before with his brother David. He liked that idea.

With his plans pretty much finalised in his mind, all he had to do now was break the news to Anne.

There can be little doubt that she was initially horrified when John first blurted out his potty plan. But for him the thought of losing everything was more than he could bear. He even claimed he thought the boys, who had moved away from home and had their own lives, would get over his 'death' in a 'month or two'.

But, surprisingly, it wasn't the plan to disappear that was the most preposterous element of his scheming.

It was what came next.

According to Bernice Saltzer, a journalist who interviewed John Darwin at length, he had given a great deal of thought to the clandestine new life he would be forced to lead on his return from the dead. Along with his list of options on how best to disappear, and where to hide out until the dust had settled, he also had to figure out the rather more difficult, and longer-term concern, of where he was going to live.

Then it came to him. I'll move back home with Anne.

He knew hiding away in one of his vacant rental properties was far too dangerous an option, as, without a body, the police were bound to check out any possible addresses he was linked to. But the house he owned next door that had been converted into bedsits did open up very real possibilities – especially with the properties' largely unused connecting doors.

Tenants tended to keep themselves to themselves and many weren't even aware who was living in the room next to them, making an empty bedsit in the basement of No. 4 the perfect bolt-hole. The rest of the time he could simply go back to living in No. 3, even cuddling up to Anne in their matrimonial bed at nights. It was risky, of course, but he was sure he could pull it off. It was a truly outrageous plan.

Having finalised his future living arrangements, John drew up a checklist of what he would need in Cumbria, such as a tent, sleeping bag, spare clothes, a torch, matches and a rucksack.

'He had already worked out where he would paddle to, how he would dispose of his canoe and how he would travel to his hideaway destination,' said Saltzer.

'He was very proud of his plans. But John knew everything would depend on Anne's help and her ability to provide a believable alibi, and that concerned him, knowing she was liable to go to pieces under pressure. He was terrified she would blow a gasket and ruin everything.'

As the days passed and the recent rainy weather improved, John and Anne talked little about the dreadful thing John was about to do. The only normal thing in their lives was the pile of bills arriving daily with a smattering of bailiffs' demands threatening eviction and court proceedings.

As D-Day approached, Anne could barely stand the tension.

'John, there must be some other way,' she begged him. 'I don't think I can go through with it. The boys will be devastated. Please don't do it.'

But John insisted there was no other way, and it was time for some mind games – unless she wanted him to end his life for real? Anne said if he did that, she would do the same by walking into the sea and drowning herself. John, no doubt mightily relieved, promised he would simply stick to his plan to disappear.

He had been keeping a close eye on the weather; conditions were starting to look perfect for his plan. On the morning of 21 March, after one last vain attempt to dissuade her husband, Anne kissed him goodbye and left for work, still not really believing she had actually agreed to go through with it. She left a note on the kitchen counter begging him to abandon the crazy plan.

Anne said she had been ill all morning, literally worried sick at the thought of what he was about to do and the lies she was going to have to tell. She was a nervous wreck but, even though she knew it was completely insane, she still assured a frantic-sounding John in one last phone call that he made to her at work at the doctors' surgery, that she would pick him up later that day, at their prearranged spot.

'I'll be there,' she said, before hanging up.

John carefully went through his list, checking off each item one last time. T-shirts, jumpers, socks, pants, spare trainers, a money belt (with cash, obviously), a torch, matches and tinted sunglasses. He stuffed what he could into the hollow ends of the red canoe in plastic bags, to try and ensure they would stay dry. Years back, when he was using the vessel regularly, John had constructed a near-watertight compartment that was perfect for getaway belongings. Even though he had already discarded a few items, which were simply too heavy or bulky to fit in, he still grimaced as he tried to lift the canoe – it seemed to weigh a ton. But it was just about manageable.

He dressed in jeans, a t-shirt, jumper and trainers. He was wearing a cheap watch he'd bought especially for his mission, leaving his usual expensive one in the bedroom, along with his wallet and wedding ring, which he'd told Anne to hide. He made a cup of coffee and stuffed a few Mars bars from the fridge into his pockets. On the side in the dining room was a security box and, inside, a carefully written set of instructions on how Anne could claim the insurance money once everyone had given up looking for him.

John went into the rear garden to feed and say goodbye to his dogs, went back inside, checked all the house doors were locked, then donned his life-jacket, which he knew was somewhat ironic in the circumstances . . . but he didn't actually want to drown, did he.

Over the top, so the bright yellow vest couldn't be seen, he zipped up a thick, quilted black cotton jacket, and, after popping his sunglasses into a pocket, he completed his attire with his black woolly hat. The sea would be cold, but he was all set.

He lifted the paddle and canoe outside, locked the front door, then, huffing and puffing, carried the heavy raft across the busy road and a further 100 metres or so to the sands, from which point he could drag it behind him. He was happy knowing that at least several walkers, hopefully vital witnesses, had seen him struggling down to the sea.

Attaching the fibreglass rudder, he waded out a little, then climbed in, but he had packed so much gear for his getaway that the canoe simply wouldn't budge. The tide was coming in and, no matter what he did, he couldn't get the damned thing to move. He pushed his hands into the sand on either side, but the boat was so heavy it wouldn't shift. He bounced up and down, rocked back and forwards like a madman, and dug his hands into the sand harder, trying desperately to get some movement. There was nothing for it but to get out and try again. It wasn't quite the smooth start to the end of his life that he'd been hoping for. It was pure Reggie Perrin farce.

'Eventually, after what seemed a lifetime, I finally caught a wave, and then another, and the canoe slowly lurched forwards,' Darwin told Saltzer.

He was off. The water was freezing and waves quickly started crashing over the side, as John paddled out to sea, south towards the pier at North Gare. He paddled hard and it wasn't long, maybe fifteen to twenty minutes, before he could see the point at which he would return to shore. The sea began to get quite choppy and he grew nervous about capsizing and actually drowning, because he'd never mastered the Eskimo roll.

By the time he made shore, both he and most of his belongings, including the tent and sleeping bag, were soaked by the waves, and matters got even worse as he tried to climb out of the canoe and drag it ashore. He was shivering, dripping wet and freezing from the biting wind blowing in off the sea. He couldn't light a fire as he knew the smoke would attract attention; in fact he was so miserable, he claimed, that he thought about calling the whole thing off and going home. But, of course, that would have been too sensible an option . . .

A few items of clothing and his spare trainers had somehow stayed dry, so he changed out of his sodden apparel. Tossing one trainer into the sea, he wedged the other in the bow of the canoe, which bobbed about in the shallow water in front of him. Then he sat hidden in the dunes for the rest of the day waiting for the light to start fading.

As it did, with as much energy as he could muster, he threw the paddle out to sea, only for it, predictably, to wash straight back to shore on the next wave. He tried again, but the same happened, so he decided to cut his losses and leave it where it was. Next was the canoe itself. He forced it downwards, so it quickly filled with water and threw in a few boulders and rocks for good measure. There was too much buoyancy for it to sink completely, he thought, but he hoped it would drift out to sea a little with the outgoing tide. *Quite why it took so long to be found remains a mystery.*

John packed what he had left into his rucksack, tying the tent to the bottom and the sleeping bag to the top, and headed over the dunes in the direction of the car park at which Anne had agreed to pick him up. As he walked from the beach, he looked over his shoulder and was pleased to see that both the paddle and canoe had vanished from view.

Anne was waiting for him, as promised. She flashed the car's headlights as she saw the outline of her husband trudging towards her. He looked like a bedraggled Milk Tray man, wearing his black zip-up jacket, jeans and woolly hat, and carrying a rucksack.

'For God's sake, John, you can't do this,' she begged her husband. 'Give it up. It's not too late.'

But John's mind was set.

He had decided to head across country by train, so told Anne to head towards Durham railway station. Anne asked why not Hartlepool, which was far closer?

'Because it's the first place they will look, silly,' he replied.

'It's bound to have CCTV all over the platforms.'

He said he planned on going to Newcastle, then across the country to Carlisle.

'Unfortunately, it will then be up to you love. I'm sorry,' he said.

Still not really believing what she was actually doing, Anne drove the twenty-four miles to Durham railway station in her Skoda Felicia. She parked in an unlit side street, wary that there were CCTV cameras in the station car park. At the last minute, John agreed to Anne's suggestion that he dump the tent and sleeping bag; they were both soaking wet and would take days to dry out properly. A builders skip was conveniently nearby.

Anne walked with him on the platform and, after carefully checking the coast was clear, they had an emotional hug goodbye, knowing it would be some time – weeks, if not months – before they saw each other again.

'I think I cried all the way home as I was driving,' Anne later recalled.

'I was frightened. I was being asked to do something I didn't want to do and I didn't know how to get out of it.

'I knew it was wrong, of course I did, and I knew I'd hurt everyone with the lies that John had concocted.'

But Anne had gone along with everything asked of her and was therefore very aware that she was totally complicit in the crime, and an equal partner in their outrageous deceit.

Sitting next to a window and keeping his head down, careful not to make eye contact with anyone, John caught a train to Newcastle, then another across country to Carlisle. He arrived just gone 10 p.m. and began looking for a cheap B&B.

John checked in using the name John Allen, the first of many aliases he would adopt in the ensuing years, and was shown to his room. Johnny Allen was a fictional character from *EastEnders* and for some reason John thought using his name would be funny. One can only wonder. He plonked his rucksack down, took off his jacket and switched on the TV as he slumped down on the bed. Catching the late news, he watched a report about a huge search-and-rescue operation going on for a missing man on the east coast. Poor sod, he thought.

Then the news camera panned to his house and he saw the location, Seaton Carew. 'The missing man has been named locally as John Darwin', reported BBC North. Blimey! He thought the police would just ask a few questions and wander up and down the beach; he never imagined there would be quite so much fuss. He glanced anxiously at the bedroom door. Would the police soon come knocking?

He knew there could be no going back. Life on the run had begun.

26

Some Father, Some Friend

T HE NEXT MORNING, while everything remained frantic at No. 3 The Cliff, in the nondescript little B&B in the county town of Cumbria, all was calm. John had slept remarkably well after a rather extraordinary day, and woke up feeling hungry. After showering, he went downstairs and ate a bowl of cereal while waiting for a hearty cooked breakfast of bacon, eggs and sausages, washed down with a nice mug of piping-hot tea.

His would-be rescuers, who had been working in shifts throughout the night, would have loved the time for such a substantial breakfast.

Then he headed off to the library to get a list of bedsits for rent in the area. He didn't appear to be overly concerned at the trail of devastation his 'death' was creating elsewhere.

John grew annoyed that everything he found for rent was more than he wanted or could afford to pay, so he decided to revert to his plan to camp. He'd spotted an Argos store where he'd be able to pick up everything he needed – and cheaply, too. Inside, John totted up the cost of his shopping list – a new tent, sleeping bag, larger rucksack and an air mattress, to soften his sleep. He was pleased to see the cost, £80, came to less than two weeks' rent at the B&B. He stopped at an Oxfam store to buy a few books costing a few pence each.

Offering another insight into John's characteristically self-centred mindset, Saltzer said John actually claimed to feel 'cheated' that his health had taken a turn for the worse and his stress levels had gone through the roof. It's as if he simply thought he would be able to stop worrying now that he'd pulled off his vanishing act. He seemed to disregard the fact that his sons and other family members were worrying themselves sick and his accomplice wife was at her wits' end. As always, John was simply obsessed with his own problems and well-being.

With his rucksack packed full of supplies, his next stop was Silloth. He wasn't sure how far it was so decided to take a bus: probably just as well as it was over twenty miles away. He asked the driver to shout out when they reached the town, then sat back for the ride along the narrow, winding lanes. Exactly what lay ahead now, he didn't know. But he did enjoy the ride.

Pure comedy would probably be the best way to describe what turned out to be John's three-week camping expedition among the sand dunes of a remote beach. His supplies were mainly pasties, baked beans, bars of chocolate and cans of coke. What occupied most of his time was the 'wretched' air mattress, which had quickly sprung a leak and steadily deflated every night, leaving a miserable John lying on the cold, hard ground. Most days, he cut a rather pathetic figure, sitting on a log next to his little campfire late into the evening, whittling away at bits of driftwood, carving childish hearts that he engraved with the initials A and D. He complained of being very lonely and so cold he was on the verge of dying of hypothermia.

While his sons and other loved ones mourned his 'death' – Anthony spent hours forlornly scouring the coastguards' and missing persons' websites – John's only concern was how quickly he could return to The Cliff. He knew if he was to stand any chance of getting away with his audacious plan to move back to his old home he would have to change his appearance as drastically as he could.

Just like Reggie Perrin, he needed a disguise. He didn't go quite as far as buying false buckteeth but his shabby new look was still pretty comical. John had already decided a staged limp would help and he started walking along the beach using a bit of wood as a walking stick as he practised his new shuffle. But it was hard going in the sand and he soon gave up, deciding he only needed to morph into limp mode when he spotted someone or when he neared town. He'd let his facial hair grow into a shaggy beard and his wispy hair was getting longer and stragglier by the day.

But his disguise still needed a few more accessories. John bought a couple of carved walking sticks at a country market, one with a ram's horn as a handle, and an Arthur Daley-style sheepskin coat and a tweed flat cap for a few pounds in an Oxfam charity store. He tried on several pairs of specs but gave up on the idea when he realised he couldn't see anything – and was worried he might get run over by a bus. In the end, he opted for a pair of sunglasses, which he thought made it look as if he was wearing tinted spectacles.

Pausing to look at his reflection in a shop window, he was mightily impressed at the change in his appearance. In fact, he was so pleased with his disguise he even felt confident enough to visit a local pub that evening, where he ordered half a pint of lager, one miserly drink he dragged out for more than hour as he made small talk with the barman.

John had perfected the covering story about his new identity. Sticking to the name John Allen, he was a retiree from York on a walking holiday along the coast. He was camping along the dunes for a few days before moving on. Bidding the barman good night, John limped out of the pub and off towards a telephone box half a mile away. He had given Anne the number and she was scheduled to call at 9 p.m. The arrangement was that if she didn't call because she had unexpected visitors and couldn't get out, she would try again at the same time for the next few days, until she did get through.

John was ten minutes early and hovered nervously outside wondering whether Anne would ring. She did – but sounded terrible. The police, relations, friends and, most importantly, the boys, had all been questioning her and she was telling lie after lie to everyone. She wanted John to come back and hand himself in and for it all to be over with.

'Please,' she begged him, tearfully. I really can't carry on doing this for much longer. Have you any idea what it's like, how hard it is?'

But going back to face the music, and almost certainly being sent to prison for his crimes, was not something that particularly appealed to John.

'No love, I can't,' he said. 'Trust me, it will all be all right. We'll work it out. You just need to stay calm.'

Anne knew she was wasting her breath: nothing would change John's mind. They said their goodbyes, Anne promising to call again in a couple of days.

John didn't sleep well that night and woke up cold and stiff, the mattress having deflated during the night as usual. A breakfast of cold meat pie, Mars bar and flat coke did little to lift his spirits. He was as miserable as sin and feeling very sorry for himself. How long could he last living like this, he asked himself? How long would his money last? Maybe he would just die of hunger or freeze to death one night? Or maybe Anne would actually turn him into the police, something that had crossed his wife's mind more than once? Life on the run was no fun at all.

Self-pity crashed over him like the waves over his canoe.

***

Six weeks after John disappeared, an early-morning walker spotted a broken-up red canoe being tossed around in the waves tumbling ashore at Blue Lagoon Sands at the mouth of the River Tees. After dragging it out of the water and up onto the beach, the man immediately called 999.

'I think I might have found the canoe that bloke from Seaton Carew disappeared in,' he told the operator.

Hartlepool's inshore lifeboat was launched and Coastguard and RNLI volunteers searched the coastline for several miles in each direction, while a police spotter plane flew overhead. A yellow waterproof jacket was discovered a little further along the shore . . . but there was no sign of a body.

Anne was at home when she received a phone call from her police family liaison officer, Detective Constable Ian Burnham, saying he had some bad news and would she mind making her way to the police station to see if she could identify a dark red canoe, with toggles at either end, that had just been washed ashore. A shiver ran down her spine; she hated any contact with the police and knew she would again have to put on another grief-stricken performance.

Her sons had recently returned to their respective homes in the south . . . but she wasn't alone.

'They think they've found the canoe,' she said, turning to address the man sitting opposite her as she put down the phone. 'And they want me to go and identify it.'

In a truly breathtaking move, John had returned to the family home just three weeks after staging his death: it was risky beyond belief, almost unbelievable. Truth was, he would have come home earlier had he been able to. He couldn't wait for the boys to leave and return to their homes so he could get back to his. He hadn't liked roughing it one bit, although it had only been for a paltry three weeks. He wanted to be back in his own bed again and Anne to be fussing over him, as she always did. The boys had stayed with their mother for as long as they could, but both had jobs and – albeit, shattered – lives to return to. Mark left first, then Anthony. John was delirious: he could go home. Darwin appeared to have a total lack of empathy towards his grieving sons.

Anne drove herself to the police station and with trembling lips and tears in her eyes – she was getting very good at playing the grieving widow – nodded, as she confirmed the canoe, battered and holed and with the name her husband had christened it, *Orca*, painted on the side, next to a transfer of a mother and baby killer whale, was the one that just a few short weeks ago had been sitting in the hallway of her home.

Inspector Martin Cook, of Hartlepool Police, told local journalists later that day, 7 May, that members of the family had identified Mr Darwin's canoe.

'It was in two or three parts,' he said. 'The family has attended. There's no sign of Mr Darwin.'

The officers who had comforted Anne throughout her ordeal felt for her. They knew any lingering hopes she had that her husband might have somehow miraculously survived were gone. Anne drove home and told John what had happened, then tearfully called the boys to break the news. Mark sobbed as he told her that it felt like he had lost not only his father but also his best friend. Anthony was distraught.

Some father. Some friend.

For three weeks after his disappearance, the boys had stayed with their mother to offer what comfort they could. For all of them, the days seemed to pass in a blur.

'Mam didn't eat, drink or sleep much,' Mark recalled.

'She wandered around the house in a daze like the rest of us. She was in a terrible state and kept saying, 'I think he's dead, we're never going to see him again.' She was in a state of panic. I barely left her side.

'She would just sit and stare out of the window and cry. I was numb with the pain, but I wanted to be strong for her. She needed someone close; she looked so helpless.'

★★★

Anne had picked up John and bought him home as soon as the boys had gone.

'He was getting desperate,' Anne recalled. 'He was finding it very hard.'

She had told him it was still far too early, but after one call in which he tearfully begged her to come and get him, she relented. Mark had left a day or two earlier and Anthony had returned to his home that morning, so for the first time since his vanishing act, the house was empty.

Anne drove across country to Cumbria and revealed that her husband had changed so much in just three weeks that she hadn't even recognised him as she sat waiting at their prearranged pick-up spot.

'I remember watching an elderly gentleman walking towards the car and walk past,' she said.

'Then he came past the car a second time and, as he passed, he glanced towards me and I immediately recognised him.

'He had grown a beard and he was wearing baggy clothes that I didn't recognise, which he later told me he had bought in a charity shop.

'He had lost a lot of weight. I was pleased to see he was alive, but I was also very angry with him.

'I said to him, "Now is the time to put an end to this – we have to stop." But he said he couldn't. We had come this far and the worst was over.

'I told John we should tell the boys because they were grieving, but he said we couldn't tell them. If we did they were likely to persuade me to tell the truth.'

John also said it would implicate them in their crimes and that was the last thing any of them wanted. For Anne, it meant the lying would continue.

Back in Seaton, Anne had dropped John around the corner from The Cliff and, clad in full disguise, he had shuffled up to the front door of No. 4 and let himself in using the key code, 3501. But as he entered, he was horrified to see his wife standing in the hall corridor talking to Tommy, one of the tenants he knew well. Tommy stared intently at his recently deceased landlord as he limped past and uttered a gruff 'night'. Both John and Anne were convinced Tommy had seen through the not overly convincing disguise. But he said nothing. Somehow John had got away with it. It wouldn't be for the last time.

Once Anne had unlocked the connecting door to No. 3 and John had crept back into his old home, he wanted a hot bath and something to eat: he was starving. No sooner was he 'home' than he was quizzing Anne on how she was getting on with claiming the insurance. Anne couldn't believe what she was hearing. The stress of lying in such a terrible way to her sons and everyone else had taken its toll. She was a bag of nerves and furious with him for even bringing it up so soon after coming home. He had only been gone *three weeks*; what on earth did he expect?

'I haven't done anything,' she yelled at him. 'Nothing. Nothing at all. How the hell could I?'

John knew it would be unwise to push things further; for now, anyway.

For practical reasons, John needed a proper new identity. He had kept his long shaggy beard, unkempt hair and disguise outfit for when he decided it was safe to venture outside.

But he knew that to get on with his life, he needed to be someone who actually existed: he needed a new name. How else would he ever be able to get a driving licence, a passport, or even join the local library? After all, John Darwin was supposed to be dead.

It was the matter most on his mind when, just three days after he returned, Anne received a call from the police that sent her into a blind panic: the next day a team of officers would be coming round for a renewed top-to-toe search of her house, looking for any clues they might have initially missed.

It seems strange that the police were telegraphing their visit, but, as Anne wasn't exactly a crime suspect and there was no evidence of any wrongdoing, it's likely they were just being kind and gentle on a woman they believed to be a grieving widow.

Having had advanced warning, John and Anne quickly set about methodically walking through every room, making sure there were no tell-tale signs of his being there. Since returning, John had spent most of his time in No. 3 with Anne but had regularly used a bedsit on the ground floor of No. 4 and then Room 12, the room partly across the top floor of her home, which was actually part of next door. He knew there might soon come a time when he would have to rush through one of the connecting doors in a hurry. He made frequent trial runs to help eliminate the risk of errors when he had to make that quick getaway for real. He also devised a secret code of knocks for the connecting doors so both could be sure the coast was clear. One knock followed by three in quick succession, then one more, meant it was safe to enter No. 3. They also used hand-held radios to communicate.

With the police coming the next day, John knew it was far too dangerous, and too early, to risk hiding next door: he wasn't happy at all, but realised there was only one thing to do – disappear again.

After the last disastrous camping expedition, taking to a tent again wasn't an option, so John told Anne he'd head north for an hour, to Morpeth, the county town of Northumberland, and lie low in a B&B for a week.

Incredibly, despite knowing the police would soon be knocking on the door in the morning, John didn't even leave that night. Anne changed the bedding, putting the dirty linen in the washing machine, and told John he couldn't sleep with her in the marital bed that night as she didn't want any give-away indentations in the fresh sheets. John didn't fancy a night in the hovel next door, so, after packing a ruck-sack with a few things, ready for a quick exit in the early hours, he curled up on a sofa in the drawing room and tried to get some sleep.

He woke with an idea about his new identity and quickly printed out two copies of a tenancy agreement for the bedsit he was using in No. 4 (Room 12), one for him and one for Anne. He used another fake identity, Karl Fenwick, although quite why he picked that name is not known. Maybe it was because Fenwick is a large department store in Newcastle, or maybe it was because Mr Fenwick closes his shop after refusing to serve furs to Cruella de Vil and is never seen again. With John, it's hard to know.

He printed and cut out the name and taped it on the front door of Room 12.

It was still dark and time to go. Anne unbolted the connecting door to No. 4, checked the coast was clear, and John tiptoed to his hideaway to collect his disguise garments and a walking stick. He crept down the stairs, and adopted his staged limp as he quietly shuffled out of the door and off down the street towards the bus station. As soon as he had gone, Anne went to the bathroom to check he'd put the toilet seat down: after all, he was a man and she was leaving nothing to chance.

Just one hour later, a team of police officers arrived to start their search. Talk about dicing with death.

John decided to spend the first night in Durham, booking into the Durham Light Infantryman pub, just a few hundred yards from the surgery where Anne worked, in the Gilesgate area. After a pint in the bar, he retired early, had a good night's sleep, and in the morning enjoyed his favourite full cooked breakfast before heading to the station to continue his journey to Morpeth, on the banks of the River Wansbeck. He found a cheap B&B and booked in under his pseudonym, John Allen.

Unbeknown to the police at the time, Anne actually had two telephone lines into the house, only ever plugging a handset into the socket of the second, unlisted line when she needed to secretly make or receive a call. John had set times to call, and he knew if there was no answer, it was because Anne had someone with her in the house, so hadn't plugged the phone in. The deception was very sophisticated.

John called at the agreed time that night and found Anne, once again, frantic with worry. The search had been far more extensive than she had imagined. Four police vans had arrived just over an hour after he left, and teams of officers, wearing blue forensic overalls, went through every room of the four-storey house, including the loft and the converted chapel in the back garden.

One of the first things they did was search the bedroom, carefully pulling back the duvet – obviously there were some who still felt there was more to John's disappearance than met the eye. Officers went through every drawer, bagging up dozens of letters and bills, tenancy agreements, receipts, and taking away John's prized computer. Anne was incensed they had even been through her underwear drawer.

She panicked when they went into No. 4 through the connecting door on the ground level and was mightily relieved they hadn't searched all the bedsits, probably because they would have needed search warrants. The whole experience left her badly shaken.

Back in Morpeth, John was finalising plans for his cunning new identity – and very soon he was reborn as John Jones. If it was good enough for the Jackal, he chuckled to himself, it would certainly be good enough for the wily old John Darwin.

27

The Inquest

JOHN WAS YET to discover the big flaw in his masterplan: resurrecting John Jones was a lot easier than killing John Darwin.

He had whined like a mammy's boy, pleading to return from his 'camping exile' in Cumbria, and as soon as he walked through the front door, he'd wanted to know how the claims were progressing. Furious when Anne told him she hadn't started, he'd badgered her to make the calls, writing instructions as the conversation unfolded with whoever was at the other end of the line. Each time the answer was the same – 'not without a death certificate'.

The man who enjoyed puzzles and loved reading and research had not considered insurance and pension companies refusing to pay a penny until a death certificate was produced. The coroner would have to officially declare John dead before Anne could claim the money that would free them of debt and make a new life possible.

John Darwin may have been a legend in his own lunchtime, but he couldn't extract money from the faceless administrators. Al Capone, John Gotti, The Krays would have found a way; the little man from Seaton Carew took it out on his wife.

The coroner, Malcolm Donnelly, respectfully explained to Anne that in the case of a missing person, any request for an inquest had to be personally sanctioned by the Home Secretary. Such cases were relatively rare, just a handful a year, he said, and everyone would first have to be satisfied the police believed that the case was closed.

Anne was despondent. John was livid. The police should just fuck off.

The faked death may have been his idea, but Anne had fast become the backbone of the deception, playing her own, vitally important role in the growing number of crimes they were committing.

That August, DC Burnham called Anne to say a body had been found off the coast of Hartlepool and would she mind coming to see if the body was John's.

'She broke down and sobbed,' said DC Burnham, who had been the family's main police contact since John's disappearance.

'I asked if she wanted me to come and pick her up, but she insisted she was fine and would make her own way.'

The detective, a plain-speaking 'colliery lad' who had spent fifteen years working the mines before joining the police force, described Anne as 'not cold, but reserved and very private'. Some people dealt with their grief by lying on the ground, kicking and screaming hysterically, but she was at the opposite end of the spectrum.

'As a police officer you're naturally suspicious about most things, and we were of course all suspicious about her husband's disappearance, but the police can only follow the evidence,' he added.

'There was no body, his bank or credit cards were checked and hadn't been used, and although we knew he was in some debt, we had nothing to go on.'

As Anne drove to the meeting point, DC Burnham got a call to say that identification had been found on the body and it definitely wasn't Darwin.

'I called her and as she was driving asked her to pull over,' he explained. 'I told her the body was that of a lad from Northumberland who'd taken his own life, so she didn't need to identify it.

'She started sobbing again and said she knew it sounded awful, but she'd really hoped it had been John so she could have had closure and start picking up the pieces of her life again. I felt for her. She came across as very genuine. She was obviously a pretty good liar.'

As the weeks passed, Anne became increasingly convinced John's plan had been an unmitigated disaster. She had managed to persuade most of the credit card companies to suspend payments until an inquest had been held, and the bank had agreed to keep the mortgage on interest-only repayments. But she was still struggling to pay the bills and was warned if she didn't keep up with the insurance premiums, she wouldn't be able to make a claim in the future – and that was something the Darwins could ill afford to happen. The boys offered their mother what money they could to help, but Anne wouldn't accept.

She was at her wits' end, wondering when the deception, snowballing by the day, would be over. The delay in the inquest covered her in paranoia: every knock at the door was the police or the bailiffs; each ring of the telephone carried the news that their lies had been uncovered; cars parked across the road weren't members of the public going for a walk or admiring the view, but undercover detectives or insurance investigators. She never answered the door until she knew who was there, ignored the phone until the answerphone kicked in, and closed the curtains to stop snoopers looking into her house.

Anne and John argued frequently and gradually the rows got worse. Anne was struggling with harbouring a man the world believed to be dead. John hated being banished from the marital home into the bedsit, but if Anne bolted the door, which she did with increasing regularity, there was nothing he could do about it. The bedsit was cramped and needed more than a lick of paint to rid it of the smell of its previous occupant, a chain-smoking alcoholic. John painted the room three times but couldn't get rid of the stench.

Bored out of his brains, he began painting other vacant rooms, shuffling around and pretending to be Anne's odd-job man 'Tom'. On a trip to B&Q in Stockton to buy paint, the first store assistant he saw was a former principal officer from Holme House prison. John pulled his collar up, kept his head down and shuffled past unnoticed. But the incredible risks he was taking almost imploded when a few weeks later one of his former tenants, Lee Wadrop, recognised him beneath his thin disguise and asked: 'Aren't you supposed to be dead?' Flustered, Darwin told him: 'Don't tell anyone about this.' Astonishingly, Mr Wadrop didn't tell a soul. Some people don't want to get involved; others simply don't 'grass'.

If Anne had family or guests staying, John was forced to head off into town to buy food or other provisions, again taking huge risks when he believed they were being watched. But he continued to get away with it and the longer he did, the more his confidence grew. On one occasion, John's heart nearly stopped when, walking back to his house from Hartlepool, he spotted his brother and father walking directly towards him along the sea front having visited relatives who lived in the town. Astonishingly, he shuffled past unrecognised.

Seeing people he used to work with or who knew him became a regular occurrence. He really was the invisible man, he arrogantly told himself.

In November, eight months after John disappeared, the police decided to make a fresh appeal for witnesses: *there were obviously some who believed Darwin might still be alive.* Anne was questioned by police press officer Charlie Westburg, a former journalist, who was tasked with drafting a news release seeking new information.

In the release, sent to all local and national media, Anne was quoted as saying: 'All I want is to bury his body. It would enable me to move on. It's difficult to grieve without bringing things to a close, but as it is I'm in limbo and there's nothing I can do.

'I know everyone involved in the search, particularly the Coastguard, did everything they could to find his body. I just hope that even now his remains will be recovered.

'People die, have a funeral, they have a headstone, there is something to mark the fact they existed on this earth, but without a body I don't know how we can mark John's life.'

Westburg gently asked the question that was still troubling a number of senior officers: had her husband faked his death?

Anne was adamant a tragic accident was the only explanation, adding: 'That's the only way I have been able to cope with it. *I have no reason to think he would have left and stage-managed this.*'

Westburg asked for a photograph of John to accompany the release and was thrown when Anne said she didn't have any. Not one, he asked? No, John hated his picture being taken, Anne responded. A woman without a single photograph of her husband. *Really?*

***

For months, Anne had been leaning heavily on a friend from the doctor's surgery, Irene Blackmore. They had met two years earlier when Irene was hired as a receptionist. Anne was her boss and quickly took her new colleague under her wing, for which Irene, somewhat of a loner, was eternally grateful. Irene had suffered a family bereavement earlier that year and was one of the first to visit Anne after hearing about the canoeing tragedy.

Gradually, her visits became more frequent and the two women would spend hours talking to one another and sharing their thoughts in front of an open fire in the drawing room, often until late in the evening. Sometimes she would stay the night, infuriating John, who would be consigned to his shabby bedsit next door. Anne was grateful of the company but also relieved to be rid of her husband for a few hours.

After a miserable Christmas in his cramped little bedsit, the relationship deteriorated to such an extent that Anne banned him from the marital bed completely. 'Playing dead' was not all it was cracked up to be. But on the plus side, he didn't have to lie to anyone.

'Relax, love, the worst is over,' he would tell Anne in his condescending manner.

'Who for?' she would respond sharply. 'Maybe for you, but not for me. I'm having to lie to everybody, every minute of my life. Can't you understand how hard that is?'

John never had time for his wife's histrionics and would simply roll his eyes and shuffle off to the cellar, where he would spend hours playing on his computer.

For Anne, everything she did or said involved deception. Every time someone visited, she would have to play the grieving widow, putting on an act and gratefully accepting people's kindness and consoling words. She came across as someone struggling to cope, which she was – *just not for the reasons people thought.*

John devised an ingenious warning code using their living-room curtains for when he went out: dangling freely equated to safety, tied back was a warning that Anne had unexpected visitors and he should lie low until the danger had passed. It kept their secret alive on more than one occasion. It often crossed Anne's mind to leave the curtains tied back on a more permanent basis . . . life was so much easier when John was not around.

Norwich Union had been suspicious about Darwin's disappearance from the moment Anne submitted her claim, given that a body had never been found. In February 2003, after drawing a blank on their own investigations, they called in an expert, John Saunders, who ran his own specialist investigation company. He'd previously investigated the 'deaths' of three other men who had been reported missing at sea. All three were now behind bars having been convicted of fraud. One was found hiding in a hole under his wife's bed, along with a DIY fake-your-own-death kit. His wife was also jailed. Another's 15-foot rowing boat had been found washed ashore. There had been a huge air-sea rescue search but a body was never found. It transpired the man's wife had picked him up from the beach and helped him disappear, keeping it a secret from their three sons. Another wife who had aided and abetted her husband's disappearance. Another man who had been heavily in debt and boosted his life insurance coverage in the months running up to his disappearance. You could say . . . another John Darwin.

Saunders, who had travelled to eighty-three different countries across the globe investigating thousands of suspicious claims, sent a colleague to interview Mrs Darwin.

'We knew it was fishy from the outset,' said Saunders.

'When someone disappears soon after taking out a life insurance policy and you find out they're in considerable debt, you just know. My colleague didn't believe Mrs Darwin for a minute.'

But towards the end of February, everything suddenly changed. Mr Donnelly announced he would be holding an inquest. He had sought permission from the then Home Secretary, David Blunkett, after being assured by the police that the case was pretty much closed and the chances of finding John had, sadly, long passed. The new appeal for witnesses had drawn a blank.

On 22 March, to mark the anniversary of John's disappearance, Anne and her sons decided to have a small, private ceremony at the water's edge in North Gare. They huddled together in the blustery winds and stared out at the sea, before each threw their offerings of flowers into the choppy water. Anne's were white roses.

The inquest was set for a few weeks later, 10 April. Initially delighted with the news, Anne became panic-stricken at the thought of giving evidence and being cross-examined in court. John, however, was cock-a-hoop. But in the days running up to the inquest he kept a low profile. He could not afford to have his cover blown at this late stage.

Anne was a bag of nerves, convinced, as ever, that something would go badly wrong. The boys and their partners were coming to stay at No. 3 for a few days, so it was imperative John shut himself away in his No. 4 'foxhole', as he often referred to it. From there, on the eve of the inquest, he would undoubtedly have heard the voices of his sons through the walls as they chatted with Anne late into the night. The deception continued to be breathtaking.

The morning of the inquest was a sombre affair. Neither Anne nor the boys were looking forward to it – though for very different reasons. For the boys, it would mark the end to any glimmer of hope that their father had miraculously survived. For Anne, giving evidence would be a case of adding to her rapidly increasing portfolio of monumental lies and deceit – this time in a courtroom. She had been dreading the day – and having to lie publicly in front of the boys – for weeks.

'John used his bedsit. I used to lock the doors, but they were only bolted and the boys could have easily walked through to the part of the house that John was using at any time,' said Anne.

'Initially I said I couldn't go through with it. I could not go and sit through an inquest and ask for probate because there was no will.'

But Anne did go through with it, once again carrying off the role of grieving widow with her usual aplomb. As one of the officers involved in the investigation later recalled, it was a role worthy of an Oscar.

In presenting their evidence to the coroner, the police said there were four possibilities.

1. John Darwin had staged the whole affair.
2. He had committed suicide.
3. He'd had an accident and died.
4. He had died at the hands of persons unknown.

Options one, two and four were then discounted. As his passport, credit cards and mobile phone had all been left at home there was 'less than a one per cent chance' that the disappearance had been staged; there was no evidence to prove he had planned anything, not one person the police had spoken to said he appeared suicidal and there was nothing to link anyone else to his death. The police therefore concluded a tragic accident was the most likely occurrence, whether through a heart attack (he was known to have angina), or having got into trouble in the canoe and drowned. Mr Donnelly agreed an accident was most probable and recorded an 'open verdict', declaring

John Darwin to be 'missing presumed dead'. Cause of death on the certificate was given as: 'Probably encountered difficulties as a result of which he died.'

The Darwins knew the death certificate, issued by the Maritime and Coastguard Agency because the accident happened at sea, meant there were no more obstacles in the way of the life insurance and pension payouts. Just as importantly for John, his love-life took a considerable turn for the better. He said Anne's diminished stress levels resulted in his all-important sex-life returning to normal after he was allowed to return to the marital bed.

Saunders was informed of the verdict by Norwich Union, which decided to terminate its investigation.

'It was taken out of my hands,' he recalls. 'They wanted to move on.'

One morning soon afterwards, naked and arrogantly gazing out of his bedroom window at the spot from which he'd vanished, Darwin chuckled to himself at how easy it had been. He'd moved back home and the glare of attention that had briefly awakened the sleepy little seaside town from its slumber had long since fizzled out. He knew poor old Anne was still living on her nerves, lying to all and sundry, but he was impressed with the way she had surpassed herself in playing the grieving widow. She'll be all right, he told himself, it will just take time. Now, with him having officially been declared missing, presumed dead, the police had seemingly lost interest. And all that lovely money would soon come rolling in . . .

He had bloody well pulled it off.

And, of course, he was delighted. For him, all the deception had been worthwhile: he'd won the golden ticket. He had always been confident of getting away with his disappearing act and he'd been proven right. It did dawn on him, however, that with Anne now officially a 'widow', there was nothing to stop her from leaving him and marrying someone else. It crossed his mind a few times but he didn't dwell on it. She had, after all, already passed her loyalty test with flying colours. He was feeling so pleased with himself that morning he decided to play a CD by his favourite band, Abba. The sound of 'Money, Money, Money' resonated around the house . . . '*in a rich man's world . . .*'

On 16 May, the first cheque arrived in the mailbox: £25,000 from his accidental death policy (AIG would only pay 50 per cent because his body had never been found). Days later the Norwich Union mortgage protection insurance policy paid out £137,400.72. The mortgage overdraft shrank from £215,455.74 to £78,055. Monthly payments fell from £1,735 to £826.

Then came £40,000 from the teachers' union; and a further £41,518.93 from her husband's prison pension. Money arrived from the Department of Work and Pensions Welfare Bereavement Fund and further payouts from the prison and teacher pension funds. The cheques kept on coming.

The total received was just shy of £250,000.

As the money came in, the credit card debt was paid off. Not wanting too much money sitting in Anne's bank accounts, John told her to invest £120,000 in Premium Bonds, even cruelly dragging their unwitting sons into their fraudulent scheming. On John's instructions, Anne gave both Mark and Anthony £30,000 to buy Premium Bonds on her behalf, a move which would later throw them under a cloud of suspicion.

Reducing the global mortgage so considerably also meant they could start selling off the rental properties, once tenants had been served notice. The first one sold for £21,510. Another, bought for £7,000, sold for £32,000 – a handsome profit. Soon they were all sold. The stockpile of cash kept on growing.

That August John opened a Lloyds TSB bank account in the name of John Jones. Another useful form of identification. He used the same branch where he had banked as John Darwin. He described himself as a labourer. His employer? One Mrs A. C. Darwin. His address: 4 The Cliff.

He had more front than Blackpool. Or should that be Seaton Carew . . .

28

Cedum the Saviour

DEEP DOWN, JOHN had always known that to have an existence he could enjoy he would have to move abroad. He didn't want to be the shuffling, shaggy-bearded John Jones, or Tom the odd-job man in scruffy work clothes, for much longer. He wanted his freedom back.

With his shiny new John Jones passport, a whole new world had opened up. He began giving serious thoughts to the next stage of his life, but where could he and Anne move without attracting too much suspicion?

He avidly watched any travel programmes and one on Cyprus caught his eye. The climate was good and although property in the Greek-governed south was expensive, the north, governed by Turkey, looked a much better bet, with both housing and the cost of living far cheaper. It was not too far from home for Anne, but far enough away that visitors wouldn't suddenly turn up on their doorstep unannounced, which is why they had ruled out places like Brittany.

In early 2004, he and Anne decided to check it out. Anne told family and friends she had decided to get some sun and escape for a while, which was understandable. She said she was flying from Manchester Airport, but in fact drove to Manchester with John, then caught a train to London, where they flew from Gatwick.

Anne was a bag of nerves. It was the first time John had used his John Jones passport and she was convinced he would be stopped and arrested for travelling with fake documents or they'd bump into someone who recognised them. But the journey was uneventful.

They stayed in a small hotel in the harbour city of Kyrenia, in Northern Cyprus. Their days were split between lazing by the pool and visiting potential properties and plots of land to buy. They put down £500 on an acre plot that took their eye, but the deal eventually fell through, and, because of the complexities of buying in the north, John pretty soon gave up on Cyprus and turned his thoughts elsewhere. Ironically, he considered the estate agents he'd dealt with to be a 'bunch of cowboys' who didn't know what they were doing.

★★★

'You'll never guess who I've been playing with today?'

Anne looked at John quizzically. They are sat in the kitchen of No. 3.

'The boys! But don't worry; they have no idea it's me!'

John chuckled. Anne is beyond horrified.

Two years after his 'death' and addicted to playing online fantasy games, John has – astonishingly – used his character to befriend and pit his wits against his sons, who are both active players of the online game *Asheron's Call*, a kind of *Dungeons & Dragons* reality game fighting virtual 3D monsters in an exotic, far-off land. Of course, the lads have no idea who the mysterious druid who has befriended them really is. John knew his sons' online identities from playing under a different name before he 'died'. He admits to Anne that maybe it's a little cruel, but says he finds it hard to break all ties and so, despite telling Anne he'll stop, he carries on regardless.

It is quite possible that the fantasy world in which Darwin lived for so many years actually made him lose touch with reality. His addiction to false identities is undoubtedly the reason his frauds went undetected for so many years. But his fascination for fake names and a fantasy life was not something borne out of his need to disappear. Long before he even thought about doing his now infamous vanishing act, John honed his skills at living in a fantasy world through playing on his computer.

He had been playing *Asheron's Call* for years. After staging his death, it became an addiction. He spent hours lost in a world of make-believe playing against thousands of fellow gamers pretending to be people they weren't. They had fake names, money to buy and sell property, and the power to cast spells on opponents. Characters died – but could come back to life. *Sound familiar?*

John's reality world would be the perfect training for what was to follow in real life. For when the time came to fake his own disappearance, one of his first acts had been to carefully create a false identity so robust it would give him access to credit cards that would never need to be paid back and a passport that gave him the freedom to travel and disappear.

He struck up dozens of online 'friendships', including one with a thrice-married American woman, Kelly Steel, which has to count as among the strangest chapters in John's increasingly bizarre life. Ludicrously, he considered himself a bit of a ladies' man and was soon chatting to women from all over the world; from Sweden, Australia, Hong Kong and one from New York called Maria, who lived in The Bronx. He joined another reality game, *American Farmer*, where the goal was to amass wealth.

That May came a major scare – and an almighty let-off. John had grown so cocky about not being recognised he regularly spent time gardening or pottering about in the front yard. Prison officer Dave Smith was driving his dark blue Audi A3 along the sea front in Seaton Carew after a walk along the prom with wife Denise. As he passed The Cliff he did a double-take. Smith worked at Holme House prison and whenever he was in Seaton drove past Darwin's house out of nothing more than curiosity. Half the officers didn't believe their 'irritating and loathsome' colleague had really died at sea; he'd never once mentioned his supposed love of canoeing. Stood in the walled front driveway of the house was a man Smith was 100 per cent sure to be John Darwin. He was gobsmacked.

'I said to Denise, "Christ, that's John Darwin!"' he recalled.

'He had a long shaggy beard and looked a right mess, like a bloody caveman, but I knew it was him. Denise told me not to be daft. I told her I was deadly serious. I was 100 per cent sure it was him. I turned around as soon as I could and pulled up outside his house to take another look. I couldn't believe my eyes.'

Smith, a former coalminer, like many of his colleagues, immediately reported his sighting to the police. At some stage, the police called Anne. Panicked, but thinking on her feet, she said it must have been one of the tenants. Fearing his cover was about to be blown, the pair quickly agreed he needed to disappear again until the threat of being discovered had passed.

The Darwins were frantic with worry. John told Anne he had

been considering the United States as a possible new home for them, and decided to take up the offer of his online friend Maria, who had invited him to stay if he was ever visiting. John flew to the Big Apple, landing at JFK Airport. and spent two weeks as her guest. He thought it all quite exciting.

While there, John was in constant touch with Kelly, a forty-one-year-old mother-of-three from Kansas who described herself as 'lonely and bored'. They had first begun chatting online in the winter of 2003 while playing another game, *EverQuest*. Kelly's character was Guurg, a male frog, which had reached a critical point in the game and was in dire need of extra points, but for that she required the services of a druid. Luckily for her, there was one online at the time – the romantically named Cedum – who accepted her invitation to play.

Cedum the saviour was none other than 'John Jones'. Cedum claimed he was a widower and seemed fascinated with Kelly's rural life, telling her he had always harboured an 'American dream' to buy land, marry a pretty girl and settle on the other side of the Atlantic. He said he was a former teacher and prison officer and ran a property rental business. He said his wife was dead and he'd never had children. *Nice touch John*. He was having similar flirty conversations with women from Arkansas, Nebraska and Louisiana.

As he and Kelly got to know each other, they began discussing business opportunities. She suggested renovating a farm and raising cattle. John was impressed when she told him she knew everything there was to know about horses and was well versed in bookkeeping and accounts. She said if he was prepared to invest some money, she could open an equestrian centre and they could split the profits.

In May 2004, after looking at photographs of the property on the Internet, and without telling Anne, he cashed in £30,000 of Premium Bonds and wired Kelly $50,000 from his John Jones bank account. For a man who had always been so meticulous in his affairs, to entrust such a large sum of money to a woman he barely knew and had never met defies belief. Maybe he wasn't thinking with his brain.

The alarm bells only sounded when he discovered the money had gone into a joint account held by Kelly and her ex-husband. But he didn't allow the reality of suspicion to cloud the dream. Kelly told John she had bought a ten-acre farm in Kincade for $26,500, and used some of the funds on renovations. She would keep him informed of progress in regular emails and when they chatted, and flirted, online. He tried to keep his conversations secret from Anne by wearing headphones, but she frequently heard him giggling like a pathetic schoolboy.

John and Kelly flirted to the extent that she sent pictures of herself in various stages of undress, so it seems certain he had more than just property on his mind when in early June he decided to once again fly to the States to view the investment property, which he had eventually told Anne about. She was naturally furious and incredulous at what he'd done. Having repeatedly heard his online flirting, she questioned his intentions, but was getting to the point of being past caring. John decided he'd go for three months. Anne was delighted to have him from under her skin.

John arrived in Kansas itching to see his new investment – and to get to know Kelly better. He excitedly checked out everyone in the greetings hall, certain he'd recognise her from one of the photographs she had sent. But there was no one who seemed even remotely to fit the bill. Then he noticed a woman standing among what looked like a 'small group of hillbillies', waving in his direction. John gulped. Kelly looked very different in the flesh. But it seems neither was particularly impressed.

The Conman meets the Clampetts springs to mind.

'He was such a weird kind of guy, he instantly creeped me out and it made me uncomfortable to be around him,' Kelly later revealed.

'After I picked him up from the airport I took him back to my home, where he said he wanted to change his clothes.

'I showed him to my daughter's bedroom and left him to get on with it.

'When I walked back past the room, there he was standing fully naked, with the door wide open. I shouted at him, "Dude, that maybe all right in Europe but it's not what we do here. Shut the damn door!"

'He is the creepiest, oddest and most frightening man I have ever met.'

John moved to a small motel. The next day Kelly picked him up and drove him to see the property at Kincaid.

'While we were there, he began asking me about the widows or single women in the town, and could I help him find a new wife, because that would help him get a visa and to stay in the US,' said Kelly.

'It seemed like such a weird request for him to make. He also talked about the need to get some kind of business interest in the US so that he could try to get a work visa and citizenship that way as well. He seemed extremely well researched in what he needed to get done.'

John's account of the affair was entirely at odds with Kelly's, describing what she bought as a world away from the idyllic Kansas ranch he had envisaged. He described the investment as 'Crapsville' and demanded his money back. He hired a lawyer, who discovered the farm had been purchased solely in Kelly's biker ex-husband's name and that she had thousands of dollars in gambling debt. Needless to say, no money was forthcoming and he and Kelly parted on acrimonious terms.

Before leaving Kansas, John opened an American bank account. He couldn't believe how easy this deception lark was becoming. He walked in, filled out a few forms, handed over his John Jones passport and ten minutes later had a US bank account.

He returned to England and claimed that, after one further phone call, he gave up on his ill-advised investment and wrote the money off as a bad lot. In truth, he began sending Kelly threatening and sinister emails saying he had friends in 'the mob' who would 'do anything for a few hundred dollars'.

'Basically, he threatened to kill us, to have us tortured first, to harm my animals, to burn down the property,' claimed Kelly.

You have to question what he was thinking.

Kelly said the chilling emails, which she later sent to Cleveland Police, left her scared for her life. She went to her local sheriff's office and then contacted the FBI. A special agent advised her that the emails were nothing more than crank threats and that she should tell John the FBI was investigating. Kelly did just that – and never heard from him again.

John's American dream was over and he was forced to write off £30,000 of his ill-gotten gains.

Eventually, he sheepishly told Anne the money was gone.

'Part of me wished he had just gone – disappeared for good,' she later said.

That October, as pamphlets about emigrating to various countries across the globe continued to drop through the letterbox at The Cliff, John turned his attention to the sea. His latest plan was to buy a boat in which to sail around the world. Such a voyage would be a huge undertaking for even the most experienced of sailors; with virtually no sailing experience, John knew next to nothing about rigging, winds, tides or navigation. But, as ever, he wasn't the kind of man to let such minor details get in the way of his dreams, even if his wife couldn't swim . . . and hated being at sea. He decided to make up for his shortcomings by signing up for an online navigation course and a shipping game. This sailing lark isn't too complicated at all, he thought. He'd already disappeared once at sea, now he could do it again.

He flew to Greece to look at a yacht, but it didn't meet his requirements. Then in November he flew to Gibraltar where he had seen a Solaris catamaran advertised for sale. After exchanging a few emails with the seller, boat dealer Robert Hopkin, John agreed he needed to see the 60-foot boat, named *Boonara*, for himself. Within days, he made an offer of £45,000 for the 1970s-diesel-powered catamaran, which was followed up by Anne making a £1,000 transfer from her bank account as a deposit. But Robert recalled how the deal fell apart when John flew into a rage over some of the contents of the boat not being included in the sale. He was also infuriated at the red tape he was encountering while looking into registering as a boat owner, and so turned his attention away from a life on the ocean waves.

'He went mad and before I knew it the deal was off,' said Robert.

Hardly surprisingly, John lost his deposit. Everything he touched ended in disaster. John Darwin was many things but he was no King Midas.

29

Panama!

JOHN AND ANNE'S big plan to start a new life abroad was always going to be much more than just a scheme to run away from justice. Over more than three years, they had learnt hard lessons from their mistakes and this time they were determined to get it right. It had proved impossible to register as boat owners in Gibraltar, it was too difficult to develop in Cyprus, and John's attempts to invest in Kansas had been an unmitigated disaster. Where to live was the most burning question on his mind on a daily basis.

He had looked at France and Spain but quickly ruled them out as being too close to home; ordered books about emigrating to Canada and Norway, neither of which he felt would be safe places for someone living on a false passport; and felt Argentina was too far away. That left Central America and, in particular, Belize, Guatemala, Costa Rica and Panama.

Aha! Panama, thought John: an exotic Central American location that, according to one guidebook, attracted 'adventurers and entrepreneurs, schemers and dreamers, misfits and full-on nutcases'. An ideal home, it would seem, for a man who was without doubt bordering on bonkers and appeared to tick every box. It's as if they were somehow meant to be together.

Panama was the setting for a number of thriller and spy books, including John le Carré's *The Tailor of Panama*. John – a man considered a complete bore by virtually everyone he had ever worked with – rather liked the notion he would soon become, in his misguided eyes, an international man of mystery.

Ironically, for someone so keen on keeping himself hidden away, he was incredibly indiscreet on online forums that could have been read by anyone. A January 2006 posting on the *Viviendo en Panama* (Living in Panama) reveals he had spent at least six months researching

Panama but still knew relatively little about a country he was thinking of making his new home.

Over the coming weeks and months, he signed up with more than a dozen online forums specialising in everything from Panama health-care to a bizarre site praising an automatic chicken-plucking machine. On every one he hid behind his fake identity. Within two weeks of asking for basic information about Panama's climate, John was dreaming of a new home in the rainforest. He sent off a request to Panama Realtor estate agents for information about a service they offered to erect log cabins.

But first there was the small matter of selling The Cliff properties, not helped by the 'flying freehold' of No. 4, which extended over the top floor of No. 3. He needed that bedsit – which he had started using rather than the dingy basement one – to be reclaimed by No. 3, and decided that completely separating the houses would make them easier to sell. It meant all the connecting doors would have to be blocked off – and he'd lose his escape-route-cum-bolt-hole. A team of builders and plumbers was hired to separate the utilities and re-establish the house as two individual properties. John also decided to spend £16,000 on a new kitchen for No. 3 to make the house more marketable.

For months, he had been scheming on how best to avoid paying tax, or at least as little as possible, when they sold the houses. On 3 May, Land Registry records show that the two houses, together worth nearly half a million pounds, were sold by Anne Catherine Darwin, of Seaton Carew, to one Mark Darwin, for the give-away price of £30,000 – money that she had given him to invest in Premium Bonds for her.

As described earlier, there is no suggestion Mark knew the real reason for the sale, and it's even quite possible that Anne wasn't fully aware what John was doing. Anne also asked Anthony to cash in his Premium Bonds and repay the £30,000 she had asked him to invest for her. Both sons had unwittingly been used as money launderers by their scheming parents.

★★★

Long before dawn on an English summer's morning, 12 July 2006, John and Anne left Seaton Carew on the start of an adventure that would, once again, change their already extraordinary lives for ever.

They had spent the previous day packing suitcases and carefully running through their meticulous checklist of things needed for a two-week holiday in the sun. Not that this was any run-of-the-mill package deal to the Spanish Costas or the Canary Isles; they were headed for the Republic of Panama with, unbeknown to a soul in the world, thoughts of beginning a secret new life together more than five thousand miles away in Central America. Poor old John must have felt a little miffed he was 'dead' – it was the kind of trip he would have loved to have been able to brag about.

With Anne having told everyone she was jetting off alone across the globe, the last thing she needed was to be seen leaving home with a mystery man in the early hours of the morning. It was imperative she and John slipped out while it was still dark, at an hour when their tenants and any nosey neighbours would be soundly asleep.

Neither slept well. John lay awake conjuring up colourful images of the exciting and exotic country awaiting them. Anne was a bag of nerves, convinced they would be rumbled. Both had travelled in Europe and John had visited the United States, but this was something very different for both of them. This was Panama – its very name oozed adventure.

When the alarm sounded at 4 a.m., they were already awake and it wasn't long before they were showered and dressed. Anne tiptoed down the four steps of her sea-front home, had a good look around, glanced up at the windows of the neighbouring houses, then, satisfied that nobody was awake, quietly went back inside, where John, disguised in his hat and glasses, was waiting. They grabbed their luggage, loaded it into the boot of the Range Rover and slowly set off across the gravel drive, trying to make as little noise as possible.

Anne's stomach was in knots by the time they reached Newcastle Airport after the forty-five-minute drive from Seaton. Walking quickly through the near-deserted terminal, several feet away from John, she kept her head down, terrified someone would recognise them. Unlike her far more assured husband, she was a natural worrier and dreaded the thought he would be stopped and arrested for travelling on a fraudulent passport. He told her to stay calm and everything would be fine; Anne growled through gritted teeth that she was trying her best. As it was, they coasted through security and arrived three hours early for their flight.

John had chosen a fairly obscure route, flying first to Paris with Continental Airlines, on to Caracas, the capital of Venezuela, with Air France, then finally boarding flight CM 0222 with the Panamanian state carrier, Copa Airlines, to Panama City. The reason he chose the route was simple: it was the cheapest one going.

'I was absolutely terrified we might bump into someone we knew,' said Anne. 'That was my biggest fear.'

Guide books, relocation pamphlets and hours scouring the Internet had not prepared them for the frenetic Tocumen International Airport. It was a massive shock for a middle-aged British couple who were far from well-trodden travellers. Even manoeuvring their way through the bustling airport and finding the Budget rental car desk was no easy feat. Anne was feeling very uncomfortable in such strange territory and quickly began wondering whether the trip had been such a good idea after all.

'Over the years we were married, and long before any of this business started, John often talked about a hankering to move abroad,' she later recalled.

'As the years went by, it was always a different country. He changed his mind so many times I lost count.'

Of course, it was not by chance that John had opted to visit a country long considered an ideal refuge for those needing to disappear off radar. Memories of former dictator Manuel Noriega, who had been jailed for seventeen years on drugs charges, may have been fading, but the country was still plagued by rampant corruption, used by drug barons as a transit state for the trafficking of cocaine, heroin and marijuana . . . and known to all in crooked financial circles as an attractive, no-questions-asked centre for the laundering of ill-gotten gains.

John knew the country prided itself on financial discretion, and its status as a tax haven made it very difficult for anyone to discover anything about 'salted away' assets. The more he read about Panama, the better it sounded.

The country's new mood of confidence was reflected in a five-billion-dollar project to double the width of the Panama Canal – the country's biggest revenue-earner. The figures were certainly impressive: the economy was growing at a rate of more than 8 per cent a year; a seventy-eight-storey luxury apartment and hotel complex was being promised as one of the tallest buildings in Latin America; and even developer and then TV personality Donald Trump, later to become the forty-fifth president of the United States, was investing there.

The country was already home to more than six thousand, mainly retired, Britons lured by good healthcare and land and property that was ridiculously cheap. What's more, expatriates were allowed to buy a new home without having to pay property taxes for twenty years and were also offered a string of incentives, including 25 per cent reductions in airfares and even discounts in restaurants.

To maintain secrecy, the government allowed numbered bank accounts with no names attached and set fines of $5,000 and up to six months in jail for anyone who disclosed banking information. Panama was the Switzerland of Central America.

In advance of their visit, John had identified certain locations to consider from property websites. But what really caught his eye was a number of articles about the emergence of eco-tourism in a country where tourism, generally, was still in its infancy. It was the perfect place for him to start afresh and allow him to grow rich beyond his wildest dreams.

He had read that there were miles of totally unspoiled white sandy beaches, 1,500 largely uninhabited islands, unexplored jungles and cloud-covered rain forests, where you could swim in chilly mountain streams. Even John's 'death', a forced result of his disastrous property dealing, hadn't dampened his enthusiasm for big ideas. He still planned to be a man of property, with acres of land he could call his own. He would bounce back in style and was already making plans to establish an eco-resort, with scattered log cabins and the offer of horse riding, boating and trekking for the guests who would come flocking. He wished he'd thought of it years ago.

Before jetting off, he had corresponded by email with Mario Vilar, president and managing director of a relocation and land agent company, MoveToPanama.com, and had asked for help in finding accommodation for his upcoming visit. The company, owned and operated by Mario and his wife Karina, specialised in relocation services and John felt it was an ideal place to seek information about the country he felt sure would offer them a safe haven.

Mario's meticulous record-keeping shows that the trip was a last-minute decision.

'Are these dates available and what is the total cost for the two of us?' was the brusque query he received just eleven days before John and Anne arrived. The message was a request for five nights' accommodation from 7 to 12 July. It was sent by John Jones, who said he would have one guest with him. He gave his address as 4 The Cliff, Seaton Carew.

Mario replied that the total cost would be $170, including a $25 taxi ride from the airport. John declined the taxi, explaining he had already arranged a rental car, but confirmed his reservation for the room. The old romantic was taking his wife to the country that might become their new home – and spending just over ten pounds a night on the cheapest bed and breakfast he could find.

Mario arranged for the Darwins to stay with his parents in their fourth-floor apartment in the middle-class neighbourhood of Via Argentina. It was clean and comfortable, although they had to share a bathroom. It gave John and Anne an ideal base from which to explore the city and surrounding countryside.

In between looking at half a dozen prospective properties, mainly ranches set in acres of land, they visited the city of Santiago, in the province of Veraguas, and the Bocas del Toro Archipelago, a group of seven largely undeveloped islands on the Caribbean Sea in the north-west of Panama, and home to the country's most famous beaches to which tourists were drawn to swim, dive, snorkel, surf or simply relax. John was thrilled that there were no symptoms of the hay fever that had dogged him all his life. Anne, less fortunately, slipped while traversing a steep ravine as they viewed a 270-acre plot of land, and ended up caked in mud, though unhurt.

At the end of their trip, they met Mario in his seventh-floor suite in a high-rise building in the heart of Panama City's banking district, and, as they were about to leave, he asked if he could have his picture taken with his new British friends. The Darwins had little time to think or make an excuse. Anne gave a big toothy grin as she stood between John and Mario. They were both conscious that keeping a low profile was imperative, but nevertheless agreed to the photograph. After walking out of Mario's office, they didn't give it another thought.

What harm could possibly come of it? Little could they have imagined how badly that seemingly innocent holiday snap would come back to haunt them seventeen months later.

Anne found herself pleasantly surprised by Panama. She was enthralled by the countryside and thoroughly enjoyed visits to the Panama Canal and the capital's historic old town, with its charming bars and restaurants in shaded squares along cobbled alleyways. John and Anne had seen enough of the country to make them believe it really was somewhere they could make a fresh start.

Before leaving, the Darwins couldn't resist a trip up Panama's longest river, the Chagres, in what else . . . a native Indian canoe. Then they flew home to England and back to their extraordinary double lives. Anne the grieving widow, and John the invisible man.

30

Living the Dream

As soon as she had unpacked, Anne was on the phone to her sons, her family and closest friends, telling them all how much she had enjoyed her trip. She and John had already decided that although they had failed to find the perfect spot to live, Panama seemed to fit the bill in every respect.

'I felt like I was reborn,' she excitedly told them. 'It was all so refreshing. I'll definitely be going back.'

She told them she particularly liked Panama City centre because she felt safe wherever she went. It was a far cry from the nearby cities of Middlesbrough, Newcastle and Sunderland. There were no menacing gangs of hooded youths lurking on street corners and, even wandering around at night-time, she had not felt in the least bit threatened. Police officers were armed and Anne believed that was a deterrent which obviously worked well. Perhaps they should arm officers in English cities she pondered?

After spending hours on the Internet researching their future home, John found something he described as a 'eureka moment'. It was possible to buy property through a corporation for reasons including 'confidentiality, estate planning, anonymity and to protect your property against any kind of legal proceedings or situations with creditors or recoveries aimed at a natural person's estate'. They could set up a corporation and even if their fraud were ever rumbled, their property investments would be untouchable. It would be secretive, anonymous and beyond the reach of the British authorities. He was beyond excited. 'I've bloody well hit the jackpot,' he told Anne.

Within a few months, he and Anne would be investing their fraudulently obtained cash in an exciting and exotic country, and her friends would be wondering what on earth had given the quietly spoken doctors' receptionist such a daringly ambitious new lease of life.

John was fired up for the prospect of a new life in Central America, and he and Anne began the serious business of preparing to leave for good. They agreed that Anne should start talking about the country more and more so that, when the time came for them to make their move, it wouldn't be quite such a shock for the boys or her nearest and dearest.

Anne was determined that if she was to move abroad, she should learn the language, so she ordered several teach-yourself-Spanish books. She would spend at least an hour a day, usually early evening, learning basic sentences to help her with shopping, getting about and ordering meals in restaurants. She tried to get John involved but he wasn't really interested. He continued to spend hours on the Internet looking for likely properties and land. He also ordered expensive new camera equipment using Anne's credit card. *Viviendo en Panama* was now in full swing.

Just before visiting Panama, John had used his John Jones alias to sign up for an online money transfer service. Having played the penny share market from the spare bedroom of their house in Witton Gilbert, he knew the value of a good exchange rate and hated the thought of being at the mercy of overnight bank transfers. With a passport, a birth certificate, credit card statements, a few emails and a telephone interview, he was able to sign up with an international currency transfer company offering a live online feed of international interest rates and 'efficient currency services that the new global economy demands'.

He was able to get a secure password and the freedom to ship his cash abroad at the best rates at any time of the day or night. After barely touching the cash they'd made for more than two years, there was now a flurry of activity. When the exchange rate was right, he moved the money.

Less than a month after returning from Panama, John cashed in £40,000 of Premium Bonds held since the previous May in the name of John Jones and transferred the money to his John Jones Lloyds TSB account.

The next day he started playing the money markets using his new online account. Lloyds TSB would only allow a maximum of £10,000 to be transferred on any single day – so on five separate days between 10 and 18 August, John shipped £41,000 through the foreign exchange brokerage into his Commerce Bank account in Kansas. On top of $1,000 he'd moved as a test transaction in June, he now had almost $78,000 salted away in the United States.

Importantly for John, despite the rigorous anti-money-laundering regulations that were in force, the transfers failed to trigger any of the financial services sector alarms. No one noticed that a man posing as a child who had died fifty-six years earlier was moving large amounts of money between two of the world's biggest economies.

Despite the unavoidable conclusion that he and Anne were getting deeper into the territory of organised crime – complete with conspiracy, fake identities, fraud, money laundering and offshore investments – John seemed to think it was no big deal.

In early 2007, Anne decided to tell the boys that she was seriously thinking of emigrating. She was fed up with windswept Seaton Carew, the house held too many memories of their father, and every day she couldn't help but look out over the very spot from where he had set off on his ill-fated canoe outing. It was as if her life was on perpetual hold. She was going to put both houses, Nos 3 and 4 The Cliff, on the market to see what the interest was – it was the only way she would ever be able to get on with her life, she said.

Mark, who admitted to being shocked, recalled: 'I thought she wanted a clean break, to close a chapter, to no longer look at the sea or the house. The house seemed like a millstone around her neck. I was pleased she was getting on with her life.'

Anthony recalled his mother saying she was emigrating to Panama permanently because the country was 'fun, Catholic and they speak Spanish. The weather and climate were good and there were a fair number of ex-pats.' He was convinced she would very quickly realise she'd made a mistake and move back closer to home. Both he and Mark had told her on numerous occasions they were concerned about her safety, as were other members of the family. Neither son felt the move would be permanent. Anne made it sound as if she were telling them she was moving to live a few hundred miles away in a bungalow on the south coast – not the other side of the world.

Anne also decided it was time to tell her good friend Irene about her plans. It was one of the hardest things she had to do because they had grown very close and had come to rely on each other, particularly as Irene had suffered a bereavement – although hers was genuine. She decided to tell her in an email, rather than face to face.

'I feel like I'm letting you down and abandoning you,' she wrote.

'That doesn't mean to say that I won't leave without a heavy heart, but I have come this far and am determined to see it through. It certainly won't be easy for me to say goodbye to everyone. I don't have to tell you how much life has been a struggle; you alone have shared more than anyone else. I will miss you but I have to do this for myself; it feels the right thing to do.

'Perhaps I'm the one being selfish now, but there are times when I've felt at the beck and call of everyone and his neighbour, and it's now time for me before life passes me by and it's too late. I need a challenge and an adventure. This may prove to be too adventurous and if it does I won't be too proud to admit it and return home, I just hope to have some fun on the way.'

Irene thought Anne was potty and asked what on earth her family would think. But, once she was over the initial shock, she wished her friend well and promised she would come and visit. Everyone just seemed to accept that Anne wanted to start afresh and that moving abroad was her way of dealing with the grief. It's beyond belief that no one tried to talk her out of it.

Despite having money in an American bank account and the impending sale of the two houses, 3 and 4 The Cliff, John couldn't resist one parting shot at the banks he blamed for his downfall. The Yorkshire Bank had refused to extend his credit four years earlier – in his mind, forcing him to fake his own death – and now Lloyds TSB was offering loans.

In June, he arranged for Anne to pay him £1,825 in three instalments to make it look as though she was his employer. He went along to his local branch and, armed with documents that appeared to prove he was John Jones, he posed as Anne's handyman in an interview for a loan. Without any further checks, the bank signed off on a £10,000 loan – which he agreed would be paid back in monthly instalments. Within two weeks every penny had been converted into dollars and wired to Kansas. Lloyds TSB never saw its money again. Eighteen months later, when asked why he'd taken out the loan and not paid it back, John simply claimed the bank deserved it. It is hard to have a lot of sympathy for them.

After all their careful preparations, the date for John's big move to Panama was dictated for them by the sale of No. 4. By the spring of 2007 John and Anne had salted away $130,000 – roughly $80,000 in the John Jones bank account in Kansas and $50,000 in an offshore account she had opened in Jersey – but they knew it wasn't enough to provide for them in Panama.

They needed hundreds of thousands of dollars to fund their new life in the sun, and in March of that year Gary Hepple and his wife Angela became the providers. Gary had no idea that the small, neatly dressed woman he had bought a house from was actually a skilled and experienced fraudster working in cahoots with the scruffy odd-job man who had been decorating the front bedroom when he first looked around No. 4 The Cliff.

Nor could he have guessed that the £160,000 he handed over would be converted to dollars and spent on property in the steamy heat of Central America within a few weeks of the transaction. All he knew was that the house he'd bought was a bargain – even if it was in a dreadful state.

John arranged budget accommodation in Panama City, booked cheap flights and instructed Anne to start emailing estate agents to arrange viewings of properties that they now knew they could afford.

Anne flew out to join him a week later, on 15 March 2007 – the day the sale of No. 4 was finalised. John had found a cheap hotel, the Costa Inn, on Avenida Peru, in a somewhat sleazy area of the city, where armed police guarded shops from robbers during the day and £15-a-trick hookers prowled the streets for business at night. Not quite the same rosy pictured Anne painted of life in Panama City, although her apartment was a twenty-minute drive away.

For some reason, John brazenly checked into the ninety-room hotel under his real name, paying £30 a night for a small double room. The arrival of the balding Englishman, who spoke barely a word of Spanish and was travelling alone, didn't go unnoticed by locals. In his dingy fifth-floor room, he set up his big-screen Hewlett Packard computer and spent hours surfing the Internet for remote properties to buy. When Anne arrived, the hotel staff found out a little more about their guests, as she was more forthcoming.

'She liked chatting to us and said that they both liked it here so much they were looking for a house to buy and wanted to spend the rest of their lives here,' said one waitress.

'She was a very nice lady who liked to talk a lot by using the little Spanish she knew. She was always joking and asking where we thought it was best to live in Panama. She said they were looking at the area of Colon where she had fallen in love with the coastline.'

John and Anne arranged to meet a string of estate agents and relocation experts, but in between appointments, they spent as little time at their hotel as possible – it was budget accommodation by anyone's standards. With all their money earmarked for their new life together, they were making savings wherever they could. They knew that Gary Hepple's money would convert into well over $300,000, but planned to spend all of that, and more, on property.

Until they could sell No. 3, money – even stolen money – was tight. Instead of going back to the Costa Inn, they got into the habit of returning to a dirt-cheap coffee shop they had discovered when they had stayed with Mario Vilar's parents.

Anne took to one estate agent, Diana Bishop, straight away. She felt Diana, a Panamanian who was born and raised in the canal-zone, was someone who really understood exactly what she and John were looking for. Diana found an apartment they liked in a city suburb called El Dorado – where I would first meet her after being sent to Panama following John's mysterious reappearance.

Anne was particularly pleased because there was a small Catholic chapel within walking distance. That had always been one of her top requirements when looking for the right apartment, *good honest Christian that she was* . . .

Under John's instructions, and with the help of her lawyer, Beth Ann Gray, she formed the corporation, Jaguar Properties, referred to earlier, which was used to buy the two-bedroom, fully furnished apartment for US$97,000.

Buying property through a corporation was the best way of

ensuring the names of its directors could never be discovered and that the property would be protected from any overseas asset claims. John said it would be a nice touch to make Mark and Anthony directors, as well as her – another move that would later make Cleveland Police highly suspicious that the boys had been accomplices in their parents' fraudulent scheme.

Shortly afterwards, Diana showed the Darwins a two-storey house with a swimming pool and nearly 500 acres of land – the plot the Darwins would buy on the shores of Lake Gatun, in Escobal, two hours from Panama City – which she believed would be ideal for the eco-tourist destination they had talked about so much. They spent more than two hours walking the grounds, which comprised swamps, streams, valleys, meadows and out-and-out jungle. At the end of the visit, they signed 'agreement to buy' papers.

'Of course, at that stage, I had no idea John and Anne were married,' Diana later explained.

'Anne told me she was a widow, that she had two sons and that John was her partner, so I accepted what she said at face value.

'She was a really nice lady and I had no reason to doubt her. They seemed very happy together and looked like any other couple visiting Panama to buy land.'

Anne wrote an email to her family, which must surely have left them wondering about her new-found business acumen.

'The estate agent says it's an absolute bargain and I know she is right because others I have looked at are for more money and less land.' Then she added:

'Hopefully she can explain about carbon credits for trees. It's something I'm interested in as you can get paid just to keep your trees, and as I have acres of them I hope to get some. Everybody who has heard about Escobal wants to visit. I only hope I can maximise its potential. It will make an excellent nature reserve and will take a lot of planning. Eco-tourism seems to be the way forward.'

Anne flew home via Caracas and Paris, arriving at Newcastle Airport on Air France flight 5851L on the morning of 2 April.

Ten days later, John, who had stayed on at the Costa Inn, got the keys and moved into their new apartment. But setting up a new home for a man who was used to being waited on hand and foot wasn't easy and he quickly grew grumpy as he struggled with basic domestic chores. Communication was also a major problem and he was forced to use a web translation site to write down questions he needed to ask. But then not being able to understand the answers because everyone was 'babbling away incomprehensively' in Spanish was equally as frustrating. He dismissed the locals as stupid for not speaking English.

Life didn't get any better for him when he discovered the apartment was infested with fleas. He emailed Anne a picture of what he believed to be flea bites, telling her: 'I'm sure I've got fleas.'

His regular emails to her were often saucy and full of sexual innuendo. It seemed John was growing increasingly frustrated at being alone in more ways than one. He occupied his mind by concentrating his attention on his 'Master Plan'.

On the morning of 14 May, John Darwin sat down in front of a laptop he'd bought as John Jones and logged on using the name Peter Fenwick. The man who'd become an expert at being somebody else had created a fake identity for his own fake identity. Just as in the online fantasy games, it was all about staying hidden from your enemies and remaining at least one step ahead of those who would eventually be trying to catch you out. He figured that if the cops couldn't work out what had happened to him, how on earth would they ever catch up with the fictional John Jones, let alone the even more mysterious Peter Fenwick? Exactly which one of his characters he'd chosen to be that particular day is unclear. It had all become a game to John.

He opened a new workbook in Excel, clicked on 'Save As' and typed out, 'Jaguar Lodge', the name of both his Master Plan and the home he was going to build in Colon that was to be the centre-piece of all his dreams.

As he stared at the blank spreadsheet on the laptop screen in front of him, John chose the most obvious starting point for a man driven by an obsession with money and created a new worksheet entitled 'income expenditure'. He listed the cost of everything: utilities, staff and everyday living necessities. He accounted for how he would invest every penny of his fraudulently claimed money.

As for Jaguar Lodge itself, it would be a 'magnificent house' set in acres of jungle on the edge of the rainforest, with plenty of accommodation for all the family . . . including room for not one, but two, maids. After all, John felt he had reached the time in his life when he should be waited on hand and foot. He designed graphics for how the extensive two-storey building would look, complete with doors to a rooftop terrace with its own kitchen; high, arched windows from all rooms, with, of course, absolutely no bars anywhere to spoil the view: he'd had enough of them as a prison officer.

There would be mosquito nets on all the windows, a TV and games room, a library and office; the list went on and on. The spreadsheet was so detailed, he even made a list of the animals they'd need to get his eco-centre up and running: six horses, twenty cows and twenty sheep, with money set aside for veterinary bills. They'd need fruit trees to ensure their guests enjoyed the freshest of produce every day. Initially, he wanted five banana trees, three lemon, ten mango, five pejibaye (or peach palm), one fig and, for some reason, 100 guava, plus many other varieties; coconut, melon, passion fruit and avocado to name but a few.

From the day of its creation, the Jaguar Lodge spreadsheet would become central to every move in the fraud that had by now engrossed the Darwins' lives. John would pore over it for hours on end, adding diagrams, maps and costings. It would eventually include links to relevant websites, legal advice and the all-important interest and exchange rates that were so vital for the efficient laundering of their stolen cash.

As far as he was concerned, it was the beginning of the end of more than five years of hiding and looking over his shoulder. Its creation marked the day he was going to start plotting every last detail that would allow him to live a life of luxury in sunny Central America, with all the annoying bits of the wet and windy north-east of England removed. In Panama, there would be no more rent to collect, no irritating tenants, and best of all, with hundreds of thousands of dollars in the bank, no debts ever again.

The Jaguar Lodge spreadsheet took months to complete, and it was work that was constantly interrupted by a barrage of infuriating problems. John quickly discovered that plotting the final stages of a complex scam in an exotic foreign country, when you are thousands of miles from your partner-in-fraud, short of cash, incapable of holding even a basic conversation with the Spanish-speaking locals, and deluged by the tropical rains, was not very easy – and it didn't help if the neighbours whose wireless Internet connections you were stealing kept turning them off.

A patchy Internet connection, that only seemed to work in the evening while the laptop was being dripped on under the balcony shelter, was a warning of the difficulties ahead as the Darwins tried to keep an open line of communication between Panama City and Seaton Carew. It would plague their conspiracy for months.

31

'Filthy Rich Gringos'

HAVING ALREADY COMMITTED to a new life in Central America, John suddenly became alarmed at learning of changes to visa requirements for foreign nationals wanting to emigrate to Panama.

Anyone wanting 'permanent resident status', without exception, would in future need a 'Certificate of Good Conduct' letter from the police force in their home country, stating that they were of good character.

Without that, foreigners would only be able to visit on a ninety-day tourist visa, like the one John currently held. He knew getting a reference letter from Cleveland Police would be an impossibility for John Jones, as he didn't exist. It was a huge conundrum. But rather than make him lose heart, he simply decided he'd have to tinker with his Master Plan; the plan that would end all their problems and safeguard their ill-gotten gains once and for all. He told Anne she would need to get a good conduct letter from the police for her permanent residency visa – while neglecting to mention his own dilemma. He wrote and sent an email from Anne's account to the Panama Consulate in London seeking further clarification.

There was another issue. He was approaching the end of his permitted ninety-day stay on his tourist visa. He discovered in an online article that many 'permanent tourists' living in Panama solved the issue by 'border hopping' – leaving the country for a few days as the visa was about to expire and returning with a new one. He decided to book a trip to neighbouring Costa Rica. From there, he emailed Anne a photograph of a big heart he had drawn in the sand for her and told her to hurry up and sell the houses so she could come back to join him . . . and 'I can bonk you until you are silly'.

That the Darwins were committing to a new life in Panama without being even close to solving their visa requirements was unbelievable.

Back in England, Anne knew she had to tell Mark and Anthony that she had made up her mind about emigrating, and broke the news to them on a weekend visit to Hampshire.

'Again, they were pretty shocked when I told them I had finally decided to leave England, but they were very supportive and promised they would come and visit,' Anne later told me.

Asked what John planned to do when they visited, Anne continued: 'I don't know really. I hadn't really thought that far ahead. I suppose he would have had to disappear again.'

Throughout June, John was becoming increasingly excited about the land at Colon and keeping Anne busy with an ever-growing list of things to do and what she should bring with her now that they were, in his words, 'filthy rich gringos'. John's 'jokey' list of what to bring said much about his character. It included: 'Cards; 2 hot lips; Connect 4; Something hot, soft and wet; Scrabble; No need to bring a poker . . . I've got one; Travel set games (think it has backgammon in); Set of boobies; Deodorant; Aftershave; Bikinis; Your one brain cell . . . because I want to bonk you until you are silly.' It seems Anne still stirred the familiar feelings of desire in him after thirty-five years of marriage.

Anne ordered two skips to dump some of the belongings, mainly junk, that wouldn't be needed in Panama. Plant hire owner Edika Ward advised her to move the Range Rover so that it didn't get knocked and was surprised to be asked if she wanted to buy it. Anne said she was moving abroad and would take £10,000. Edika, sensing a bargain, offered £5,000, which Anne readily accepted. John's pride and joy was off-loaded at a knock-down price.

A few weeks later, Anne returned to Panama and moved into the apartment with her husband. Once again, after nearly six long years of hiding, they could openly live together as man and wife.

Anne said: 'I came back out again in July. It was lovely and I thoroughly enjoyed it. For the first time in years, John seemed relaxed and happy again. He changed back into the person I married. It was as if our marriage was reborn – as if a huge weight had been lifted off our shoulders. It was the first time I had felt normal in many years: not having to look over my shoulder the whole time.'

Life, now, was certainly a little bit different for the Darwins of Seaton Carew. Because they had not yet sold their home in England, they had purposely bought a fully furnished apartment, deciding it was a far cheaper option than having to start from scratch. They found local stores where you could buy jeans for $5 and bras for $1. John loved hopping on and off the buses that ran day and night.

The couple quickly settled into their new way of life, usually rising early, around 6.30 a.m., and starting their day with a leisurely breakfast on the patio of yoghurt and fresh fruit: peaches, melons, mangoes, papaya – Anne's favourite – and bananas. The patio furniture was an aluminium table and four chairs.

Anne would potter around the apartment, usually in her bikini, tidying up as she went, then make the most of the tropical climate by sunbathing on the terrace overlooking the city for an hour or so, before the heat of the morning sun became too unbearable. John would either sit and read or move inside and beaver away on his computer, feverishly checking the latest bank interest rates while tinkering with his Master Plan.

Anne never once looked at it. She was too busy marvelling at the exotic, brightly coloured birds she saw from the terrace: parakeets and tiny hummingbirds – all very different from Seaton's squawky seagulls, which were forever leaving their mark on The Cliff.

Not that the show from the Darwins' balcony was anything compared with what was in store at Escobal, the rugged land they had now, after four further visits between them, agreed to buy at a cost of $389,000. In time, they planned to spend a further $100,000 building a villa where they could eventually live while developing their eco-resort.

Diana Bishop added: 'They seemed very happy. They loved being out on the land and they were really looking forward to building their dream house there and starting an eco-resort.

'Anne said it was perfect for a nature reserve. It was certainly viable, though there was an awful lot of hard work ahead of them.'

Anne couldn't wait to tell everyone at home about her exciting new life, sending a long email to her friends and family, although tell-tale spelling mistakes and John's distinctive punctuation, such as repeated exclamation marks, suggest that large parts of it were almost certainly written by him. It seems amazing no one cottoned on.

Anne returned to England alone, arriving at Newcastle on 31 July, where her brother Michael and his wife Ann were waiting for her. Very soon afterwards, in early October, Anne found a buyer for No. 3, which had been on the market since February. John Duffield paid £295,000 and eventually got the keys on 19 October, two days after Anne had moved out.

With the house sold, Mark and Flick and Anthony and Louise travelled north to help clear out and prepare for her move. She said she wanted the boys to have some of their dad's personal belongings. Mark chose a pair of black onyx cufflinks and his father's watch. Anthony took his wedding ring, pocket watch, passport and ration book. He also selected some books, one of which was *The Shelters of Stone* by Jean M. Auel.

It was only after his father's arrest that he realised the paperback had been printed in 2003 – a year after his dad had 'died'. Another of the books had an American sticker on it and Anthony realised it must have been bought while his 'deceased' dad was on his US travels.

But at the time of the handover of their father's personal belongings, the boys were both sad and emotional. Their mother, meanwhile, was playing the role of grieving widow with her usual theatrics.

'It was a heart-wrenching moment,' Mark would later recall. 'It was like the final ending. We all cried together. She said she still missed Dad every single day and this was the last thing she had to give, now she was leaving the house and the life they'd had there. It was like a goodbye to his memory.'

It was at this time that Anne first told the boys that, because she was a foreigner, she had needed to set up a company to buy the land, and had therefore decided to make them directors of Jaguar Properties, each getting fifteen of the company's one hundred shares. The boys were amazed at their mum's resourcefulness and thanked her for her generosity. Of course, they had no idea the 'gesture' would make them prime suspects in their parents' outrageous fraud.

Anne said her goodbyes to her sons, elderly parents and other relatives, and on 19 October flew back to Panama via New York's Newark Airport. To say everyone was shocked is an understatement. John had by then visited their new land several times, walking along cattle tracks bare chested and clutching a machete to clear his route.

With the sale of No. 3 complete, Mark arranged to wire $322,400 to his mother's HSBC account in Panama City. The Darwins invested some of that money in a second-hand Toyota Land Cruiser.

But it wasn't long before the thrill of living in an exciting new city was overshadowed for Anne by John's constant demands to make sure their money was being properly invested. He wanted the proceeds of the sale of No. 3 to be put in different accounts where they would maximise interest rates and give them money to live off. The process, which entailed physically going into the banks, always left Anne, who had to do the dirty work, as everything was in her name, very flustered. She just wanted to put it into the one account she already had and be done with it. It caused a lot of tension.

'It worried me that I was still on a widow's pension in England, and that, in my own mind, I didn't really know if I was even going to stay in Panama,' she said.

'I didn't even have a Panamanian visa, although I was going to apply for one. We spent the entire fortnight, it seemed, trying to sort out the bank accounts. It was not a happy two weeks. The honeymoon period was over.'

It was also when John dropped his nuclear bombshell.

He told her that because of the change in the law for permanent residency visas, he was going to go back to the UK – and reinvent himself as John Darwin. He would claim he had amnesia and could remember nothing about the last seven years. He could never get a permanent residency visa in the name of John Jones without a letter from Cleveland Police saying he was a person of good character.

And that could never happen because John Jones was dead.

He had also read that the Panamanian authorities were cracking down on so-called 'permanent tourists' by replacing the current ninety-day visas with ones valid for just thirty. He couldn't afford to travel to Costa Rica every month and, anyway, if the authorities were cracking down he was bound to be caught out. He was fucked! He had no choice other than to return to England and resurrect John Darwin.

'Pretending you are dead is easy,' he later said. 'Coming back to life is slightly more difficult.'

Anne couldn't believe what she was hearing. Or that he'd known about it for four months without telling her.

'I think he thought that if he went back saying he'd lost his memory and remembered nothing for the last seven years it would all be fine,' she said. 'I thought it was completely crazy.'

With Anne in complete shock about John's crazy new plan, he suggested they take a holiday. They went to Costa Rica for a week. They checked into the thirty-eight-bedroom Hotel Jaguar on Playa Negra – John undoubtedly choosing the hotel because of its name. They relaxed, sat around the pool reading, walked on the beach and went horse riding. John took the photograph of Anne that she later sent to Anthony after his dad's miraculous resurrection. She said the hotel's gardens were giving her inspiration for the land she had bought in Escobal.

While there, they received an email saying their shipment of personal belongings from England would be arriving on 7 December, slightly earlier than they had anticipated. Anne knew she would have to get moving with her own visa application. She needed paperwork saying she had applied for a visa in order for the shipment to be allowed into the country.

'We talked about John going back to England and he asked me when would be a good time to go back with his story about having amnesia,' said Anne.

'I said: "There will never be a good time." He said the decision was mine and if I wanted him to stay he would. I really didn't think he would get away with it. But if it wasn't going to work, I would rather it didn't work sooner rather than later.

'John thought he could pick up the pieces of his life. We talked about what he was going to say.

'He wasn't quite sure, other than he had decided he would claim he couldn't remember anything after a holiday we had in Norway in 2000. I was worried because John was tanned from six weeks living in Panama and asked him how he was going to explain it.

'He said he didn't want to look like he had been incarcerated indoors all those years. I think he thought he would get away with it, and he would come back and we would live happily ever after.'

He told Anne it would take 'six months at most' to sort things out – and he'd be back as John Darwin. *Talk about wishful thinking.* But John's mind was made up. Anne bought him a single Air France flight to Heathrow, via Paris, for Friday 30 November.

'I had a worried feeling inside me as I drove John to the airport, and when he left it was quite emotional,' said Anne.

'I was being left in Panama on my own and he was going home with this story, which I didn't think anyone would believe for one moment. Would he be arrested? How will the boys feel? Will they see through his story? Here we go again . . .'

After he left, Anne sent John an email saying she hoped everything went well with the family and that she was missing him already. She ended it with the words 'don't leave me'.

After landing, John took the Heathrow Express to Trafalgar Square. It was about 3.15 p.m. as he emerged onto the crowded streets of the capital. Deciding he would have no more use for his John Jones passport, he ripped it up and scattered the pieces in a dozen different waste bins as he strolled down Oxford Street. *RIP John Jones.*

Later that evening he walked into the West End Central police station and uttered those immortal words: 'I think I'm a missing person.'

32

'Take Them Down'

GIVEN THAT HER story had more twists and turns than a snowy Alpine pass, it was perhaps inevitable that Anne's assurance that she was ready to hold up her hands, tell the police the whole truth and take whatever punishment was coming her way did not happen. For a month after being arrested, she continued to deny being in on the deception from the start.

But even after her confession, there was to be one last roll of the dice. Lawyer Nicola Finnerty delved into the statute books and found a way for her to fight the charges with the exceptionally rare defence of 'marital coercion' – offering her a glimmer of hope of avoiding prison by laying all the blame on her husband's 'bullying' ways. Hutch had warned his team during the interview sessions with Anne that a Not Guilty plea remained a possibility.

It was such a rare defence that, up to its abolishment in 2014, when the Law Commission said it was 'no longer appropriate' and a relic of a bygone age, there had been only five reported cases in the last 100 years. For it to be successful, Anne's defence team would have to demonstrate two things: that John was physically present (at her side) at every step of each crime being committed; and that through coercion or intimidation he was able to leave her with no choice but succumb to his will. Anne was well aware that both were untrue.

On Monday 14 July 2008, at Teesside Crown Court in Middlesbrough, Anne denied nine charges of money laundering and nine of deception. The saga of greed, deception and lies was now outlined in graphic detail to a packed court over eight days.

John, for once having taken the sensible option, had already pleaded guilty to seven charges of obtaining cash by deception and a separate passport offence. Nine charges of using criminal property, which he denied, were allowed to lay on file.

Opening the trial in Court 11, Andrew Robertson QC, prosecuting, told the jury that while the initial idea may well have been John's, it was not only a scheme in which Anne played an equal and vital role, but also a role that she played with 'superb aplomb'.

Somewhat inevitably, the defence began falling apart from the opening day. First came evidence that proved Anne was not even in the same country as John when some aspects of the crimes were committed, hence he could not have been physically 'at her side'; and second, a string of loving emails between the couple undermined any possibility that she had been totally coerced by her husband. She had admitted during her police interviews that John was neither violent nor threatening.

A number of emails between the couple were read out to the jury. One, sent from Anne just hours after John left Panama to return to the UK, told him how much she missed him. Another, dated 30 October 2007, said she hopes he had a good flight and adds: 'Love you, missing you already. xxxxxxx'

Mr Robertson, who appeared to have modelled himself on John Thaw's *Kavanagh QC*, said Anne had shown a considerable amount of 'guile, convincing pretence, persistence and guts' to see it through. John, after supposedly disappearing, had simply to keep his head down so that the falsity of his disappearance would not be rumbled by anybody. Anne was the one who had to take all the positive steps. But she coolly kept her nerve, knowing the rewards were going to be considerable – sufficient not only to discharge their debts, but to finance a potentially idyllic life abroad and together.

In truth, the defence of marital coercion never stood a chance. Yes, her lawyers had been the ones who came up with the idea, but it was Anne's decision to plead Not Guilty and fight for her liberty. Day after day, judge and jury listened as she wriggled and squirmed, repeatedly changing her story as she told lie after lie. It made very uncomfortable viewing – and bold newspaper headlines.

Anne even removed her wedding ring in a gesture presumably to show that the relationship with John was dead. But it left many wondering whether it was simply another part of their elaborate charade – trying to fool the world into believing their marriage was over while all along they were secretly plotting to reunite in

Panama once they were free to return to the riches they had left behind.

Because their mother pleaded Not Guilty, the boys were forced to attend court and relive the horrendous ordeal that had blighted their lives. Such was their contempt for their deceitful parents, they agreed to give evidence for the prosecution; evidence that would ultimately help condemn them to a far sterner sentence than their lawyers had predicted. Dragging the boys into court was entirely Anne's fault. It was a shockingly bad decision and one that she later described as the most horrendous experience of her life. *Some might call it payback.*

The boys, ashen-faced and smartly dressed in dark suits and ties, told the court they found their mother's deception heart-breaking and hard to believe.

'I couldn't believe the fact she knew he was alive all this time and I had been lied to for God knows how long,' said Mark, who described his feelings of extreme trauma and anger.

As he left the box he gave his mother a look of contempt. His eyes were dark and cold, and it sent a shudder down Anne's spine. She sensed the hatred.

Asked how he felt at the deception, Anthony scratched his head: 'Upset, betrayed . . . I don't know . . .' He looked genuinely perplexed. He had no idea about his parents' financial woes. He described his relationship with them as 'close and easy, which is why it hurts now so much to know they didn't feel they could trust us with their problems'.

Anthony told police that as he got older he didn't always see 'eye to eye' with his father and their relationship could at times be 'rocky'. But he said these differences of opinion never got out of hand or led to a major fallout. His parents always seemed to have a good relationship, though his dad was very much the boss, the 'driving force' behind things.

'Mam never seemed to stop Dad from doing what he wanted,' he told them.

After they finished giving evidence, Mark and Anthony sat listening intently to the rest of the proceedings from the public gallery. It was only then that they discovered their mother had been part of John's disappearing act from the outset. They had previously believed she only found out he had returned from the dead a year later. It was another savage twist of the blade to their stomachs.

The prosecution said it had all been very much a husband and wife team effort – and they should each pay accordingly. By cashing in the pension and life insurance policies, the fraud amounted to £250,820.75. But, said the prosecution, by the time the fraud was uncovered in December 2007, the amount of money, land and property owned by the couple amounted to more than double that.

Had they been forced to sell their properties and cars at the time John vanished, they would have barely had enough to pay off their debts. As it was, by staving off bankruptcy and selling their property portfolio, they had more than doubled their money and were sitting on a small fortune.

Irene Blackmore took the stand. Asked how she felt about being so cruelly deceived by her – now – former close friend, she was asked if she felt very bitter and let down. 'Yes, very,' said Irene. 'Devastated.'

The jury of nine women and three men took less than four hours to convict Anne on all counts. Four hours to consider eight days of evidence suggests what the jury thought of Anne's defence.

John was led into the dock for sentencing. At Anne's request, a custody officer stood between them. They were instructed to rise and stood four feet apart as Mr Justice Wilkie passed sentence. They looked straight ahead, their sons sitting impassively in the public gallery.

The judge told the Darwins: 'Although the sums involved are not as high as some reported cases, the duration of the offending, its multi-faceted nature and in particular the grief inflicted over the years to those who in truth were the real victims, your own sons, whose lives you crushed, make this a case which merits a particularly severe sentence.'

While the judge accepted Anne was initially reluctant to proceed with the plan, he said she soon played her part 'efficiently and, I am satisfied, wholeheartedly'. There were audible gasps in court as he went on to pass sentence. John would serve six years and three months, while Anne, who had forfeited any reduction in sentence by trying to shift all the blame onto her husband, got longer still – six years and six months.

In the dock, Anne was numb, struggling to breathe and control her emotions. She had been expecting two to three years at most. In front of her, those sat in the prosecution benches were all smiles, handshakes and gentle back-patting. John was told that had he pleaded Not Guilty he would have been sentenced to ten years. He would later claim he had researched the matter thoroughly and expected two years at most.

As the judge concluded his summing up with the words, 'Take them down', the Darwins were led away to the cells. Their sons showed no emotion as they watched from the public gallery.

Amid a scrum of journalists outside court, Detective Inspector Andy Greenwood said he was pleased with the guilty verdicts but admitted the Canoe Man story was still far from over. The police were concentrating efforts on recovering the money and assets salted away in Panama. But with no bilateral agreement between the UK and Panama for crimes other than murder, investigators knew that the cash and property might be difficult, if not impossible, to recover.

Would the Darwins have the last laugh?

Their Panamanian pot of gold might not be recoverable. Could they one day return to the sunshine and pick up the pieces of their lives with their squirrelled-away assets? They still had two bank accounts, in Anne's name, containing £271,000. As well as the cash, the couple owned a £23,000 Toyota Land Cruiser, a £60,000 flat in Panama City, and a £200,000 derelict farmhouse sitting on almost 500 acres of tropical jungle – all in the name of an untouchable Panamanian corporation. Then there was the £25,000 John had invested in a run-down ranch in Kansas, bought during his ill-fated relationship with Kelly Steele, though that was probably a lost cause. In Anne and John's minds, a return to Panama was not out of the question.

'I don't think we have really got to the bottom of everything here today,' said DI Greenwood.

The police probably weren't the only ones with that thought . . .

33

Sorting Fact from Fiction

E VEN AFTER THE trial, there remained a number of intriguing questions that continued to puzzle virtually everyone. While trying
to see through the blizzard of lies and half-truths Anne offered in
defence of her actions in court, both prosecutors and the judge
seemed uncertain about the couple's true motives and, in particular,
the most baffling question of all: exactly why John had flown home
to the UK in December 2007, having got away with his audacious
disappearing act for very nearly six years.

He had no debt, hundreds of thousands of dollars tucked away in
a number of foreign bank accounts, a fancy jeep, an apartment and
land on which he planned to build an eco-tourist centre that would
make him rich beyond his wildest dreams. Why risk everything with
a hair-brained scheme to walk into a London police station claiming
amnesia?

The perceived wisdom of many was that the Darwins had fallen
out in Panama, probably because one or both of them was having an
affair, and he had stormed home determined to seek revenge and ruin
her. The theory was well wide of the mark. John would later *joke*:
'Anne did have a boyfriend in Panama – me!'

It was John's fake identities that had shielded vital evidence from
the scrutiny of the lawyers at Anne's trial. The Jaguar Lodge Excel file
that the police had copied onto a CD, was, like all Microsoft Office
documents, registered to a particular user, in this case, another of
John's pseudonyms, Peter Fenwick.

When Cleveland Police discovered the name's existence, they
were less interested in John's sense of humour than in the possibility
that his latest alias might actually have his own bank accounts and
assets hidden in Panama: a fully-fledged John Jones mark II. But
whatever use Peter Fenwick might have been to John in the long

term, in the nine months that he was living in Panama, his new alias was indelibly recorded on every Microsoft Office document he created.

John's scheming and dreaming were all there, hidden away in the Jaguar Lodge file. It was just a matter of fathoming them out. After the file was introduced as evidence during Anne's trial, it was hardly mentioned again. But the detail it contained was absorbing.

Jaguar Lodge was complex and intricate down to every last detail. It was designed to guarantee the three most important things in his life: the security of the fraudulently obtained cash he and Anne had stockpiled; his return to Panama with his old identity re-established (a rethink forced by changes in visa requirements); and a safe and prosperous retirement in Central America, a place the Darwins could live out the remainder of their days in sunshine and luxury.

The goal was simple: to evade justice for ever.

Meticulous in its preparation over many months, the project to reinvent his whole life was laid out lovingly in full colour. It included computer-generated graphics, a flow chart marked with explanatory notes, and a detailed business plan that plotted every penny of John and Anne's illicit cash and future expenditure. Arrows pointed out important sections and carefully pasted links could be clicked on for more information from relevant websites. Different colours were used to plot the best options – green being the best, red the worst. There were always alternatives in case Plan A didn't work out.

With John and Anne both established as liars, it's hard to know which of their claims while being interviewed by police could be believed. John told detectives that he had planned to return as John Darwin even before he disappeared in 2002, while they both insisted he always wanted to pay back the cash.

John claimed in an interview after being freed: 'I treated the crime as basically borrowing the money off the insurance companies. I knew I would come back one day. I knew I would have to pay the money back. I have two sons and I wanted to be part of their lives again. I knew at some stage they would have children. And I would be a grandparent. I didn't want to miss out on all of that. So yes, I came back because of that. I didn't expect to be treated so harshly by the courts. But that's another story.'

As usual, though, his claims were hollow. The uncomfortable truth for both was the transfer of all that stolen money to Panama. If they really intended to pay it back, why tie it up in secret US-dollar accounts in Central America, thousands of miles from the companies they had defrauded? Panama was chosen because it prided itself on 'financial discretion' – with much of the money invested in property purchased in the name of what John believed to be an untouchable corporation. He had zero intention of paying it back.

As for not wanting to miss out on his sons' and grandchildren's lives, in the years to come that would prove another hollow claim. Even today, he's not even met all his grandchildren and hasn't seen a single member of his family for at least the last seven years since moving to live with his new young wife and her children in the Philippines.

The best indication of John's real intentions lie within the gradual development of his Jaguar Lodge Master Plan. Under the heading 'timetable', he detailed the various options for the resurrection of John Darwin. The original plan was for Anne, who was technically a widow, to apply for an investor's visa by depositing the required $200,000 in a 'time-locked' deposit in a bank for two years, which would grant her permanent residency.

Then all she had to do was marry her dashing companion John Jones and he too would be granted the same privilege as his spouse. How any of them would have been able to keep a straight face at the altar is anyone's guess. And no matter that they would both be committing yet another serious fraud, only this time on the other side of the world: it was simply a means to an end as far as John was concerned.

But then he discovered he would need a 'good conduct' letter from his local constabulary in the UK no matter what visa he was applying for. John Jones would struggle with that – he didn't exist. It was back to the drawing board. Reinventing John Darwin was literally the only other option he could come up with.

Without the Internet – patchy or not – it's doubtful whether John and Anne could have managed the plotting and scheming that took place between April and October 2007. Claims that Anne was an unwilling, coerced victim of John's crimes appear far-fetched once their complicated use of technology is examined. John set up at least five secret email accounts to enable their fraud. As well as emails, they were avid, and very careful, users of instant messaging. When John popped up in the messaging window on Anne's computer he was hidden behind yet another – this time, rather startling – alias. Few people would have guessed that a balding, middle-aged fraudster would have called himself 'Sexy Beast', but he did.

Internet telephone access was the final piece in their high-tech fraudsters' jigsaw. The technology that allowed them to talk over the Internet for a few pence a minute wasn't very reliable, but for fraudsters watching their pennies it had an irresistible attraction.

Using all three methods of communication, John and Anne chatted and messaged and emailed late into the night as they plotted together – with John logged on using his stolen wireless connection in the tropical heat and Anne burning the midnight oil in Seaton Carew. Their combined use of web-based email and instant messaging was inspired.

On some days, in the course of plotting to sell the family home as quickly as possible, they were using several email accounts simultaneously. John and Anne logged into her 'public' email account – the one that friends and family knew about – at the same time as they were logged into the 'secret' accounts that were only used for fraudulent purposes. This shared access, using the same email space at the same time, despite being thousands of miles apart, was an extremely efficient way to work together.

An email that John had written and saved in the draft folder would be opened by Anne, tidied up and sent off to insurance companies and banks as if she had written it. Crucially, the email could never be traced back to Panama through the hidden IP address information in the email's header. It was an ingenious method of working together that required real teamwork and displayed the sort of dedication to detail that helps to explain why their criminal activity went undetected for so long.

By the time Anne had arrived back in Panama in early December, John had decided he was going to head home to England, putting the latest updates to his Jaguar Lodge plans into effect by claiming amnesia. And after their brief excursion to Costa Rica, that's exactly what he did. Before coming home, there was no massive row with Anne, as was speculated during her trial.

'It was simply a case that John didn't have a better plan,' said Anne.

'I was all in favour of him going back, but to claim that he was going to have amnesia, I really thought that was going to be a difficult story for anyone to believe. I said I wasn't certain it would work.'

But John had made up his mind and that, as ever, was that.

'It was up to him,' she shrugged. 'He was going to play out this charade.'

John had little regard for the police; after all, he had managed to disappear and then return to live in his own home, right under their noses, just over three weeks later. He'd fooled them once and he was convinced he could do it again. They'd just be glad to get him off their hands as quickly as possible.

As for the boys, he felt they would be so thankful he had returned from the dead, they'd barely question what had happened and would welcome him back with open arms. Although he would have some explaining to do to the insurance and pension companies, he believed they too would accept his story and let them off because the claims had been made in 'good faith'. At the very worst, they would accept a deal to repay some of the money over a period of time.

Besides, all his, or rather Anne's, assets were safely tucked away in Panama in the name of an untouchable corporation. As soon as the dust had settled, he would return to Panama as John Darwin, with a new passport and a letter of good conduct from the police. He and Anne could get their visas and settle down to a nice quiet life in the tropics. The boys could come and visit whenever they wanted. John and Anne could simply pick up where they'd left off, developing an eco-retreat that would make them wealthy beyond words. One day he'd sell it for a small fortune and be that millionaire he'd always dreamt of being: it would just have taken a few more years than he boasted.

It never actually crossed John's mind that as well as repaying the proceeds of his crime, he would also have to give back all the profit he made as a result of his deception – and that would leave him right back where he started before he disappeared, without a penny to his name.

***

Two of the most puzzling questions that remained were why the Darwins agreed to *that* picture being taken in the first place and why they then allowed it to be posted on the web. John was living a secret life, Anne was hiding him and they were travelling together illicitly. Whatever possessed them after successfully hiding John's existence from their own children and the outside world for more than five years?

To answer the first question, you have to travel to Panama City, to Mario Vilar's office. Sitting in one of the chairs that John and Anne had occupied on that fateful day in 2006, Mario was asked to demonstrate how he had persuaded the secretive couple to pose for the camera. Next to Mario's office is a small reception area that is, as often as not, staffed by his wife Karina. No sooner had the question been asked than she appeared through the open doorway, with a small digital camera in her hand and a broad smile on her face.

'It was me!' she explained. 'I asked them if they would mind standing up against the window with Mario.'

It seems highly likely that John, considering himself something of a ladies' man, was only too willing to impress the tall, blonde and vivacious Karina. His excuse was that he didn't want to arouse suspicions by saying no. He later haughtily claimed he hadn't been concerned because 'most people in England hadn't even heard of Panama before *my* story'.

'They said that was fine,' smiled Karina, 'and I took the picture.'

In a flash, quite literally, John and Anne's fate was sealed.

The answer to the second question – why they would allow the picture to be posted on a website – is fairly straightforward: Mario and Karina never actually told them it would be.

'We might not have mentioned it,' Karina admitted.

The Darwins would come to regret having met someone as efficient as Karina, who made two simple decisions that ultimately sealed their downfall. First, before pressing the shutter, she had set the camera to burn the date onto the image as it was taken, and then she typed her clients' names into the 'save as' box as she uploaded it to the office computer. With 'John' and 'Anne' in the photograph's filename, it was uploaded to the company's web server and added to the gallery page of 'Move To Panama' and the company's happy customers. In no time at all, the automatic archiving systems used by Internet search engines had logged the words 'John' 'Anne' and 'Panama' and stored them with the website's address.

The photograph stayed there, unnoticed, for almost eighteen months until our armchair detective typed those three words into Google and blew apart the Darwins' lies. It gave police incriminating evidence that could not be questioned: John and Anne were guilty of fraud. All the hours John had spent planning every last detail of his and Anne's future on the Jaguar Lodge Excel sheet had been for nothing.

It is quite possible that the fantasy world in which John lived for so many years actually made him lose touch with reality. Sorting fact from fiction was one of the toughest jobs for the detectives tasked with trying to establish the real reason he'd come back from the dead.

It seems that living his life as somebody else became so normal for John that he became convinced he could get away with just about anything. He considered himself such a whizz at deception that his planned resurrection would be as believable as his 'death' and the police would never be able to figure out his true intentions.

Could he actually have got away with his amnesia story? Tony Hutchinson knew from the moment he walked into the police station it was 'bollocks'. But maybe, just maybe . . . had the photograph of John and Anne posing happily together in Panama in 2006 not appeared, who knows? A cold case review was underway and it's possible the police would ultimately have caught up with the deceitful Darwins. But with no bilateral treaty between the two countries for fraud, had John managed to return to Panama as the resurrected John Darwin, he would have been beyond the reach of British authorities.

Darwin certainly hadn't counted on the discovery of that 2006 picture when mapping out his blueprint for the future. Not for a moment had he dreamt his web of lies would be completely undone by one simple piece of evidence.

Just as Anne predicted when John first came up with his idea of faking his death, both had indeed ended up behind bars.

34

'Hideous, Lying Bitch'

Tony Hutchinson is walking along the front at Seaton Carew. It's a jeans and t-shirt day; the beach is packed, colourful spinnakers are unfurled on the yachts in the club race. He passes The Staincliffe, a hotel owned by very good friends many years ago. He points out Darwin's former home to his companion.

'The air of superiority he carried walking into a police station and expecting nothing more than a warm welcoming committee displayed an incredible level of arrogance,' says the now retired detective superintendent.

'The little big shot who was prepared to sacrifice his sons and other family members at the altar of greed and pride. Absolute vermin who got what he deserved.'

Hutch leans against the blue railings, watches the inshore RNLI lifeboat speed past. He has nothing but admiration for them and buys from their shops in Seahouses and Whitby whenever he visits. For the RNLI alone, the search for the man who wasn't missing cost almost £30,000, with two crews from Hartlepool each spending more than fifteen hours out at sea. In total, the operation is estimated to have cost more than £100,000.

'We didn't buy his pathetic amnesia fantasy for one minute,' he says.

He has little sympathy for Anne Darwin, agreeing with the trial judge that she 'played her part efficiently and wholeheartedly'.

Youngsters are running around, some are in the water, parents and grandparents are enjoying the sun. Hutch grins. The north-east riviera at its best.

'She deserved to go to prison for a long time. Was the sentence excessive? I'm not convinced. Remember, she lived opposite this.'

He nods at the North Sea.

'She would have seen the night lights of the rescue crafts, heard the blades of the helicopters, all the time knowing she had taken her so-called missing husband to the railway station,' he says.

'Forget the cost for a moment; what if there had been a real distress call that night?

'She lied to the police, lied to the coroner, maintained the grieving widow pretence for years and had no intention of returning to the UK. Yet she still pleaded Not Guilty at court. You tell me if it was excessive. Did she look under duress in that photograph? Anne Darwin coerced? Don't make me laugh.'

Ian Burnham, the family liaison officer who had spent more time with Anne that any of his fellow officers, was at Hartlepool police station when news of the verdict reached him. He was more philosophical than many of his colleagues. His overriding sentiment was one of 'disappointment' at having been lied to.

'When I heard the verdict I wasn't jumping for joy,' he recalls.

'When Darwin turned up after all those years it was not like I fell out of bed or anything. I was not totally surprised.

'I was disappointed Anne had lied to me. But then, as a bobby, I was used to people lying to me – it was a daily occurrence.

'I never took it personally. Sometimes I'd go to court and see people I knew to be as guilty as sin get away with it, wink at me as they left, and I'd just think to myself, no problem, I'll get you next time.

'I have no personal animosity towards Anne. I actually felt the Darwin sentences were harsh. The money amounted to about £500,000 – not a fortune really, is it? I've seen people who've done far worse get away with a lot less. The judge obviously felt they deserved it for what they put the sons through.'

The Darwin boys had remained silent from the moment of John's return. They had been pestered incessantly to give their side of the story but had steadfastly refused to say a word. That was about to change. Having been offered huge sums of money, Mark and Anthony, under the guidance of a wily old journalist, Tom Hendry, who had befriended them, decided to have their say, selling an interview to a Sunday newspaper for a reported £80,000. As innocent victims who played no part in their parents' crimes, they were free to do as they pleased.

In the interview, with the *Mail on Sunday*'s writer Angella Johnson, neither pulled any punches. Mark, once fiercely protective of his mother, said he always believed he had the best parents anyone could ever ask for. He described the mother he had always loved and respected as a 'hideous lying bitch' who went to 'outrageous lengths to con us'.

Mark thought his mother to be a wonderful woman who loved her sons and would do anything to protect them. As he sat talking on a windswept Cumbrian beach Mark told his interviewer: 'Before then I would never have traded them, I thought they were the best parents, but then they both lied to us in the cruellest way possible.'

He was sickened that she had bought Premium Bonds in his and Anthony's names, dragging them into the fray, and as things stood, he wanted nothing more to do with them. Anthony agreed with his brother's sentiments.

'It's bewildering. Nothing seems real any more,' he said. 'It's as if our whole life has been a lie.'

Mark accused his parents of tarnishing all the good times and said he could *never* forgive them for putting them through the torture of mourning. They were in it together and deserved the sentences handed down by the judge.

'They're as bad as each other,' he said. 'Dad told one nasty lie and disappeared and said he was dead, but she lied for six years, she was the face of the lies, she kept on lying even when the evidence was so overwhelmingly against her.

'She dragged us through hell by forcing a court case. They trampled over our lives for the sake of money. That is not something you do to people you love.'

Anthony recalled that on his last visit to see his parents, his dad had shaken his hand when he left. He had never done that before and it had struck Anthony as strange. It felt, now, that he had been saying goodbye. 'I suppose that by then they had hatched their devious plan and he was planning to bugger off,' he recalled.

And so, with the stinging words from their sons ringing in their ears, the deceitful Darwins began their prison sentences. Surely no amount of time could ever mend the hurt and anguish suffered by Mark and Anthony at the hands of their lying parents? As the boys headed south, to their respective homes in the Home Counties, from where they would continue to pick up the pieces of their disorientated lives, John and Anne were facing up to the reality of their new existence: a long stretch behind prison walls.

To this day, Anne rues the fact that she didn't stick to her intended script when she flew home from Panama to face the music.

'I guess I thought I had a chance,' she would later reflect.

'I really just wanted to plead guilty and have done with it, but I was told I had a real chance of defending the charges, so that's what I decided to do.

'I'll regret it to my dying day.'

35

'It's Over, I'm Not Coming Back'

I N PRISON, ANNE and John reacted very differently to the shame and humiliation of having their story of greed and deception played out in the public spotlight. Anne was sent to HMP Low Newton, in Brasside, a tough, Category A maximum-security jail, whose towering walls and grim, barbed-wired fences appeared somewhat out of place in the midst of County Durham's green fields and rolling countryside. She was known as Prisoner KP4801.

The prison housed such notorious inmates as serial killer Rose West, convicted of murdering ten young women in the infamous Gloucester 'House of Horrors', and Tracey Connelly, who drew public outrage by allowing the death of her 'Baby P', who died after suffering more than fifty horrific injuries over an eight-month period. A court ruled the child died at the hands of Connelly, her boyfriend Steven Barker and his brother Jason Owen, who also lived at the house with a fifteen-year-old girl.

To some it seemed a harsh place for a first-time fraud offender, guilty of telling some incredibly cruel lies to her sons, but a woman who, in reality, was really no danger to anyone. Others had little sympathy for her.

At HMP Everthorpe, a former borstal, near Brough, East Yorkshire, it was a different story altogether for Prisoner A1323AC – husband John. Although he was a former prison officer who would normally have been considered 'at risk' behind bars, it seemed the main risk was posed by him – of boring the life out of his fellow inmates.

Considering himself something of a celebrity inmate, John loved bragging about his canoe capers and his exotic Panamanian adventures. But few, if any, wanted to listen to his long-winded and boastful storytelling. As one former inmate put it: 'Everyone considered him a bit of a prat. He loved the sound of his own voice but no one had any time for him at all. If you saw him coming, you turned and walked the other way.'

In jails across the world, detainees avoided the hardmen fearing a beating; in Everthorpe, setting your own feet on fire was preferable to being lumbered with the tedious John Darwin. But it wasn't long before he was roughed up by an inmate allegedly paid by a lag who knew him from his prison officer days. Although the injuries were not serious, he was treated for cuts and bruises in the hospital wing, segregated, then transferred to another prison.

On the advice of their lawyers, both John and Anne appealed against their sentences, but both were denied by the Court of Appeal. Instead of showing any contrition, John, astonishingly, was resentful that Mark and Anthony had, he believed, refused his requests to help with the appeals. But, unbeknown to his parents, Mark had actually written to the Court of Appeal asking for leniency in their sentences, a remarkable gesture given what they had put him through.

'They are depriving both of us from seeing our fathers alive again,' John moaned to Anne.

The irony that he was complaining about not getting to see his own father – when he deprived his own sons of seeing him for nearly six years – seemed lost on him. In fact, he never again got to see his father Ronnie, who died in a nursing home in December 2008, aged ninety-one, after a series of strokes. John was banned from the funeral.

Relatives said Ronnie never got over the shock of discovering his son had lied to him in such a shocking way. He even cut John out of his will, leaving his entire net estate of £189,184 to his other son David and daughter Sheila. Before he died, Ronnie told how John wrote just one short message to him from his prison cell, the first contact between the pair since he went 'missing' five and a half years earlier. The note read: 'Dear Dad. Just to let you know, please don't worry.'

They were the only ten words Ronnie ever heard from his son again.

Rather than repent, John moaned to everyone that he'd made a terrible mistake in coming back to the UK. He even started learning Spanish, aiming to return to Panama when free.

'I wished we'd simply stayed together in Panama,' he said – a blatant admission that he never really intended to pay back the money.

Might he have escaped justice? We will never know.

Anne's life and actions in jail were in stark contrast to her husband's. At Low Newton, four miles outside the historic city of Durham, she kept the lowest of profiles, refusing to discuss her crimes with fellow inmates, all of whom wanted to know more about the Canoe Woman's adventures.

She immediately set about trying to repair the damage she'd done, frequently writing to the sons she'd deceived so badly and begging them for forgiveness, if not immediately, then later, when their hurt had healed a little. She knew that may never happen and that's what pained her the most: but she refused to give up on the feint glimmer of hope she held. She knew many people felt the story of her husband's back-from-the-dead gallivanting across the globe was one of pure comedy and farce, and that she was an evil, lying mother who got everything she deserved.

True as that might be, to Anne it was a tragic tale of regret and remorse that she would probably never fully recover from. She was assigned work, first as a cleaner, then in the prison gardens, where she spent her days tending to the flowers and concentrating on living as anonymous an existence as her surroundings allowed.

She would spend hours reading or writing letters, cutting a rather sad and lonely figure, with few visitors and fewer friends. The occasional letter from the handful of people who had stood by her, at least offered some comfort.

Initially, back in late 2007 and the early months of 2008, while on remand awaiting trial, Anne cut off all contact with John. She ignored his letters begging for forgiveness.

'He used to write to me. Always, every day,' said Anne.

'His letters would be repetitive and I told him to stop writing.'

But, just as he had been since the day they first met, John proved himself persistent and refused to give up on the girl he first set eyes on all those years ago on the school bus.

And, eventually, a year after they were sentenced, she finally started answering the long, rambling letters. She was torn and frequently changed her mind; after all, John was the only man she had really ever known – the father of their two children. She remained dubious as to whether prison would change him for the better. But there remained the remote glimmer of hope of a return to Panama.

'As soon as I was locked up, I knew I had to do things to change the person I'd become,' she said.

'I never really knew with John. We did have an awful lot of history.'

And then, much as she had predicted, she read a newspaper article revealing he had been secretly exchanging smutty sex letters with another woman. It was nothing short of childish filth. She cut him off immediately.

Truth is, John seemed none too bothered in seeking forgiveness from Anne or his sons – he was far too busy working out how he could cash in on his crimes, bragging to a fellow prisoner how he would 'make a million pounds' by selling his life story and film rights. He spent hours beavering away on two books; an account of his Panama adventure, and another on his prison diaries. He even designed what he saw as the front cover of the main book: a man in a red canoe paddling towards an idyllic tropical island, laden with palm trees. Knowing he couldn't directly profit from his crimes, he set about trying to beat the system by smuggling his books, written in a childish scrawl, out of jail, using a bogus law firm set up by a fellow inmate. Exactly how he planned to profit is unclear.

'I want to be able to get back into the situation we were in,' he boasted.

'Freedom and a million pounds should suffice. More would be welcome but even a little less would allow me to keep Anne in luxury for the rest of her life.'

But John's recklessness in trusting a twice-convicted fraudster to act as his 'agent' backfired spectacularly when his memoirs appeared in the *Sun* – and John never saw a penny. His dreams, as ever, were fanciful.

Far worse than that for Anne was that he also smuggled out of jail and into the arms of potential publishers her private letters: ones in which she had opened her heart and talked about a possible future together when their time was served and they were deemed fit to be released back into society. She still loved him, she had written, and couldn't imagine a future without him. But that, of course, was before his latest act of treachery; one that undoubtedly marked the end for John and Anne Darwin.

There was another huge black cloud hanging over Anne. She was told that if the Crown Prosecution Service's Proceeds of Crime team was unable to recover her assets from Panama, within twelve months the courts had the power to increase her sentence by anything between five and ten years, without parole. Everything was in her name, so this would only affect her, not John. The thought of being behind bars until she was nearly seventy was a terrifying prospect. She had instructed her lawyers in London and Panama to do whatever they could to assist the recovery, but the Panamanian authorities seemed in no hurry. Anne genuinely wanted to repay all the money and put an end to it. Was she about to pay an even heavier price for John's choice of an untouchable safe haven?

She sank into a deep depression. Struggling to cope, she reached the point when the future looked so bleak she seriously wondered if she had anything left to live for. She had been prescribed medication for high blood pressure and began wondering what would happen if she took all the tablets in one go. No more pain, anguish or humiliation. Would she drift off to sleep and never wake up, or would it be a horrible and violent end? She would be free from everything. But she thought of the pain it would inflict on the beloved boys she had already hurt so much – and she couldn't do it.

She needed help and it was agreed she should see a psychologist, Eva, with whom she built up a close relationship. It was a meeting that probably saved her life. For the first time ever, she felt able to talk about how utterly lonely and worthless she felt. She opened up about her life, the boys and her relationship with John. Having someone to listen to her helped her understand she needed to live her life independently of him. Anne asked her sister Christine, who had been a tower of strength throughout her time in jail, for her opinion. She asked Anne if she could ever really trust John again and if she believed he really loved her. It brought clarity to some painful home truths.

It was on a cold and dank morning, in November 2010, during a prisoner-to-prisoner telephone call that Anne told John that their thirty-seven-year marriage was finally over.

About six weeks earlier, she had been transferred to HMP Askham Grange, an open prison in the historic village of Askham Richard, set around a duck pond, stone cottages and a village green, six miles from

York. The move was made possible after the threat of a longer sentence was lifted because all the money had by then been repatriated from Panama.

There were acres of gardens, around which inmates were allowed to freely wander, even in the evenings, and a weekly treat was the Sunday roast, with fresh vegetables grown and nurtured by prisoners in the grounds. Life at Askham was different to Low Newton in just about every respect.

The main focus was in the reintegration of prisoners back into the community and preparing them for life after prison. Once transferred, inmates knew they really were finally on the home straight. As part of their resettlement, they were offered work placements outside the prison walls: it was a breath of fresh air for Anne.

After two years behind Low Newton's barbed-wire-topped, towering prison walls, she was finally given a taste of freedom. She was allowed to leave the prison grounds by herself, either to do her voluntary work, having found a placement with the RSPCA, or to spend the day with visitors. The only requirement was that she had to stay within a fifty-mile radius of the jail.

John always believed that, once out, they would quickly settle their – albeit considerable – differences and get back to being man and wife. Anne had finally come to the decision that the man she had known since their schooldays would play no further part in her life. In that brief and difficult telephone call, the first time they had actually spoken in years, she told him their marriage was over.

John was angry and belligerent, telling his wife not to be 'daft' and that they could still 'work things out'.

'No John, you're not listening,' she told him firmly, as he continued his rant. 'I don't want to be with you when I get out of here. It's over, I'm not coming back.'

John slammed down the receiver: Anne felt nothing but a tremendous sense of relief.

'I know it won't be long before he does something stupid again,' she said.

'He can't seem to help himself. I have to make a fresh start on my own. I've known him since I was eleven, but I can't go back to how things were. If he'd done the sensible thing, back then, and declared himself bankrupt, the shame would have been over a long time ago now. But that's not what happened and you can't turn back the clock. We have to live with the decisions that were made.'

It was as if a great weight had been lifted from her shoulders.

In November 2011, having been released, John was questioned about his feelings towards Anne in an interview with Tyne Tees television. 'I love her. I hate her. It's a fine balance,' he said.

'I'm bitter that she won't communicate.'

He wasn't yet done. In 2012, after *he* served divorce papers on the grounds of *her* unreasonable behaviour, Anne received a threatening letter from him at her home, appearing to boast he could find her whenever he wanted. Very few people knew her address. The boys, with whom she was once again in contact, assured her they would never dream of telling anyone. The letter included an old photograph of Anne with a 'copyright' symbol stuck over her face. It seemed to suggest that she was his property. Terrified he would turn up on her doorstep and harm her, she contacted her probation officer, who said she needed to alert the police. John was served with a restraining order, forbidding him from coming within two miles of her home.

Anne never heard from him again.

36

July 2015 – Forgiving the Unforgiveable

As the tourist coach edged its way along the narrow North Devon lanes, Anne gazed out of the window, admiring the lush, hilly countryside and, once again, thanked her lucky stars that the madness that had plagued her life for so many years was now behind her. That madness, or, to be precise, mad man, was ex-husband John, who, for some reason that Anne could never quite fathom out, seemed to crave the spotlight she herself so despised.

This time around, he was making national news headlines having married a Filipina half his age after a 'whirlwind romance'. Anne could only shake her head in disbelief. Although having had virtually no direct contact with him for nearly six years, she had been warned by members of her family that the story was about to break in news-papers and knew the press would be banging on her door at any moment. She was right.

At least John was, according to what she'd been told, now on the other side of the world, living with his young new bride, Mercy May Avila, in Manila, the capital of her native Philippines; the latest bizarre chapter in his almost unbelievably bizarre life. Mercy, said to be deeply religious and in her thirties, had been busy posting messages about John on her Facebook page. 'I love you so much sweetheart', was one. 'Our life is great and happy! Remember we are sign of Libra very lucky ha ha ha!' was another. *Poor girl,* Anne thought to herself. *Being married to John, she's going to need all the luck she can get.*

'I haven't spoken to him in years,' she said. 'He's very much a part of my former life and long gone now, thank goodness.

'It's his problem, his life and nothing to do with me any more. Of course, I still get to hear about all the stories that appear in the news-papers. There was one about him going back to Panama, but I really can't see it. But I guess you never really know with John. Anything is possible. I still think about Panama from time to time, and all the strange things that happened, but I have no wish to ever go back. I have plenty of regrets, and there are a few things I can laugh about now, but that part of my life is over. Thankfully, I now have far more important things to concern me.'

Anne had been fortunate. Not long after the wedding story appeared in newspapers, she had two weeks' holiday booked, so made a spur-of-the-moment decision to flee the journalists seeking her reaction to the story by joining a week-long coach tour to Devon, hundreds of miles away, in a part of England she had never before visited.

In fact, it was the first time she had ever holidayed alone (her time alone in Panama could hardly be classified as such), and although she had been slightly nervous at the prospect, she was now very much enjoying her first proper holiday since being freed from Her Majesty's pleasure. The weather was glorious as the coach, packed with fellow tourists from the north-east, ventured on day trips to such places as Bideford, a picturesque port town on the estuary of the River Torridge, and the quaint village of Combe Martin, on the north-west edge of the Exmoor National Park.

Anne felt invigorated: she loved the anonymity of being with people who knew her as simply a divorcee, taking a well-earned break from her job working for the RSPCA in York. Although accustomed to keeping herself to herself, certainly over the last few years, she had befriended another single lady, from Sunderland, who in turn had become friendly with a retired couple. The four spent a good deal of time together, chatting and sharing the occasional meal during their outings.

'Are you sure I don't know you?' the only male in the party-of-four, who happened to be a retired police sergeant, asked Anne over a pub lunch in Ilfracombe, the pretty seaside town in which they were staying. 'You seem so familiar.'

'No, no, quite sure,' Anne reassured him. 'Maybe I just have one of those faces!'

The man smiled but continued looking at her quizzically, obviously not totally convinced. He was, after all, a former cop. Eventually, Anne was fairly sure he twigged who she was, though she was grateful he was kind enough not to mention it.

'I'm sure the penny dropped eventually, but he didn't let on,' she said.

Anne's appearance had changed somewhat in the years since her face was plastered all over the front pages of newspapers and she had been portrayed as one of the vilest women on the planet. She had made sure of that by dyeing her silvery-white hair auburn, which softened her look and, perhaps, made her appear a little younger. But it wasn't just her appearance that had changed: her entire life had taken some remarkable, some would say unbelievable, turns for the better.

'It was a lovely holiday,' said Anne. 'The weather was glorious and I had such a relaxing time.

'I had been planning to go to my sister's, but at the last minute, when all the stories started appearing in the papers again, I booked a trip and decided to brave it on my own.

'I knew it had been coming for some time through the family, but it was still a shock to see the story in the papers and have all the press banging on my door again. I will never get used to that.

'The stories about John's wedding were all pretty ghastly. I needed to get away. I was so physically and emotionally drained. Even today he seems to enjoy courting controversy and being the centre of attention. As more time passes, and I stop looking over my shoulder, the harder it gets when something like this happens, or there's another story about John doing this or that . . . it's like being hit with a brick.'

On the day she travelled back to York, Friday 3 July 2015, Anne Stephenson, having reverted to the use of her maiden name following the divorce, celebrated her sixty-third birthday. No party, no fuss; her fellow travellers unaware.

She preferred to keep the news to herself. But there were calls on her mobile, wishing her a happy birthday, from the two most important people in her life: Mark and Anthony, the sons who had once so publicly disowned her.

Astonishingly, the boys she had so heartlessly betrayed had let their mother back into their lives, forgiving her for what many said was unforgiveable. It had been a long, difficult and emotional journey, but, as the saying goes, time had proved the greatest healer.

The pain and suffering Mark and Anthony endured over six years is well documented. Deception doesn't get a lot worse and few could have blamed the Darwin boys for cutting their devious and callous parents out of their lives for ever. But Anne never lost hope or gave up trying to heal the wounds.

Her letters begging forgiveness from Mark and Flick and Anthony and Louise had started as soon as she returned from Panama. From her prison cell while on remand awaiting trial, she pleaded with them to try and understand why she had lied, why she hadn't dragged them into the deception – although, of course, by making them directors of Jaguar Properties and involving Mark in international wire transfers and the sale of her home in Seaton Carew, that's exactly what she did.

She told them she couldn't even begin to imagine how they must be feeling after all the trauma of the last few weeks, and that she understood if she was the last person on earth they wanted to hear from.

'But I need to tell you both how sorry I am for the pain and anguish,' she wrote. 'There is no excuse for the pain and heartache you have been caused.'

Her early letters went unanswered and for several years, while their parents were locked up, serving their time, virtually nothing was heard of the brothers – two young men left to try and pick up the pieces of lives shattered by almost unimaginable deceit. Indeed, for the first two years of Anne's imprisonment, Anthony completely shunned his mother, ignoring her every letter. Mark, however, despite his angry public condemnation, did start corresponding with both his parents in the months after they were jailed. The untold story of family forgiveness is a remarkable one, given the pain and angst the Darwins put their sons through.

Twice, Mark travelled north to see Anne at Low Newton, each time spending two hours with her at an allocated visiting time. On his second visit, this time with Flick, Mark told his mother they were getting married the following month. But her joy at their wonderful news was short-lived when he pointedly told her it was 'a shame' that neither of his parents would be there to support him.

It wasn't until a few months before Anne was transferred to Askham, as the summer of 2010 drew to a close, that Anthony, with wife Louise at his side, finally followed his brother's lead and visited his mother.

He had written several letters, but she hadn't seen him in over two years and that had been nothing more than a fleeting glimpse out of the corner of her eye before she was led away to the cells after being sentenced.

It was during that visit that the couple broke the news to Anne that she was a grandmother for the first time. But Anne's joy was quickly brought crashing to earth when Louise asked her: 'How could you have done this to your own sons?' Anne was filled with shame.

Two months after being transferred to Askham, Anthony wrote asking if he could visit again.

Anne walked nervously down Askham Grange's gravel drive, barely daring to believe he would be there waiting. But he was. So too was Louise. They had driven 200 miles north from their home in Hampshire to introduce Anne to her first grandchild.

Anne's heart missed a beat as first she spotted Anthony, then Louise standing alongside him – holding their newborn baby.

'I walked out the gates and there was Louise, holding her baby son,' said Anne.

'I just burst into tears. I didn't even know Louise was coming. She walked over and put my grandson in my arms and I cradled him. It was hard to believe what was happening. It was all too much to take in.'

It was, indeed, an incredible gesture, given that, by helping John stage his disappearance at the very time Anthony was about to ask for Louise's hand in marriage on their ill-fated trip to Canada, Anne had ruined what should have been one of the happiest days of her daughter-in-law's life.

Mark and Flick, heavily pregnant at the time with the couple's first child, visited as the months to Anne's release drew ever closer.

'Mark was very worried about where I would go when I was released and Flick very kindly suggested I could even stay with them and help look after the baby,' Anne said.

'It was an incredibly kind gesture. I thanked her but said no. I said I didn't want to bring any more unwanted attention from the media on them, or any of my family come to that.

'They have all been through more than enough already because of what John and I did, and it would have been totally unfair to thrust any of them back into the spotlight again.

'I really am just so happy that they have forgiven me. That's more than I could have ever asked for.

'Mark said he couldn't bear to think of me walking out of prison alone, but I told him he must stay away and I'd deal with whatever attention came my way. I was dreading being part of the media circus again, but I felt, hopefully, it wouldn't last for ever. I didn't want anyone else to be a part of that.'

With the Darwins' Panama City flat now sold, Mark agreed to fly to Central America to recover some personal, mainly sentimental, belongings his parents had left behind, including a gold chain given to Anne by her parents. He flew alone and visited the apartment where, in December 2007, his mother had been found cowering behind the door after the story of the back-from-the-dead Canoe Man first surfaced. It must have been an incredibly strange experience for Mark, who spent several hours inside, sifting through his parents' belongings. He called both of them in jail, to check he had what they wanted, before flying home to the UK with paperwork, jewellery and family photographs.

Anne actually chose to spend her last Christmas as a prisoner inside Askham, rather than accept offers from members of her family to spend it with them.

'I would have been allowed out, but I chose to stay at Askham. I really didn't want to impose on anyone,' she said.

'Christmas was very nice, most of the girls went home, so the place was quiet; there was a lovely peaceful atmosphere. The building was decorated and the food was good and we all received a present on Christmas Day from one of the local churches.'

On Wednesday 9 March 2011, having served three years and three months of her sentence, Anne, wearing the same red coat in which she was arrested at Manchester Airport, was released on licence from Askham Grange. She spent the first six weeks in a halfway house bail hostel in Leeds, which she didn't enjoy, especially as she had been told that journalists were frantically looking for her, then found a tiny but adequate ground-floor apartment in a converted house on the outskirts of York, in an area called Heworth Village. The RSPCA had agreed to give her three days' paid work a week, so her life had suddenly taken two very good turns for the better.

'At long last I'm free!' she wrote in one of the many letters we had exchanged since returning from Panama.

'My landlady is very nice and it's great to have my own space and privacy at last.'

Meanwhile, John, who had been released from Moorland open prison in Doncaster, seven weeks earlier, moved straight back to the scene of his crimes. He found refuge with perhaps his one true friend, his old classmate Paul Wager, in Easington, County Durham, just thirteen miles from Seaton Carew. And it wasn't long before he was photographed walking a friend's dog along the very beach from which he staged his death. The Canoe Man appeared to love being straight back in the limelight.

***

Anne's home today is a small but comfortable flat in a pretty North Yorkshire village with peaceful views over farmland. There's a marketplace, a good range of shops, tea rooms, several pubs and restaurants – just about everything anyone living the village life could need. She's retired from her job with the RSPCA. Mark and Flick and Anthony and Louise, each now the proud parents of two children, are regular visitors and she travels to see them whenever she can. It's more than Anne could have ever dreamt possible

Even as Anne's elderly father Harry died in November 2013, John – with his impeccable timing and eighteen months prior to meeting his Filipina wife – was making front-page headlines having flown to the Ukraine to meet a girl less than half his age he met on an Internet dating site. It's certain that the twenty-five-year-old blonde who said she was looking to marry a wealthy foreign husband had no idea that the man who wooed her, boasting he could satisfy any woman in bed, would be a balding, penniless ex-con with an incredibly dubious history.

As he arrived back in the UK, he was promptly arrested and thrown in jail for twenty-eight days for breaching his parole terms by leaving the country without authorisation. It does seem amazing that the authorities hadn't, at the very least, confiscated his passport. After all, he did have a rather well-documented history of disappearing.

The press attention that naturally followed really was the last thing Anne needed at that particular time of her life.

'I had far more important things to worry about than his latest stupid antics,' said Anne.

But, as she was staying with her elderly mother, Catherine, while arrangements were made for her father's funeral, at least she wasn't at home or work, so journalists quickly gave up trying to find her.

'Everything that happened was so hard for Mam and Dad to understand,' said Anne.

Her mother had been virtually housebound before her father's death, but after his passing, she deteriorated and has since died.

Anne remains grateful that they did manage to visit her in prison a number of times; twice at Low Newton and once at Askham. On another occasion, several months before her release, they were waiting to greet Anne when she was allowed out to spend the weekend at a relative's home.

'It was wonderful spending some time with them both,' she recalled.

'I know how hard it was on them. They were quite frail and I could see in their faces how much I'd hurt them and the pain I'd caused. They were times after I was initially locked up when I wondered if I'd ever see them again.

'I was allowed to make calls with the phone cards I bought in prison, so I rang Mam every week to see how they were doing.

'She would put the call on the speaker phone (just as Anne did when her sons used to phone her, so that their 'dead' father could secretly listen in) and we chatted for a while. Dad would just listen. Sometimes I'd say, 'Are you still there, Dad?' and he'd say, 'Yes love, I'm here.' He didn't say much but it was reassuring to know he was there.'

As Anne returned from her summer holiday in Devon, the Crown Prosecution Service obtained a court order ensuring John would have to forfeit his pension funds, worth £40,000, after they matured – the very last penny of his known assets. He was left with precisely nothing.

The property in Panama had been sold and the money from the various accounts repatriated under Proceeds of Crime Orders. DC Dolan from Cleveland's Economic Crime Unit, working with the High Court-appointed Receiver, the Crown Prosecution Service and Anne's Panamanian lawyer, ensured that the total sum of her remaining 'realisable assets' – £591,838 – was accounted for. A further £88,000 had been spent and could not be recovered. John acknowledged his role by offering a nominal £1. There was no hidden pot of gold as many people believed.

Thirteen years after John faked his death, the persistence of the asset recovery teams had ensured he and Anne would be left penniless – in a far worse state than they would have been had John taken the sensible option and declared bankruptcy in 2002. It truly was the end of the Panamanian dream.

Money was one thing, forgiveness another.

Despite the boys welcoming Anne back into their lives, the Darwins' legacy is not a tale of a family once again happily reunited. The boys remain angry with their back-from-the-dead father for the embarrassment he continues to heap on them and the family. Mark is still in contact, but it's believed Anthony refuses to speak to him.

After being released, John signed up for several different online dating sites and, according to journalists who interviewed him, was in regular contact with dozens of women from all over the world. It's believed that's how he met Mercy Mae. The pair married in 2015.

He will no doubt be loving his latest adventure in the Philippines. He's never shown remorse to the sons who once worshipped him. Asked after his release if he'd given their feelings much thought before disappearing, he responded: 'As far as I was concerned they had moved away from home, contact was less and less, and they had their own lives to lead. We were here by ourselves, we couldn't talk to them about problems and we thought less of it. It wasn't the foremost in our minds.'

On Facebook, he lists his favourite quote as: 'Live life to the full each day *and have no regrets*.' It sums him up rather well. He revels in his Walter Mitty infamy, seeing himself as an irresistible sex symbol, and arrogantly believing he is smarter than everyone else. Bernice Saltzer, who spent several weeks interviewing Darwin for a possible book collaboration, before they fell out and the project was scrapped, described him as 'deeply unpleasant, sleazy and unrepentant'.

'One day he flirted with a pretty young waitress who brought us coffee,' she said.

'She was just doing her job, but he smirked and said, "Did you see the way she looked at me?" He was completely deluded with a total lack of self-awareness. He was not pleasant to be around.'

***

The year 2021 marked the tenth since the Darwins were freed on parole after serving half of their six-year-plus sentences. Having served their time, do the couple who put the bucket and spade town of 'Seaton Canoe' on the map for all the wrong reasons really deserve a second chance?

John, who turned seventy-one in August (2021), is probably a lost cause. He has little or no contact with his family. Journalists who've tracked him down say he refuses to talk unless, as obsessed with money as ever, it's for payment, which is forbidden under the Proceeds of Crime Act. He continues to live in the Philippines with Mercy Mae, who is twenty-three years his junior and a mother-of-three. Both declined to be interviewed for this book.

Mark and Anthony, however, decided their mother deserved redemption, and after what they endured, who is anyone to question their decision? For the brothers, the horror of what they went through is a cruel act of betrayal that no parents should ever inflict on their children. Anne begged forgiveness, repeatedly telling the boys how sorry she was for deceiving them, and is genuinely contrite for the terrible lies she told. It's quite possible neither son will ever really understand how she could have done what she did. But they have nevertheless accepted how devastated she was at the distress she caused and, after a lot of soul-searching, decided to make their peace.

Mark describes his mother's road to redemption as a long and tough journey for them all. Today, he loves his mother – just not in that child-hood, all-encompassing way. His bitterness and fury have long passed. But while he has forgiven her, he will never understand – or forget.

'We have normal conversations, the sort of ones mothers and sons do,' he says.

'If one of the kids is sick, I'll ask Mam what she thinks I should do. We try to stay on safe subjects, though. That said, what she did isn't the elephant in the room. And believe it or not, we can even, at times, joke about it. In a black humour sort of way.'

His feelings towards his father are a lot more complicated. Having him alive, and in his life in some way, is much more preferable to him having died. Not that it negates what he did in the slightest. Could he do what his parents did to him? Never, he says. Never ever.

Whether Anne's punishment really fitted the crime is open to debate. Hutch, like many, has no doubts she got her just deserts and points out that both were refused leave to appeal against their sentences.

It is worth bearing in mind, however, that Mr Justice Wilkie's sentences were far harsher than those meted out to others who have defrauded financial institutions or the Treasury on a far, far grander scale.

The judge said the boys were the real victims, which emotionally, of course, is true. But lying to family members and causing them misery is a moral – not criminal – offence. Yes, it should be taken into account when sentencing, but wrecking a family one way or another is not uncommon and very rarely indictable. Anne isn't a danger to society. Six years-plus for a £250,000 insurance and pension fraud seemed, to me, to be excessive.

Anne Stephenson, now sixty-nine, is a woman who made some terrible choices in life: agreeing to help with the scheming of the arrogant, deluded and emotionally bullying John Darwin has to be by far the worst. The mental anguish she caused those she loved most will haunt her for ever.

'Not having the courage to stand up to John will always be my biggest regret,' she told me when we last met in October 2021.

'In prison I learned to have the courage to end my relationship with him and to finally stand up for myself. I'm sure there are many other women who have found themselves in similar situations with overbearing husbands. I would urge them to be strong and have the courage of their convictions.

'I still think about John from time to time; we were together for many years. But I don't miss not having him in my life, not at all. I have the boys and their families and I'm sure many people think that's probably more than I deserve. I could not be more thankful.'

Today, as Anne says, she is back in her sons' lives as a mother and grandmother; the boys who were so heartlessly betrayed have no regrets about rebuilding their relationship. The past is the past, as far as both are concerned. Canoe and Panama are words they would rather forget and both have made clear that their life today is nobody's business but their own.

***

Whenever John makes headlines, as will doubtless continue for years to come, he causes a huge amount of distress to his sons and his family, for whom he callously seems to have so little regard.

For Anne, it means another round of being thrust back into the spotlight she so despises. And when it happens, the same thing always crosses her mind.

With a hint of a smile she says:

'Sometimes I wish *I* could just disappear . . .

Acknowledgements

Special thanks to all the outstanding journalists and police officers who helped in the research of this book. Each played an important role in what has gone down in folklore as one of the most mind-boggling tales of deception of recent times.

From the *The Mirror*, first and foremost, Jeremy Armstrong, and his colleagues, past and present, Anthony Harwood, Jon Clark, Stewart Maclean, Paul Henderson, Martin Newman and Ian Down.

From the *Daily Mail*, Gerry Hunt, for the call that set me on my way, and Natalie Clark.

Photographer Steve Dennett, my good friend, curry lover, and travel companion, and Matheus Sanchez, for his timely linguistic skills.

My fabulous fellow author Tony 'Hutch' Hutchinson, and his former officers and friends at Cleveland Police, especially Ian Burnham, Iain Henderson, Gary Dolan, Steve Rowlands and Jim McArthur.

Craig Clark-Darby, formerly of the Metropolitan Police.

A special thanks to Dave Nath, of Story Films, producer Alison Sterling, director Richard Laxton, and screen writer extraordinaire Chris Lang, for brilliantly bringing to life this outrageous story in the ITV dramatisation starring Eddie Marsan, Monica Dolan and, of course, David Fynn, who had his work cut out playing me.

The wonderful Shirley Patton, from ITV Publications, and Nick Mattingly at ITV Productions.

From Hodder, thanks for the calmness shown by our Editor, Cameron Myers, and the wisdom of his colleagues Nick Fawcett and Steven Cooper.

I'm eternally grateful, as ever, to my guiding light, my journalist father and mentor Don, for his patience, help and thoughtful advice with this book and throughout my career – and my family for putting up with me.

And for those who can't be mentioned, for one reason or another, many thanks for your valuable help. You know who you are!

Picture Acknowledgements

Getty Images: 1, top. 3, middle.

The Mega Agency: 1, middle, bottom. 3 top, bottom. 4, top left, middle, bottom.

Dean Chapple/The Mega Agency: 8, bottom.

Cleveland Police: 2, top.

MoveToPanama.com: 5, top left.

Splash News: 2, bottom. 5, top right. 6, middle, 7 top, middle.

MirrorPix/Daily Mail: 5, bottom.

ITN Productions: 6, top.

North News & Pictures: 6, bottom. 8, top.

Les Wilson: 8, middle.